Analysis for Marketing Planning

McGraw-Hill/Irwin Series in Marketing

Alreck & Settle
The Survey Research Handbook
Third Edition

Anderson, Beveridge, Lawton, & Scott
Merlin: A Marketing Simulation
First Edition

Arens
Contemporary Advertising
Ninth Edition

Arnould, Price & Zinkhan
Consumers
Second Edition

Bearden, Ingram, & LaForge
Marketing: Principles & Perspectives
Fourth Edition

Belch & Belch
Advertising & Promotion: An Integrated Marketing Communications Approach
Sixth Edition

Bingham & Gomes
Business Marketing
Third Edition

Cateora & Graham
International Marketing
Twelfth Edition

Cole & Mishler
Consumer and Business Credit Management
Eleventh Edition

Cravens & Piercy
Strategic Marketing
Seventh Edition

Cravens, Lamb & Crittenden
Strategic Marketing Management Cases
Seventh Edition

Crawford & Di Benedetto
New Products Management
Seventh Edition

Duncan
Principles of Advertising and IMC
Second Edition

Dwyer & Tanner
Business Marketing
Second Edition

Eisenmann
Internet Business Models: Text and Cases
First Edition

Etzel, Walker & Stanton
Marketing
Thirteenth Edition

Forrest
Internet Marketing Intelligence
First Edition

Futrell
ABC's of Relationship Selling
Eighth Edition

Futrell
Fundamentals of Selling
Eighth Edition

Gourville, Quelch, & Rangan
Cases in Health Care Marketing
First Edition

Hair, Bush & Ortinau
Marketing Research
Second Edition

Hawkins, Best & Coney
Consumer Behavior
Ninth Edition

Johansson
Global Marketing
Third Edition

Johnston & Marshall
Churchill/Ford/Walker's Sales Force Management
Seventh Edition

Johnston & Marshall
Relationship Selling and Sales Management
First Edition

Kerin, Hartley, & Rudelius
Marketing: The Core
First Edition

Kerin, Berkowitz, Hartley & Rudelius
Marketing
Seventh Edition

Lehmann & Winer
Analysis for Marketing Planning
Fifth Edition

Lehmann & Winer
Product Management
Third Edition

Levy & Weitz
Retailing Management
Fifth Edition

Mason & Perreault
The Marketing Game!
Third Edition

McDonald
Direct Marketing: An Integrated Approach
First Edition

Mohammed, Fisher, Jaworski & Paddison
Internet Marketing: Building Advantage in a Networked Economy
Second Edition

Monroe
Pricing
Third Edition

Mullins, Walker, and Boyd
Marketing Management: A Strategic Decision-Making Approach
Fifth Edition

Nentl & Miller
SimSeries Simulations:
  SimSell
  SimSales Management
  SimMarketing
  SimMarketing Research
  SimCRM
First Edition

Pelton, Strutton, Lumpkin & Cooper
Marketing Channels: A Relationship Management Approach
Third Edition

Perreault & McCarthy
Basic Marketing: A Global Managerial Approach
Fifteenth Edition

Perreault & McCarthy
Essentials of Marketing: A Global Managerial Approach
Ninth Edition

Peter & Donnelly
A Preface to Marketing Management
Ninth Edition

Peter & Donnelly
Marketing Management: Knowledge and Skills
Seventh Edition

Peter & Olson
Consumer Behavior
Seventh Edition

Purvis & Burton
Which Ad Pulled Best?
Ninth Edition

Quelch, Rangan, & Lal
Marketing Management Text and Cases
First Edition

Rayport & Jaworski
Introduction to e-Commerce
Second Edition

Rayport & Jaworski
e-Commerce
First Edition

Rayport & Jaworski
Cases in e-Commerce
First Edition

Richardson
Internet Marketing
First Edition

Roberts
Internet Marketing: Integrating Online and Offline Strategies
First Edition

Spiro, Stanton, Rich
Management of a Sales Force
Eleventh Edition

Stock & Lambert
Strategic Logistics Management
Fourth Edition

Ulrich & Eppinger
Product Design and Development
Third Edition

Walker, Boyd, Mullins & Larreche
Marketing Strategy: A Decision-Focused Approach
Fourth Edition

Weitz, Castleberry & Tanner
Selling: Building Partnerships
Fifth Edition

Zeithaml & Bitner
Services Marketing
Third Edition

Analysis for Marketing Planning

Sixth Edition

Donald R. Lehmann
Columbia University

Russell S. Winer
New York University

McGraw-Hill Irwin

Boston   Burr Ridge, IL   Dubuque, IA   Madison, WI   New York
San Francisco   St. Louis   Bangkok   Bogotá   Caracas   Kuala Lumpur
Lisbon   London   Madrid   Mexico City   Milan   Montreal   New Delhi
Santiago   Seoul   Singapore   Sydney   Taipei   Toronto

 **McGraw-Hill
Irwin**

ANALYSIS FOR MARKETING PLANNING
Published by McGraw-Hill/Irwin, a business unit of The McGraw-Hill Companies, Inc., 1221
Avenue of the Americas, New York, NY, 10020. Copyright © 2005, 2002, 1997, 1994, 1991, 1988
by The McGraw-Hill Companies, Inc. All rights reserved. No part of this publication may be
reproduced or distributed in any form or by any means, or stored in a database or retrieval system,
without the prior written consent of The McGraw-Hill Companies, Inc., including, but not limited to,
in any network or other electronic storage or transmission, or broadcast for distance learning.

Some ancillaries, including electronic and print components, may not be available to customers
outside the United States.

This book is printed on acid-free paper.

1 2 3 4 5 6 7 8 9 0 FGR/FGR 0 9 8 7 6 5 4

ISBN 0-07-286596-2

Editorial director: *John E. Biernat*
Sponsoring editor: *Barrett Koger*
Editorial coordinator: *Scott Becker*
Executive marketing manager: *Dan Silverburg*
Media producer: *Craig Atkins*
Project manager: *Kristin Puscas*
Senior production supervisor: *Sesha Bolisetty*
Coordinator freelance design: *Artemio Ortiz Jr.*
Lead supplement producer: *Cathy L. Tepper*
Senior digital content specialist: *Brian Nacik*
Cover design: *Artemio Ortiz Jr.*
Typeface: *10/12 TimesNewRoman*
Compositor: *GTS—New Delhi, India Campus*
Printer: *Quebecor World Fairfield Inc.*

Library of Congress Cataloging-in-Publication Data

Lehmann, Donald R.
    Analysis for marketing planning / Donald R. Lehmann, Russell S. Winer.—6th ed.
      p. cm.—(McGraw-Hill/Irwin series in marketing)
    Includes index.
    ISBN 0-07-286596-2 (alk. paper)
      1. Marketing—United States—Management. I. Winer, Russell S. II. Title. III. Series.
HF5415.13.L395 2005
658.8′02—dc22

                                   2004053843

www.mhhe.com

To our families,
colleagues,
and students

Contents

Preface   ix

Acknowledgements   xi

About the Authors   xii

Chapter 1
Marketing Planning   1

Overview   1
Definition and Objectives of Plans   1
Frequent Mistakes in the Planning
    Process   4
What Makes a Good Planning System:
    Some Empirical Results   7
Is Planning Worthwhile?   7
The Planning Process   8
Approaches to Planning   8
Steps in the Planning Process   9
Components of the Marketing
    Plan   11
The Executive Summary   11
Situation Analysis   11
Marketing Objectives/Strategy   12
Supporting Marketing Programs   13
The Rest of the Plan   13
Example   13
Two Case Studies   16
Energy Bars (ca. 2002)   16
Personal Digital Assistants
    (ca. 1999)   18
Summary   21
References   22
Appendix   Marketing Plan Outline   23

Chapter 2
Defining the Competitive
Set   25

Overview   25

Levels of Market Competition   28
Definitions   28
Overlapping Market Segments   33
The Impact of Metamediaries   33
Product Strategy Implications   33
Illustrations   36
Methods for Determining
    Competitors   38
Managerial Judgment   38
Customer-Based Measures   39
Summary   44
Competitor Selection   45
Enterprise Competition   47
Summary   49
References   49

Chapter 3
Industry Analysis   51

Overview   51
Aggregate Market Factors   52
Category Size   52
Market Growth   53
Product Life Cycle   53
Sales Cyclicity   55
Seasonality   55
Profits   55
Category Factors   56
Threat of New Entrants   56
Bargaining Power of Buyers   58
Bargaining Power of
    Suppliers   59
Current Category Rivalry   60
Pressure from Substitutes   61
Category Capacity   61
Environmental Analysis   62
Technological Factors   62
Political Factors   64
Economic Factors   65

Regulatory Factors 65
Social Factors 66
Illustrations 70
 Energy Bars 70
 Personal Digital Assistants 73
Summary 74
References 75

Chapter 4
Competitor Analysis 76

Overview 76
Sources of Information 82
 Secondary Sources of Information 82
 Primary Sources of Information 88
 Other Sources 89
 Some Sources with Ethical
  Considerations 91
Analyzing Product Features 92
Assessing Competitors' Current
 Objectives 93
 Determination of Competitor
  Objectives 93
Assessing Competitors' Current
 Strategies 95
Marketing Strategy 95
 Comparing Value Chains 96
 Marketing Mix 97
 How to Assess Competitors'
  Strategies 98
 Technology Strategy 100
Differential Advantage
 Analysis 102
 Ability to Conceive and Design 102
 Ability to Produce 104
 Ability to Market 104
 Ability to Finance 104
 Ability to Manage 104
 What to Do with the Information 104
Assessing a Competitor's
 Will 106
Predicting Future Strategies 107
Illustrations 110
 Energy Bars 110
 Personal Digital Assistants 114

Summary 118
References 118

Chapter 5
Customer Analysis 120

Overview 120
What We Need to Know About
 Customers 121
 Who Buys and Uses the
  Product 121
 What Customers Buy and How
  They Use It 127
 Where Customers Buy 129
 When Customers Buy 130
 How Customers Choose 130
 Why They Prefer a Product 135
 How They Respond to Marketing
  Programs 140
 Will They Buy It (Again)? 140
Segmentation 141
 Desirable Criteria for
  Segments 142
 Methods for Market
  Segmentation 143
Illustrations 158
 Energy Bars 158
 Personal Digital Assistants 160
 Motorcycles 162
Summary 164
References 165
Appendix 5A Economic Value to
 the Customer (EVC) 167
Appendix 5B Latent Class
 Methods 169

Chapter 6
Market Potential and Sales
Forecasting 170

Overview 170
Definitions 170
Market Potential 171
 Overview 171
 What They Are Used For 172

Information Sources   172

New or Growing Product
Potential   174

Mature Product Potentials   175

Methods of Estimating Market and
Sales Potential   175

Analysis-Based Estimates   175

Area Potential   178

Sales Potential   179

Sales Forecasting   179

Overview   179

Level of Accuracy Needed   181

Judgment-Based Methods   181

Customer-Based Methods   185

Sales Extrapolation Methods   188

Model-Based Methods   191

What Methods Are Used?   192

Using Regression Models for
Forecasting   192

Developing Regression
Models   199

Recognizing Uncertainty   199

Nonlinear Relations   199

Share Forecasts   201

Forecasting Really New Products   201

Illustrations   202

Forecasting Energy Bar Sales via
Regression   202

PDA Sales   204

Using Forecasts   205

Combining Forecasts   206

Gaining Agreement   206

Why Not Just Go to the Web?   207

Summary   207

References   207

Appendix   Time Series Regression
with Seasonal Factors   209

Chapter 7
Developing Marketing
Strategy   212

Overview   212

Benefits of Strategy   212

Elements of a Marketing Strategy   214

Setting Objectives   214

Selection of Strategic Alternatives   217

Increasing Sales/Market Share   217

Increasing Profitability   219

Summary   220

Positioning: Choice of Customer
Targets   221

Positioning: Choice of Competitor
Targets   222

Positioning: The Core Strategy   223

Cost/Price (Value) Strategy   224

Nonprice Strategy   224

Managing Brand Equity   228

Measuring Brand Value   233

Relation to Customer Strategy   236

Marketing Strategy over the Life
Cycle   236

Introduction Strategies   236

Growth Strategies   238

Maturity Strategies   239

Strategies for the Decline Stage   239

Summary   240

Illustrations   240

Odwalla Energy Bar   240

Handspring   241

Summary   241

References   242

Appendix A   245

Index   249

Preface

RATIONALE

Many marketing books deal with marketing on the strategy level, addressing issues such as what business to be in. Others focus on operating-level product/brand management decisions involving the marketing mix or its individual elements (e.g., price, advertising/communications) whether the focus is strategic or tactical. In either case, sound decisions generally stem from sound analysis. This book focuses on the analysis needed for marketing decisions. It is structured around the basic planning document, the marketing plan.

This book evolved from a course given at the Columbia Business School called Marketing Planning and Strategy. In the mid-1970s, the marketing faculty at Columbia realized that traditional marketing management courses in business school curricula were fine for preparing MBA students for senior-level marketing positions, but did not equip them with the tools necessary for first jobs with titles such as "assistant brand manager" or "product manager." It was felt that students needed a "hands-on" course that would prepare them for the data collection and analysis tasks that often fall to junior-level managers. Interestingly, having a basic template for analysis proved beneficial for strategy-based courses as well.

The exercise of actually developing a marketing plan is highly integrative as it brings together concepts learned from marketing research, marketing strategy, finance, operations, and policy courses. Despite the advent of the Internet and the resulting development of new job titles, terminology, and technology, the need to develop sound analysis and planning is as important as ever.

This book does not attempt to cover all aspects of the marketing plan. We focus on the analysis of information pertaining to a product's environment, customers, and competitors. Chapter 1 contains an overview of an operating marketing plan. As such, the book can be used as a companion text to books on strategic marketing management, which tend to focus more on what to do after the type of analysis treated in this book has been completed, as part of a product/brand management course, or as a general reference for practitioners. Over the previous five editions of the book, we have been surprised and gratified at the wide variety of courses and contexts for which the book has been adopted.

OUTLINE OF THE BOOK

The book has seven chapters. The first six provide specific analytical methods and data sources that can be useful for each of the analyses discussed in the chapters. Perhaps as important, they also provide some useful formats for summarizing the information. Chapter 7 then relates the concepts to the development of marketing strategy. The chapters are:

1. **Marketing Planning.** In this chapter, we present the rationale for planning, pitfalls that should be avoided, and an outline of a complete marketing plan.

2. **Defining the Competitive Set.** One of the most challenging decisions faced by marketing managers is that of defining the competition since the set of competitors can usually be constructed as narrowly or as broadly as desired. This chapter discusses methods for defining different levels of competition.

3. **Industry Analysis.** Fundamental criteria for evaluating a product's position in the market are aggregate factors such as market growth rate, industry factors such as barriers to entry, and environmental factors such as regulation.

4. **Competitor Analysis.** Monitoring strategies of key competitors and anticipating their likely moves are key to the development of successful marketing strategy. This chapter covers how to analyze competition in terms of competitors' objectives, strategies, and capabilities, and most important, how to predict future actions.

5. **Customer Analysis.** At the core of modern thinking about marketing is a customer orientation. In this chapter, we discuss the key information required to monitor customer behavior.

6. **Market Potential and Sales Forecasting.** In this chapter, we describe methods for estimating the potential size of a market and predicting future levels of sales and/or market share.

7. **Developing Marketing Strategy.** Rather than leaving the reader "hanging" after the discussion of the situation analysis, we have included a chapter outlining how the concepts developed earlier in the book can be used to develop a marketing strategy.

We have incorporated several changes into this sixth edition:

- We have expanded the chapter on customer analysis (Chapter 5). Since customers are both the key to a successful business and at the core of marketing, we felt some additional material was warranted. This includes some newer material such as the lifetime value of a customer.

- We also expanded the discussion of marketing strategy (Chapter 7). We present a measure of brand equity based on sales and prices and discuss customer-based strategy (acquisition, retention, expansion, and deletion).

- Of course, any marketing book has to include the Internet. Although the core of a product manager's job has not changed, the Internet has certainly affected a number of activities. The outline of the marketing plan, for example, now has sections for website design.

- One of the features readers liked best about the earlier editions is the pair of running examples. The two examples in the sixth edition are energy bars and personal digital assistants (PDAs).

Acknowledgements

We would like to acknowledge our former students at Columbia, Vanderbilt, Berkeley and NYU who have stimulated our thoughts and given us incentive to improve our understanding of marketing planning. Over the years, we have received valuable comments from the reviewers and colleagues at our current schools and other universities. We also want to thank our team at McGraw-Hill—Barrett Koger, Scott Becker, and Kristin Puscas. As always, we thank our families for their patience. A special thanks also goes to Kris Lehmann for her outstanding editorial and word processing assistance.

We hope you find the book useful.

Donald R. Lehmann
drl2@columbia.edu

Russell S. Winer
winer@stern.nyu.edu

About the Authors

Donald R. Lehmann

Donald R. Lehmann is George E. Warren Professor of Business at the Columbia University Graduate School of Business. He has a BS degree in mathematics from Union College, Schenectady, New York, and an MSIA and PhD from the Krannert School of Purdue University.

His research interests include modeling individual and group choice and decision making, empirical generalizations and meta-analysis, the introduction and adoption of new products and innovations, and measuring the value of marketing assets such as brands and customers. He has taught courses in marketing, management, and statistics at Columbia, and has also taught at Cornell, Dartmouth, New York University, and the University of Pennsylvania. He has published in and served on the editorial boards of *Journal of Consumer Research, Journal of Marketing, Journal of Marketing Research, Management Science,* and *Marketing Science,* and was founding editor of *Marketing Letters.* In addition to numerous journal articles, he has published several books including *Market Research and Analysis, Analysis for Marketing Planning, Product Management,* and *Meta Analysis in Marketing.* Professor Lehmann has served as Executive Director of the Marketing Science Institute and as President of the Association for Consumer Research.

Russell S. Winer

Russell S. Winer is the Deputy Dean and William Joyce Professor of Marketing at the Stern School of Business, New York University. He received a B.A. in Economics from Union College and an M.S. and Ph.D. in Industrial Administration from Carnegie Mellon University. He has been on the faculties of Columbia and Vanderbilt universities and, most recently, the University of California at Berkeley. He has been a visiting faculty member at M.I.T., Stanford University, New York University, Cranfield School of Management (U.K.), the Helsinki School of Economics, the University of Tokyo, and École Nationale des Ponts et Chausées. He has written three books, *Marketing Management, Analysis for Marketing Planning* and *Product Management,* and has authored over 60 papers in marketing on a variety of topics including consumer choice, marketing research methodology, marketing planning, advertising, and pricing. He is a past editor of the *Journal of Marketing Research,* the current co-editor of the *Journal of Interactive Marketing,* and is on the editorial boards of the *Journal of Marketing,* the *Journal of Marketing Research,* and *Marketing Science.* He has participated in executive education programs around the world, and is currently an advisor to a number of startup companies.

Marketing Planning

Overview

Definition and Objectives of Plans

Developing a marketing plan is a key activity. In fact, some people believe the development of the annual marketing plan is the single most important activity of a product manager (Stasch and Lanktree, 1980).

Marketing planning has become a major activity in most firms. A survey by Hulbert, Lehmann, and Hoenig (1987) found that over 90 percent of marketing executives engaged in formal planning. These executives spent, on average, 45 days each year on planning, relying most heavily on information from the sales force, management information systems, and internal marketing research. The development of marketing plans, which are generally annual and focus on a product or one or more product lines, is thus an important function for marketers, one that is believed to improve both coordination and performance.

The marketing plan can be divided into two general parts: the situation analysis, which analyzes the background of the market for the product, and the objectives, strategy, and programs based on the background analysis that direct the firm's actions. While most books and the popular press concentrate on the latter, incorrect or inadequate analysis often leads to poor decisions about pricing, advertising, and the like. The next few chapters of this book are devoted to the critical task of providing the analysis on which to base an action plan—in short, the marketing homework.

What is a marketing plan? A working definition is:

A **marketing plan** is a *written* document containing the guidelines for the *business center's* marketing programs and allocations over the *planning period*.

Several parts of this definition have been emphasized and merit further explanation. First, note that the plan is a *written* document, not something stored in a marketing manager's head. This characteristic of marketing plans produces multiple benefits. Requiring that the plan be written calls for disciplined thinking. It also ensures that prior strategies that succeeded or failed are not forgotten. In addition, a written plan provides a vehicle for communications between functional areas of the firm, such as manufacturing, finance, and sales, which is vital to the successful implementation

FIGURE 1.1 Time Horizons for Marketing Plans

Time Period	Consumer Products	Industrial Products	Services
1 year	62%	45%	65%
3 years	5	5	8
5 years	15	17	3
Long term	4	3	6
Indefinite	0	2	2
Other	14	28	16

Source: Howard Sutton, *The Marketing Plan in the 1990s* (New York: The Conference Board, 1990), p. 25.

of the plan. Also, a written marketing plan pinpoints responsibility for achieving results by a specified date. Finally, a written plan provides continuity when management turnover occurs (a significant issue for many managerial positions) and quickly introduces new employees to the situation facing the business.

A second aspect of the marketing plan definition to note is that it is usually written at the *business center* level. This is purposely vague because the precise level at which plans are written varies from organization to organization. For example, in a company using a brand management organizational structure, a marketing plan is written for each brand that is (at least nominally) a profit center. Alternatively, some companies write plans for groups of brands or products, particularly when fixed costs are difficult to allocate by individual product. Thus, while marketing planning is common, it occurs at different organizational levels. In this book, we focus on specific products or closely related product lines.

For example, Kraft develops a separate marketing plan for each brand of cereal marketed by the Post Division, such as Raisin Bran. Alternatively, one medical equipment company develops an overall marketing plan for reagents, the chemicals added to blood before it is analyzed, despite the fact that many different reagents exist. The reagents are grouped by application type, and parts of the overall reagent marketing plan are devoted to each group.

A final item to note from the definition of a marketing plan is that the *planning period* or horizon varies from product to product. Retailing, for example, traditionally has short planning cycles to match seasonality and the vagaries of fashion trends. Industrial firms and firms manufacturing consumer durables tend, more so than frequently purchased consumer product or service firms, to have longer than annual marketing plans. Automobiles, for example, have longer planning cycles because lead times for product development or modifications are longer, when there are long lead times, the plan covers several years with annual updates and the focus becomes broader than tactical issues such as promotion.[1] Other factors contributing to variation in the length of planning horizons are rates of technological change, intensity of competition, and frequency of shifts in the tastes of relevant groups of customers. The typical horizon, however, is annual, as the data in Figure 1.1 indicate.

[1] For the auto companies with brand management systems, the planning horizons could be shorter. Importantly, cycle times for new models are diminishing.

FIGURE 1.2   **Hierarchy of Planning**

Corporate
strategic
planning

Group or
sector
planning

SBU
planning

Annual
marketing
(business)
plan

The Internet has had a substantial impact on the planning cycle times. "Internet time" has come to mean that planning assumptions are often voided quickly by changes in the economic environment (e.g., how much venture capital is available), the number of competitors, regulatory shifts (e.g., privacy, Napster-type disputes on copyright protection), and technological change. Thus, the data in Figure 1.1 are perhaps somewhat out-of-date. Even if plans currently have similar horizons, there is a substantial need for frequent updates.

Often there is confusion between *strategic* planning and *marketing* planning, which are distinct in two ways. First, strategic planning usually takes place at a higher level in the organization than marketing planning. As Figure 1.2 shows, strategic planning takes place at the corporate, group, or strategic business unit levels. At these levels, objectives are broad (e.g., return on investment or assets) and strategies are general (e.g., Westinghouse divesting of manufacturing nuclear power generating plants and Disney purchasing the television network ABC). Marketing planning takes place at the business center level and has specific objectives (e.g., market share) and strategies (e.g., pursuing the small-business segment). A second difference is that, due to the long-term nature of strategic plans, they usually have a longer time horizon than marketing plans; a horizon of three to five years or more with annual updates is not uncommon.

In summary, the marketing plan is an operational document. It contains strategies for a product, but it focuses on a shorter time span than the strategic plan.

Marketing plans are specific statements of how to achieve short-term, usually annual, results.

The objectives of a marketing plan can be stated concisely as follows:

1. To define the current situation facing the product (and how we got there).
2. To define problems and opportunities facing the business.
3. To establish objectives.
4. To define the strategies and programs necessary to achieve the objectives.
5. To pinpoint responsibility for achieving product objectives.
6. To encourage careful and disciplined thinking.
7. To establish a market orientation.

The last objective is particularly important. Most marketing managers are aware of the *marketing concept* popularized in the 1960s, dictating that marketers must develop strategies that maintain a customer orientation. This customer orientation was reinforced in the 1980s by Peters and Waterman's book *In Search of Excellence* and the total quality management (TQM) movement. Today the marketing concept has been translated into a strong focus on customer retention and service. Less commonly acknowledged is the fact that a *competitor* orientation, especially in today's business environment of more competitors and shorter life cycles, is equally important. In recent years, a few books with the word *warfare* in their titles have focused on the competitive nature of marketing (see, for example, Ries and Trout, 1986). The vast majority of products and services are not monopolies; competitors often determine a brand's profits as much as any action taken by the marketing managers. In addition, in fast-moving Web-based product categories, the competitors' actions change virtually daily and need to be monitored. By emphasizing the importance of having both a customer orientation and a competitor orientation, the marketing plan focuses on the two most important components of the strategy development process. This is consistent with recent research at the firm level showing that a significant and positive relationship exists between a firm's degree of market orientation (as measured by customer and competitor orientation plus interfunctional coordination) and performance (Deshpandé, 1999). One would think that, at this point in time, all companies would be interested in researching their customers and competitors. However, a study by Day and Nedungadi (1994) suggested that a large percentage of companies do not study either customers or competitors. In their sample, 41 percent of the companies admitted to paying little attention to what customers believe or what competitors are doing. Another 30 percent studied only customers and 13 percent studied only competitors. Thus, only 16 percent of the companies in their sample analyzed both customers and competitors.

Frequent Mistakes in the Planning Process

Unfortunately, not all organizations attempting to develop marketing plans have been pleased with the process. The Strategic Planning Institute and the authors have identified the most common mistakes in planning (generally defined) that are relevant to marketing planning as well.

The Speed of the Process The planning process can either be so slow that it seems to go on forever or so fast that managers rush out a plan in a burst of activity. In the former case, managers required to constantly complete forms that distract them from operational tasks burn out. In the latter case, a hastily developed plan can easily lead to critical oversights that impede the strategies developed.

The Amount of Data Collected It is important to collect sufficient data to properly estimate customer needs and competitive trends. However, as in many other situations, the law of diminishing marginal returns quickly sets in on data collection. Usually a small percentage of all the data available produces a large percentage of the insights obtainable. What is the "right" amount of information? Although we could say that product managers ought to collect about 10 pounds of magazine articles or visit 187 websites, no prescription for data collection effort would be sensible. One of the purposes of this book is to point managers toward the most important areas for data collection to avoid both under- and over-collecting information.

Who Does the Planning? In the late 1960s, strategic planning models developed by the Boston Consulting Group, McKinsey & Company, General Electric, Shell Petroleum, and others led to the formation of formal strategic planning groups in many major corporations. Essentially the planning process was delegated to professional planners, while implementation of the plans was left to line managers. Naturally, line managers resented the process. They thought the planners had no "feel" for the markets for which they were planning, and were managing by the numbers rather than considering market intuition gleaned from experience. As a result, hostility between the staff planners and line managers led to strategies that were either poorly implemented or ignored. Presently, poor results from staff-directed planning and recent economic recessions have led to cuts in non revenue-producing jobs, making line managers get more involved with planning, both strategic and marketing. At many successful companies, such as Emerson Electric, "the people who plan are the people who execute" (Knight, 1992). Besides leaving planning to those who will implement the plans, it is important to involve managers from other functions in the firm. This helps to ensure buy-in from all relevant parties.

The Structure Any formal planning effort involves some structure. The advantage of structure is that it forces discipline on the planners; that is, certain data must be collected and analyzed. Interestingly, many firms believe the most important result of planning is not the plan itself but the necessity of structuring thought about the strategic issues facing the business. However, an apparent danger is that the structure can take precedence over the content so that planning becomes mere form filling or number crunching with little thought for its purposes. Thus, although there must be enough structure, the process should not be too bureaucratic. A good solution to this dilemma is to use the plan format shown in the appendix to this chapter as a guide but to set a rigid timetable. A flexible format helps to prevent the plan from deteriorating into mindless paper shuffling.

Length of the Plan The length of a marketing plan must be balanced, neither so long that both line and senior managers ignore it nor so brief that it omits key

FIGURE 1.3 Lengths of Marketing Plans

Length	Consumer Products	Industrial Products	Services
10 pages or fewer	28%	23%	26%
11–20	17	22	22
21–30	18	11	15
31–50	21	17	12
51 or more	16	27	24

Source: Howard Sutton, *The Marketing Plan in the 1990s* (New York: The Conference Board, 1990), p. 25.

details. Many organizations have formal guidelines for the optimal length of plans (similar to Procter & Gamble's dreaded one-page limit on memos), so what is long for one firm may be optimal for another.

Figure 1.3 provides some data on lengths of plans. The data show an interesting U-shaped pattern: Many plans are 20 pages or fewer, and many are 51 pages or more. However, the median lengths are 30 pages for industrial products, 25 for consumer products, and 21 for service businesses. Thus, typical marketing plans are between 20 and 30 pages in length.

Frequency of Planning A potential problem occurs if an organization plans either more or less frequently than necessary. Frequent reevaluation of strategies can lead to erratic firm behavior and make the planning process more burdensome. However, if plans are not revised as needed, the product's marketing strategies may not adapt quickly enough to changes in the environment, and its competitive position may deteriorate. This has become increasingly apparent in the Internet age. Often a company adopts its fiscal year as its planning cycle. Sometimes it is difficult to determine the appropriate planning interval with precision. However, after several planning cycles and some experimentation, the appropriate amount of time becomes apparent.

Number of Courses of Action Considered Too few alternatives may be discussed, thus raising the likelihood of failure, or too many, which increases the time and cost of the planning effort. It is important to have diverse strategic options (e.g., both growth and hold strategies) because discarded strategies often prove useful as contingency plans. In fact, one job of a marketing manager is to prioritize possible marketing strategies at a given point in time. The most appropriate strategy clearly should be implemented first, and the others should become contingency plans.

Who Sees the Plan The successful implementation of a marketing plan requires a broad consensus from as many corporate departments as possible. Increasing the "buy-in" to the marketing plan increases its likelihood of success. For example, a strategy emphasizing high quality is difficult to implement if manufacturing does not simultaneously emphasize quality control. Growth objectives may be achievable only by relaxing credit policies. A common mistake is to view the plan as the proprietary possession of the marketing department.

Not Using the Plan as a Sales Document A major but often overlooked purpose of a plan is to generate funds from either internal sources (e.g., to gain budget approval) or external sources (e.g., to gain a partner for a joint venture or to secure venture capital financing). The plan and its proponents compete with other plans and their proponents for scarce resources. Therefore, the more appealing the plan and the better the product managers' track records, the better the chance of budget approval.

Insufficient Senior Management Leadership   As with many intrafirm programs, commitment from senior management is essential to the success of a marketing planning effort. Mere training is insufficient. One organization with which we are familiar did and said all the right things about implementing a marketing planning process, but frequent turnover of marketing vice presidents with different backgrounds, values, and attitudes toward the development of marketing plans prevented a successful planning effort.

Not Tying Compensation to Successful Planning Efforts   Managers are usually driven by their compensation plans. Compensation should be oriented toward the achievement of the objectives stated in the plan. If the organization rewards profit margins and the negotiated objective of the plan is market share, a fundamental conflict will arise that will lead to a concentration on margins rather than on what is best for the product at that time.

What Makes a Good Planning System: Some Empirical Results

Although few systematic studies of marketing planning systems have been published, some useful guidelines for improving planning have appeared in the marketing literature. A major component of a good marketing planning system is its thoroughness. A marketing planning process is considered to be thorough if it does the following (Stasch and Lanktree, 1980):

1. Utilizes experience from several managerial levels rather than just from product managers. Particularly in organizations in which senior marketing managers have risen through the ranks, considerable knowledge exists of past successful and unsuccessful product marketing strategies.
2. Employs a variety of both internal and external sources of information rather than just internal information. For example, the advertising agency working on the product account can often be a valuable source of information.
3. Extends over a period of time sufficient to collect and analyze the data necessary for developing the marketing strategies.
4. Employs a number of incentives for managers in addition to employment security or advancement.

Is Planning Worthwhile?

Again, few studies empirically link the quality of planning systems to performance as measured in terms of higher profitability or increased market share. One study found that strategic planning in general is not positively related to levels of performance, but firms with formal planning systems have less variation in profitability than those without them (Capon, Farley and Hulbert, 1988). Using a sample of six firms, another study found a generally positive relationship between the thoroughness of the marketing planning effort and various performance measures (Stasch and Lanktree, 1980). Although it is difficult to directly relate marketing planning to improved market performance, most managers believe planning provides intangible benefits such as a disciplined approach to strategy development and the assurance that the external environment is adequately considered.

THE PLANNING PROCESS

Approaches to Planning

In general, the planning process works as shown in Figure 1.4. Whereas the collection and analysis of data and the development of product strategies take place over a limited time frame, there is no beginning or ending to the planning process as a whole. The formal part of the process is followed by implementation, during which programs such as distribution, promotion, advertising, and the like are executed. Monitoring and evaluating both the performance of the plan and changes in competition or customers in the external environment are also continuous tasks. This information feeds back into the formal planning part of the process. This circular aspect of marketing planning ensures that the plan is not "cast in stone" and can be revised as necessary. It also guarantees that information obtained from the market concerning the performance of the plan is integrated into next year's plan.

Two general approaches to planning have been developed. In *top-down* planning, the marketing plans are formulated by either senior or middle management with the aid of staff and product management and then implemented by the latter. In *bottom-up* planning, the lower ranks down to field salespeople are actively

FIGURE 1.4 **The Planning Process**

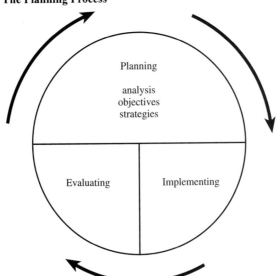

Source: Mary Ann Pezzullo, *Marketing for Bankers* (American Bankers Association, 1982), Washington, D.C. p. 32.

involved in the planning process through collecting competitor and customer information and making forecasts. The information is subject to higher-level review, but lower management personnel play key roles in the process.

Both systems have some commendable characteristics. The rationale often used for top-down planning is that higher level people in the organization, have better perspective on the problems facing the business. Field salespeople, for example, tend to consider the competitive battleground as their sales territories and not necessarily the national or international market. Bottom-up planning systems are often characterized by better implementation than top-down approaches, since the people primarily charged with executing the plan are involved in its development.

Steps in the Planning Process

In most organizations, collecting information and structuring the marketing plan require a sequential planning process. This process generally includes eight steps, as shown in Figure 1.5.

FIGURE 1.5 **Marketing Planning Sequence**

Update historical data

Collect current situation data

Data analysis

Develop objectives, strategies, programs

Develop financial documents

Negotiate final plan

Measure progress toward objectives

Audit

Step 1: Update the facts about the past. Data collected for marketing planning purposes are often provisional or estimated. For example, planning for 2005 takes place in 2004. At that time, annual data on market sales or share would be available only for 2003 at best and often only for 2002 or even earlier due to delays in the data collection process. As a result, planners often use forecasts or extrapolations of partial results. However, when new data become available, they should replace figures that were estimated or forecasted.

Step 2: Collect background data. Data collection focuses on information available about the current situation, which forms the situation analysis part of the plan. Again, lags in collecting data about an industry or product category mean that the time period of the data often does not match the period of analysis.

Step 3: Analyze historical and background data. Analyze the existing data to forecast competitors' actions, the behavior of customers, economic conditions, and so forth. Such an analysis need not be quantitative; in fact, as later chapters show, much of the analysis is qualitative and draws implications from non-numerical data. This analysis leads to delineating key opportunities and threats to the business.

Step 4: Develop objectives, strategies, and action programs. Use the implications drawn from the background data (see step 3) to formulate objectives, strategies, and marketing mix decisions. This is, in fact, the critical activity of the planning process because it outlines in detail what will be done with the product during the year (or the appropriate planning period). However, the order of the steps indicates that logical strategic thinking cannot be done without considering the facts at hand.

Objectives, strategies, and mix decisions are constrained by the company's mission, objectives and strategy, policies, resources, and legal considerations, among other factors. Thus, this part of the process generally involves (1) setting product objectives; (2) developing strategies and programs to achieve the objectives, (3) comparing programs in terms of their abilities to achieve objectives (e.g., market share) within the bounds of company policies and legal constraints, and (4) selecting a basic objective, strategy, and program combination.

Step 5: Develop pro forma financial statements. Such statements typically include budgets and profit-and-loss figures.

Step 6: Negotiate. Rarely, if ever, is the marketing plan generated from steps 1 to 5 implemented without several rounds of negotiations with senior management. In a brand management organizational structure, the plans themselves must be marketed both inside and outside marketing as managers compete for their desired portions of corporate or divisional resources. In large organizations, this negotiation process can last as long as all the prior steps.

Step 7: Measure progress. To correct the plan if the environment changes within the planning period, progress toward stated objectives must be monitored. This implies that marketing research and other information relevant to measuring the quantities stated as objectives (e.g., market share or sales) must continue to be collected.

Step 8: Audit. After a planning period, it is customary to determine variances of planned versus actual results and sources of the variances. This audit provides important diagnostic information for both current and future planning efforts and thus acts as a source of feedback on the planning effort.

The planning sequence is therefore a logical flow of events leading from data collection and analysis to strategy formulation to auditing the performance of the plan. It implies that sound strategic thinking cannot occur unless the manager has used all available information to draw implications about future market conditions.

COMPONENTS OF THE MARKETING PLAN

Although nearly every firm has its own format (see Hopkins, 1981, and Sutton, 1990, for examples), most marketing plans do have a common set of elements. The appendix to this chapter provides a sample marketing plan outline, which is summarized in Figure 1.6. This outline describes the major areas of analysis and data collection required for a "typical" marketing plan. The rationale and a brief description of each major component of the plan follow, giving an overview of the plan and a context for the planning chapters of the book.[2]

The Executive Summary

A senior manager often must review many marketing plans, so a brief summary of the marketing plan focusing on the objectives, strategies, and expected financial performance is necessary. This brief overview is useful for quickly reviewing the major elements of the plan and easily comparing product plans.

If the plan is being used as a business plan for a new product or service (e.g., an Internet-based service), the Executive Summary is crucial. In this case, other relevant information includes the business model (that is, how revenues will be generated), the amount of money needed from investors, how the money will be spent, key management, and a summary of the financial projections.

Situation Analysis

The Situation Analysis contains the data and concomitant analysis vital to developing sound marketing strategies. It is the "homework" part of the marketing plan; no strategy should be developed without first analyzing the product category in which the product competes. The Situation Analysis is composed of six major parts.

The first major section of the Situation Analysis is the definition of the competitor set or *category definition*. This involves identifying both close and distant competitors and then prioritizing them. This is an important place to start because the definition of your competitors impacts much of what follows.

The *category analysis* identifies factors that significantly impact the attractiveness of a product category (or industry if more appropriate) in which the product competes at a given point in time. Since all markets are dynamic in that

---

[2] Marketing planning software with predesigned planning formats is also available from Business Resource Software (*www.brs-inc.com*) and Palo Alto Software (*www.palo-alto.com*).

FIGURE 1.6 Marketing Plan Summary

I. Executive Summary
II. Situation Analysis
    A. Category/competitor definition
    B. Category analysis
    C. Company and competitor analysis
    D. Customer analysis
    E. Planning assumptions
III. Objectives
IV. Product/Brand Strategy
V. Supporting Marketing Programs
VI. Financial Documents
VII. Monitors and Controls
VIII. Contingency Plans

competitors, customers, technology, and sales growth rates change, the underlying attractiveness of a product category as a target for investment can also change.

Given the definition of the category, *competitor analysis* asks who the key competitors are in the market and what their likely future strategies are. Competitor analysis is becoming an increasingly important activity. A critical section of the competitor analysis component is what is often termed a *resource analysis* or self-assessment. By comparing the product to its key competitors, the strengths and weaknesses become clear.

The aim of the *customer analysis* is to guarantee that the product manager retains a customer focus at all times. This customer focus is critical to success in today's competitive marketplace. It is vital to understand not only who the customers are but also how and why they behave the way they do. As can be seen from the outline, quite a number of issues have to be resolved here.

The fifth part of the background assessment deals with a wide variety of *planning assumptions*. First, the product's market potential is a key number in making decisions about expected future category growth, resource allocation, and many other areas. Market and product forecasts and assumptions about uncontrollable factors, such as raw materials or labor supply, are also relevant.

As noted earlier, the background assessment is the homework to be done before formulating marketing objectives and strategies. It may be more enjoyable to develop the marketing strategy for a product during the next planning horizon, but the preliminary data collection and analysis are more vital because drawing implications from the background data often makes the optimal strategies apparent.

Marketing Objectives/Strategy

It is logical to follow the background assessment by the strategy portion of the plan, which includes two sections: a statement of marketing objectives (where do we want to go?) and the marketing strategy itself (how are we going to get there?).

Supporting Marketing Programs

This is the implementation part of the plan. Decisions about pricing, channels of distribution, customer service programs, advertising, and other relevant marketing programs are described in this section.

An important new part of the programs part of the plan is the company's Internet plans. Even if the plan is not being developed for a stand-alone Web business, all companies today need to think about their Internet strategy. In particular, some questions need to be addressed: How will a website integrate with our existing business? Who are the targets of the site? How can we use the website for customer retention purposes?

The Rest of the Plan

The final three parts of the marketing plan do not form a cohesive unit, but they are nevertheless important components. The financial documents report the budgets and pro forma profit-and-loss (P&L) or income statements. Senior managers, naturally, inspect the expected financial outcome carefully. In fact, the P&L statements are often the key element in securing approval for the plan. The monitors and controls section specifies the type of marketing research and other information necessary to measure progress toward achieving the stated objectives. The kind of information collected depends on the objectives; for example, if a market share increase is the objective, information must be collected in time to check for possible shortfalls. Finally, contingency plans are helpful, particularly in dynamic markets where either new products or new competitors create the need for changes in strategy before the end of the plan's horizon. These contingencies are often previously considered strategies that were discarded.

Example

Figure 1.7 shows a planning form at for Sonesta Hotels.[3] As can be seen, this company limits the plan to 20 pages, excluding exhibits. Sections IV, V, and VI cover the situation analysis. The rest of the plan describes the marketing objectives, strategies, and action programs. Note the separate objective, strategy, and program sections for different market segments (group and transient customers) and products (food and beverage). Clearly, advertising and public relations are viewed as very important to the hotel industry because they merit distinct sections of the plan. In general, the two major parts of the plan—the situation analysis and the objectives, strategies, and programs—are covered well by this structure. This company's plan differs from the general format previously described in several ways. For example, the company prefers an initial description of its differential advantage over competitors (Section II), as opposed to discussing this as part of the product positioning. In addition, as can be seen from the home page of the company's website (Figure 1.8), Sonesta integrated an Internet strategy (Section V of the plan) into its marketing plans by establishing a "Web Club" for building a community around the brand. This is now standard practice.

[3] Other examples of marketing plans appear in Willam A. Cohen, *The Marketing Plan,* 2nd ed. (New York: John Wiley & Sons, 1997).

FIGURE 1.7 Sonesta Hotels Marketing Plan Outline

***Note: Please keep the plan concise—Maximum of 20 pages plus summary pages. Include title page and table of contents. Number all pages.

I. *Introduction.* Set the stage for the plan. Specifically identify marketing objectives such as "increase average rate," "more group business," "greater occupancy," or "penetrate new markets." Identify particular problems.

II. *Marketing Position.* Begin with a single statement that presents a consumer benefit in a way that distinguishes us from the competition.

III. *The Product.* Identify all facility and service changes that occurred last year and are planned for next year.

IV. *Marketplace Overview.* Briefly describe what is occurring in your marketplace that might impact your business or marketing strategy, such as the economy, the competitive situation, etc.

V. *The Competition.* Briefly identify your primary competition (3 or fewer) specifying number of rooms, what is new in their facilities, and marketing and pricing strategy.

VI. *Marketing Data*
   A. Identify top 5 geographic areas for transient business, with percentages of total room nights compared to the previous year.
   B. Briefly describe the guests at your hotel, considering age, sex, occupation, what they want, why they come, etc.
   C. Identify market segments with percentage of business achieved in each segment in current years (actual and projected) and project for next year.

VII. *Strategy by Market Segment*
   A. Group
      1. *Objectives:* Identify what you specifically wish to achieve in this segment. (For example, more high-rated businesses, more weekend business, larger groups).
      2. *Strategy:* Identify how sales, advertising and public relations will work together to reach the objectives.
      3. *Sales Activities:* Divide by specific market segments.
         a. Corporate
         b. Association
         c. Incentives
         d. Travel agent
         e. Tours
         f. Other
         Under each category include a narrative description of specific sales activities geared toward each market segment, including geographically targeted areas, travel plans, group site inspections, correspondence, telephone solicitation and trade shows. Be specific on action plans, and designate responsibility and target months.
      4. *Sales Materials:* Identify all items, so they will be budgeted.
      5. *Direct Mail:* Briefly describe the direct mail program planned, including objectives, message, and content. Identify whether we will use existing material or create a new piece.
      6. *Research:* Indicate any research projects you plan to conduct next year, identifying what you wish to learn.

FIGURE 1.7   Sonesta Hotels Marketing Plan Outline—*continued*

    B. Transient (The format here should be the same as group throughout)
      1. *Objective*
      2. *Strategy*
      3. *Sales Activities:* Divide by specific segments.
        a. Consumer (rack rate)
        b. Corporate (prime and other)
        c. Travel Agent: business, leisure, consortia
        d. Wholesale/Airline/Tour (foreign & domestic)
        e. Packages (specify names of packages)
        f. Government/Military/Education
        g. Special Interest/Other
      4. *Sales Materials*
      5. *Direct Mail*
      6. *Research*
    C. Other Sonesta Hotels
    D. Local/Food & Beverage
      1. *Objectives*
      2. *Strategy*
      3. *Sales Activities:* Divide by specific market segments.
        a. Restaurant and Lounge, external promotion
        b. Restaurant and Lounge, internal promotion
        c. Catering
        d. Community Relation/Other
      4. *Sales Materials* (e.g., banquet menus, signage, etc.)
      5. *Direct Mail*
      6. *Research*

VIII. *Advertising*
    A. Subdivide advertising by market segment and campaign, paralleling the sales activities (group, transient, F&B).
    B. Describe objectives of each advertising campaign, identifying whether it should be promotional (immediate bookings) or image (long-term awareness).
    C. Briefly describe contents of advertising, identifying key benefits to promote.
    D. Identify target media by location and type (e.g., newspaper, magazine, radio, etc.).
    E. Indicate percent of the advertising budget to be allocated to each market segment.

IX. *Public Relations*
    A. Describe objectives of public relations as it supports the sales and marketing priorities.
    B. Write a brief statement of overall goals by market segment paralleling the sales activities. Identify what proportion on your effort will be spent on each segment.

X. *Summary:* Close the plan with general statement concerning the major challenges you will face in upcoming year and how you will overcome these challenges.

Source: Howard Sutton, *The Marketing Plan in the 1990s* (New York: The Conference Board, 1990), pp. 34–35.

FIGURE 1.8 Sonesta Hotels Website

TWO CASE STUDIES

In Chapters 2 through 6, we illustrate the concepts presented with two running examples. In these examples, objectives and strategies will be developed from background analyses. Because most product strategies, particularly those in high-technology industries, are subject to considerable change, the two examples are meant to illustrate the use of background analyses for developing the marketing plan; they do not necessarily provide current data about the products and brands involved.

Energy Bars (ca. 2002)[4]

One of the segments of the broad snack bar category is energy bars. Snack bars include such items as granola bars while health bars include, for example, cereal or diet bars. Energy bars are defined as vitamin-enriched, nutritious bars intended either to boost performance or replenish nutrients following exercise or as a complete snack or meal replacement. The energy bar category is highly fragmented with over 100 competitors and 700 brands. There are several subcategories such as energy/endurance, functional/

---

[4] This illustration is based on Monica Brown, Eleanor Huang, Jennifer Okanes, and Jennifer Wickland, "Odwalla Bar Marketing Plan," Haas School of Business, University of California at Berkeley, 2002.

nutritional, diet/weight loss, and high protein/body building. PowerBar, Balance Bar, Luna Bar, and Clif Bar are major competitors in the energy bar category.

Overall snack bar sales were over $1.4 billion in 2002; of this, energy bars were nearly $300 million with a 28 percent growth rate over 2001. Industry experts expect the energy bar category to continue to grow in the 25–30 percent range annually.

Some marketing mix information about the energy bar category is the following. Price ranges between $1 and $3 per bar. The typical price in the grocery and drugstore channel is $1.39. More specialized bars such as Ultra Low Carb and high protein tend to be priced at the higher end of the range. Promotion in this category has been the primary form of communications with sponsorships, sampling, and in-store activities being favored. Distribution for the category has expanded significantly over the last five years with the largest players in the market gaining national distribution in grocery, natural foods, drug, mass, and even club stores.

Due to the high growth rate in the category, established companies such as Nestlé, Kraft, and Kellogg's recognized the potential and acquired PowerBar, Balance Bar, and Kashi, respectively, in 2000. Coca-Cola/Minute Maid acquired Odwalla at the end of 2001, primarily for its juice business rather than for the energy bar brand. Clif Bar has decided to remain independent.

Our analyses will be conducted from the perspective of Odwalla Bar. The brand's website is shown in Figure 1.9. Odwalla Inc. was founded in 1980 to create socially

FIGURE 1.9 **Odwalla Bar Website**

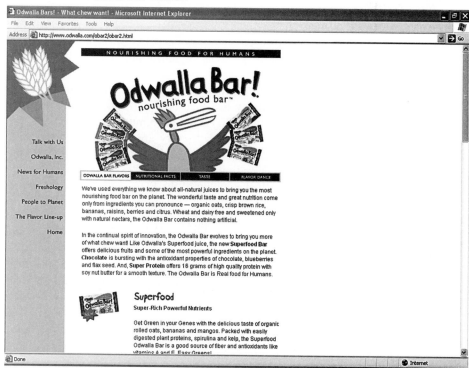

FIGURE 1.10 Reference Sources for the Energy Bar Category

AC Nielsen SPINS 2000
Advertising Age
Confectioner magazine
Consumer focus groups
Information Resources Incorporated
Interviews with category brand managers
Mintel International Group

responsible products that nourished the body with natural ingredients. After establishing a popular line of natural juices and juice-based drinks, Odwalla introduced the brand extension in the energy bar category in 1998. Although market share is difficult to determine since many energy bars are sold by retailers such as REI which sells outdoor and related enthusiast products, as of late 2002, Odwalla was the sixth-best selling bar. Sources of information used for this illustration are shown in Figure 1.10.

Personal Digital Assistants (ca. 1999)[5]

A growing need for smaller and lighter mobile computing devices to organize and store personal data and to communicate while on the road has created a market for a class of electronic devices known as personal digital assistants (PDAs). Often called by other names such as high-end electronic organizers, palmtop computers, and personal communicators, PDAs are handheld computers that combine communications, personal organization, and word processing capabilities.

PDAs generally weigh less than one pound, measure less than four inches by seven inches by one inch, and display less than one-fourth the number of pixels of a subnotebook personal computer (PC) (they have much smaller screens and less brightness). Device navigation and data entry are accomplished by using either a built-in miniature keyboard or a penlike stylus. Some PDAs support both methods of input. The well-publicized introduction in 1993 of the Apple Newton MessagePad essentially marked the beginning of the PDA product category (electronic personal organizers existed prior to 1993). However, the Newton failed in the marketplace due to a combination of high price and a set of features that did not match needs of any particular segment. Similar products by Sharp, Casio, and AT&T met the same fate.

In 1996, the market was changed dramatically by the introduction of the Palm Pilot from the Palm division of 3Com Corporation. The Pilot's designers were

[5] This illustration is based on Caroline Chi, Juan Eraso, Jennifer Lee, Mei Mei, and Frederik Pettersson, "VISOR 2000: Marketing Plan for the Year 2000," Haas School of Business, University of California at Berkeley, 1999, and Joe Conley, "Handspring Visor," Graduate School of Business, Stanford University, 2000.

FIGURE 1.11 **PDA Sales Growth**

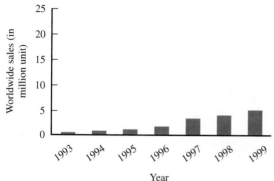

Source: *Computer Reseller News,* May 31, 1999.

determined to keep the device small, light, and inexpensive—even if that meant giving up advanced features such as e-mail and faxes. The product was designed to do the following:

- Fit in a shirt pocket.
- Perform instantly.
- Synchronize its calendar and database seamlessly with a desktop computer by pushing just one button.
- Be useful right out of the box.

To keep the price down, the product was also designed for easy manufacturing. For example, while organizers from Sharp and Casio would use between 8 and 15 screws of different sizes, the Palm Pilot used only 3—reducing part costs and complexity.

The success of the Palm Pilot was instantaneous. While Newton sales reached a total of 150,000 units by the end of 1995, Palm Pilot sales were 360,000 units in 1996 and increased to 1.2 million in 1998. The sales growth of the total PDA category through 1999 is shown in Figure 1.11. PDAs use two competing operating system platforms: the Palm OS and PocketPC (formerly Windows CE) made by Microsoft. Market shares (as of 1997) of the leading brands are shown in Figure 1.12.

In July 1998, the original Palm Pilot creators left 3Com and formed a company called Handspring. Handspring was in the business of designing and marketing PDAs that utilize attachable modules to expand, enhance, and personalize the functionality and experience that a customer has with the PDA.[6] Our analysis will take the perspective of Handspring's first product, the Visor, which was introduced in 1999. Sources used in this illustration are shown in Figure 1.13.

---

[6] In this context, a module is a piece of hardware that is attached to a PDA and contains software that enables some specific functionality such as a modem or a game.

FIGURE 1.12   **Market Share for U.S. Palmtop Market (1997)**

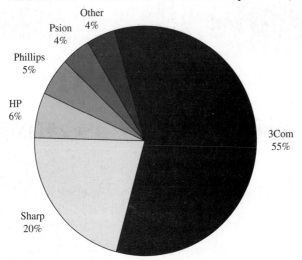

Source: Dataquest in article from *Forbes,* July 5, 1999, p. 122.

Clearly, the market for PDAs has changed significantly since 1999. In 2003, Handspring was acquired by its original parent, Palm, to form PalmOne. PalmOne sells the most popular PDA brand, the Tungsten, as well as the Treo, which was originally developed by Handspring. Other popular models are Hewlett-Packard's iPaq and Sony's Clié. More than 9 million PDAs were estimated to have been sold by 2004. Innovations such as smaller size and better functionality have led to a

FIGURE 1.13   **Reference Sources for the PDA Category**

Brandweek
Business Week
CNET News.com
CNN.com
Computer Reseller News
Electronic News
Forbes
Forrester Research reports
Fortune
Frost & Sullivan reports
Gartner Group reports
Handspring: *www.handspring.com*
The Industry Standard
International Data Corporation reports
OneSource Information Services
Pen Computing
San Francisco Chronicle

FIGURE 1.14 PalmOne/Handspring Website

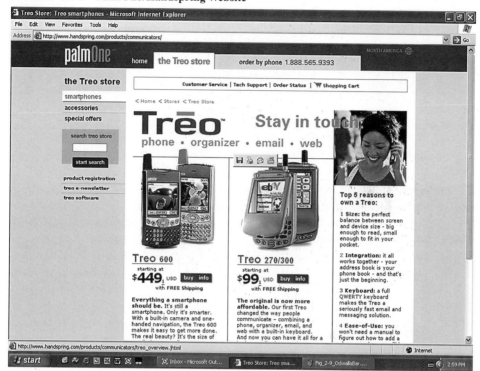

blurring of the product category lines between cellular phones and PDAs. In fact, as can be seen from the website shown in Figure 1.14, the term PDA is beginning to disappear in favor of "Smartphone." However, despite these changes, the extant category characteristics in 1999 are sufficiently similar to those currently so that the somewhat older data still provides an excellent illustration of the marketing planning tasks described in this book.

SUMMARY

The marketing plan provides a central focus for a firm's marketing activities. While product managers have responsibility for many tasks, such as arranging trade shows, checking print advertising copy, and managing distribution channel members, day-to-day tasks should have the marketing strategy as a guiding theme. This theme emanates from a careful analysis of the market, giving a marketing manager ideas on how to differentiate his or her product from the others from which customers can choose. The tasks (marketing tactics), guiding theme (marketing strategy), and analysis (situation or background analysis) are what marketing plans and planning are about.

References

Capon, Noel, John U. Farley, and James M. Hulbert (1988) *Corporate Strategic Planning*. New York: Columbia University Press.

Cohen, William A. (1997) *The Marketing Plan*, 2nd ed. New York: John Wiley & Sons.

Day, George S., and Prakash Nedungadi (1994) "Managerial Representations of Competitive Advantage." *Journal of Marketing*, April, 31–44.

Deshpandé, Robit (1999) *Developing a Market Orientation*. Thousand Oaks, CA: Sage Publications.

Hopkins, David (1981) *The Marketing Plan*. New York: The Conference Board.

Hubert, James, Donald R. Lehmann, and Scott Hoenig (1987) "Practices and Impacts of Marketing Planning." Unpublished working paper, Columbia University.

Knight, Charles (1992) "Emerson Electric: Consistent Profits, Consistently." *Harvard Business Review*, January–February, 1992, 57–70.

Ries, Al, and Jack Trout (1986) *Marketing Warfare*. New York: McGraw-Hill.

Stasch, Stanley, and Patricia Lanktree (1980) "Can Your Marketing Planning Procedures Be Improved?" *Journal of Marketing*, Summer, 79–90.

Sutton, Howard (1990) *The Marketing Plan in the 1990s*. New York: The Conference Board.

Appendix

MARKETING PLAN OUTLINE

I. *Executive Summary.* A one- to three-page synopsis of the plan providing highlights of the current situation, objectives, strategies, principal actions programs, and financial expectations.

II. *Situation Analysis*
  A. Category/competitor definition.
  B. Category analysis.
   1. Aggregate market factors.
      a. Category size.
      b. Category growth.
      c. Stage in the product life cycle.
      d. Sales cyclicity.
      e. Seasonality.
      f. Profits.
   2. Category factors.
      a. Threat of new entrants/exits.
      b. Bargaining power of buyers.
      c. Bargaining power of suppliers.
      d. Pressure from substitutes.
      e. Category capacity.
      f. Current category rivalry.
   3. Environmental factors.
      a. Technological.
      b. Political.
      c. Economic.
      d. Regulatory.
      e. Social.
  C. Company and competitor analysis.
   1. Product features matrix.
   2. Objectives.
   3. Strategies.
   4. Marketing mix.
   5. Profits.
   6. Value chain.
   7. Differential advantage/resource analysis.
      a. Ability to conceive and design new products.
      b. Ability to produce/manufacture or deliver the service.
      c. Ability to market.
      d. Ability to finance.
      e. Ability to manage.
      f. Will to succeed in this category.
   8. Expected future strategies.

    D. Customer analysis.
      1. Who are the customers?
      2. What do they buy and how do they use it?
      3. Where do they buy?
      4. When do they buy?
      5. How do they choose?
      6. Why they prefer a product.
      7. How they respond to marketing programs.
      8. Will they buy it again?
      9. Long-term value of customers.
      10. Segmentation.
    E. Planning assumptions.
      1. Market potential.
      2. Category and product sales forecasts.
      3. Other assumptions.

III. *Objectives*
    A. Corporate objectives (if appropriate).
    B. Divisional objectives (if appropriate).
    C. Marketing objective(s).
      1. Volume and profit.
      2. Time frame.
      3. Secondary objectives (e.g., brand equity, customer, new product).
      4. Program (marketing mix).

IV. *Product/Brand Strategy*
    A. Customer target(s).
    B. Competitor target(s).
    C. Product/service features.
    D. Core strategy.
      1. Value proposition.
      2. Product positioning.

V. *Supporting Marketing Programs*
    A. Integrated marketing communications plan.
    B. Advertising.
    C. Promotion.
    D. Sales.
    E. Price.
    F. Channels.
    G. Customer management activities.
    H. Website.
    I. Marketing research.
    J. Partnerships/joint ventures.

VI. *Financial Documents*
    A. Budgets.
    B. Pro forma statements.

VII. *Monitors and Controls*
    A. Marketing metrics.
    B. Secondary data.
    C. Primary data.

VIII. *Contingency Plans*

Chapter Two

Defining the Competitive Set

Overview

Chapter 1 presented an overview of marketing planning and an outline of a marketing plan that can be used in a wide variety of organizational settings. Of particular importance to the marketing plan is the background analysis of "homework," which focuses on the existing category and the competitive and customer situations. However, before beginning the analysis, a marketing manager must have a good conceptual definition of the product category to serve as the focus for data collection and analysis. This chapter provides tools to develop that category definition. In particular, we point out several possible ways to define the competition for a product or product line.

In our view, many managers tend to view competition too narrowly. For example, a product manager for a line of notebook computers would likely view other notebook computers as the major competitors. This is a natural outgrowth of the short-term orientation that pervades product management; competitor products or services that are most similar receive the most attention. However, as we argue in more detail later in this chapter, a myopic view of competition can be dangerous. For example, a parent thinking of purchasing a personal computer for a child going to college might be debating between the higher portability of a laptop versus the lower price and higher security characterizing a desktop. In this case, the two subcategories of PCs obviously compete. Other possible options include advanced personal digital assistants and tablet PCs. Thus, many different products compete for the same needs the student has for doing his or her work.

In some sense, everything competes with everything else for scarce resources, usually money. Since this concept of competition is not useful to a marketing manager, the key question in defining competition is not whether two products compete but the extent to which they compete. The degree of competition is a continuum, not a discrete *yes* or *no*. Defining competition therefore requires a balance between identifying too many competitors (and therefore complicating instead of simplifying decision making) and identifying too few (and thus overlooking a key competitor).

This chapter focuses on customer-based competition; in other words, a competitor is defined as one competing for the same customers. Competitors tangle on other

FIGURE 2.1 Bases of Competition

1. Customer oriented
   Who they are: competition for the same budget
   When they use it
   Why they use it: benefits sought
2. Marketing oriented: advertising and promotion
   Theme/copy strategy
   Media
   Distribution
   Price
3. Resource-oriented
   Raw materials
   Employees
   Financial resources
4. Geographic

bases as well. For example, Sun Microsystems and Amazon.com, although noncompetitors in terms of customers, compete for computer programmers—the same labor supply. Kodak and jewelers compete for silver—raw materials. Suppliers are also a basis for competition; in 1990, hard disk drive manufacturer Conner Peripherals sued rival Seagate Technology on the grounds that Seagate blocked Conner's supplies of a critical component. In 2000, Palm Inc. could not make enough units to meet demand because it was fighting with cell-phone makers like Nokia and Motorola for a limited supply of memory chips and liquid-crystal screens. Avon and Tupperware compete for home demonstration sales—the same channel of distribution. Similarly, frozen food manufacturers that use the freezer cabinets in supermarkets compete for shelf space. Geographically based competition is important for local retailers—for example, hardware stores—and multinational firms in the market for telecommunications equipment such as Ericsson (Sweden), NEC (Japan), and Nortel (Canada). In other words, competition exists across many dimensions. Figure 2.1 summarizes these different bases of competition.

As Figure 2.1 suggests, competitors can be defined using several criteria. Competition can exist for customers in terms of their budgets (disposable income: vacations versus financial products), when they use a product (evenings: a basketball game versus a movie), and benefits sought (cancer treatments: bioengineered drugs versus chemotherapy). Competition is also related to marketing activities such as advertising (time on network television programs) and distribution (shelf space). The battle for shelf facings in supermarkets has led to a variety of manufacturer concessions to retailers to obtain desirable shelf positions, and the struggle for shelf space occurs across as well as within traditional product category boundaries. Examples of resource-based and geographic-based competition have already been mentioned.

Another crucial competition occurs *within* a company, when different units in an organization request funds for their marketing plans. In this form of competition, the plan serves mainly as a sales document, and its financial projections often become the key to the "sale." This competition is often intentional; it puts pressure on managers to develop sound and aggressive marketing plans.

Misidentification of the competitive set can have a serious impact on the success of a marketing plan, especially in the long run. Overlooking an important competitive threat can be disastrous. For example, for many years the Swiss controlled the market for premium watches and Timex dominated the market for inexpensive watches. When Japanese firms such as Casio developed electronic watches in the 1970s, they were not viewed as a threat or serious competition in either business. Today both Timex and Swiss firms offer electronic models, and only the strong success of the Swatch brand of inexpensive fashion watches saved the Swiss watch industry.

A second illustration comes from the U.S. coffee industry (Yip and Williams, 1986). Coffee manufacturers traditionally felt free to pass along increased costs to consumers when a freeze in Colombia or another coffee-producing country restricted the supply of coffee beans. However, during 1977 and 1978, retail coffee sales dropped nearly 20 percent due to price increases. Much of this decrease can be accounted for by the concurrent rapid increase in demand for soft drinks and juices. Witness also the recent attempt by Pepsi to compete with coffee manufacturers by introducing a morning cola, Pepsi A.M. (which, unfortunately, failed). In fact, share of occasion and so-called share of stomach competition is a major consideration of food and drink producers.

Pity the owner of a small "mom and pop" video store in 2004. Strong retail competitors such as Blockbuster exist with greater selection and considerably more marketing muscle due to national advertising and direct-mail campaigns. Netflix allows you to receive DVDs in the mail. Moreover, the video store owner competes against another giant, Sony, which sells the small satellite dishes that, when combined with a home entertainment service, can deliver video on demand. In addition, every telephone and cable company wants to get into the video-on-demand business shipping video images over telephone lines (DSL) and cable modems.

Finally, the automobile industry has had to be dragged kicking and screaming into the Internet age. In 2002, over 80 percent of Acura, Audi, Porsche, and BMW buyers used the Web to research their car purchases before buying.[1] Before Ford, Chrysler, General Motors, and other car companies started developing their online businesses, companies like Autobytel, CarPoint, and CarsDirect were selling automobiles through their Internet sites. The bigger companies ignored the smaller upstarts as they thought that they would not be serious competitors. Although these Internet sellers are either defunct or have developed different business models (e.g., referrals to dealers), the new competition certainly caught the attention of the major manufacturers.

Ambiguous definition of the competition creates uncertainty in market definition and therefore ambiguity in market-related statistics such as market share. This leaves open the possible manipulation of market boundaries, particularly when compensation or allocation decisions are at stake. For example, assume an objective for a notebook computer weighing four pounds with a hard disk drive but no floppy disk drive is to gain 10 percent market share. The ability to achieve this objective depends on whether the "market" is defined as all notebook products, including floppy and

---

[1] Josef Federman (2003), "In the Driver's Seat," *The New York Times*, May 19, p. R12.

CD-ROM drives, all portable Windows-based computers, all desktop computers plus portables, and so on. A chocolate-covered granola bar could have a large share if measured in the snack bar category or a very small share if considered in the snack food category. To combat complacency, General Electric required redefining the markets in which they compete so their share was 15 percent or less.

Data from the travel industry provide an additional example of how market shares do not tell the whole story. As of late 2003, Expedia held 36 percent of the online travel booking business, with Travelocity at 24 percent and Orbitz at 13 percent (Federman, 2003; Thomaselli, 2003). However, it is estimated that just under 50 percent of the total travel market is Web based. Thus, the Internet companies face serious competition not only within their narrowly defined set but outside as well, indicating that the high market share owned by Expedia.com is only part of the story of their performance.

In this chapter, therefore, we take the view that the definition of the competitive set ultimately affects what strategy is pursued, and the definition can be too narrow or too broad for existing market conditions. Not all authors subscribe to this approach (see, for example, Abell, 1980) as some believe the corporate mission or business definition selected affects the set of competitors for a firm. In other words, the definition of competition is a decision made by a marketing manager. Unfortunately, competitors usually do not care how a company chooses to define itself or how a marketing manager defines competition, and they are thus free to compete against a firm's products even if that firm does not define itself to include them as competitors.

In this chapter, we describe several levels of competition that can be useful for conceptualizing the competitive set. In addition, we discuss methods that can help determine the competition at the various levels. Finally, we describe the notion of enterprise competition.

LEVELS OF MARKET COMPETITION

Definitions

One way to delineate the set of competitors facing a brand is to consider the proximity of other products to the physical attributes of the product in question.[2] As Figure 2.2 shows, the problem of defining competition can be viewed as defining a set of concentric circles with the product or brand in question at the center.

A product's features are defined as the presence (or absence) of a characteristic or attribute (e.g., calories, weight). The *value* of a feature is the level of the characteristic (e.g., 0 calories, 5 pounds). Thus, Coke and Diet Coke share the same features—carbonation, cola taste, sweetness, and the like—but have different values of some of the features since Diet Coke has fewer calories and is artificially sweetened.

The narrowest perspective one can take of competition is called *product form.* These products typically pursue the same market segment, and their features

---

[2] Again, the use of the term *physical* does not preclude services from utilizing the proposed method for identifying competitors. Services can also be described in terms of their actual characteristics, for example, interest rate for a mortgage.

FIGURE 2.2 **Example of Levels of Competition**

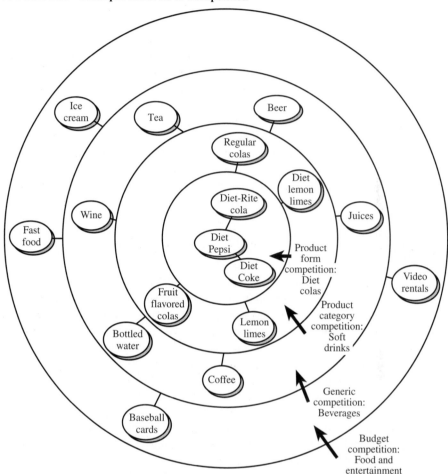

therefore have similar values. As Figure 2.2 shows, from Diet Coke's perspective, a narrow view of competition would include only diet colas, such as Diet-Rite and Diet Pepsi. These brands appeal to similar consumers: those seeking a cola taste with low calories. Similarly, Compaq, Gateway, Dell, IBM, Toshiba, and others compete in the Windows-based notebook/laptop computer category. Again, although the brands differ slightly on some characteristics, they use the same operating system and are fairly similar in weight. Apple's Ibook might not be included in this product form competition, since it has a different operating system. Interestingly, competition in the notebook market could be asymmetrical in that companies that produce Windows machines may not view Apple as a competitor, but Apple might be interested in selling machines to customers who currently have Windows-based desktop computers. To further clarify the definition of product form competition, subnotebook and tablet products comprise noticeably different sets of product form competitors.

Thus, product form competition is a narrow view of competition because it considers only those products that "look" the same as the product or service in question. This might be an acceptable perspective in the short run, as these would be the most serious competitors on a day-to-day basis. It is also a convenient definition of competition because it mimics the way commercial data services often measure market shares. For example, A. C. Nielsen, a major provider of market share information to consumer packaged goods companies (along with its main competitor, Information Resources, Inc., or IRI), provides market share information not only on the entire soft-drink category but also on the diet product segment alone. This narrow definition of the market supplied by a data collection service can have the unfortunate effect of setting an industry standard for looking at competition and market shares in a way that does not represent the true underlying competitive dynamics in the industry. Thus, the product form view, while perhaps providing the set of the closest competitors in a product feature sense, is too narrow for a longer-run view of competition.

The second level of competition is based on those products or services with similar features. This type of competition, called *product category,* is what product managers naturally think of as the industry. For example, personal computers, fast food, televisions, and the like describe sets of competitors that are aggregates, or composites, of narrower product forms. All soft drinks (Figure 2.2) form a market as well. This is, in fact, the traditional way to determine the composition of a competitive set. While somewhat broader than product form competition, this product category definition of competition still takes a short-run view of market definition. To recall an earlier example, the video store "industry" faces critical competition from the telecommunications "industry."

The third level of competition is longer term and focuses on substitutable product categories. At this level, termed *generic competition,* competition, and therefore the market, is defined as consisting of those products and services fulfilling the same customer need. Thus, soft drinks compete with orange juice in the "thirst-quenching" market, fast-food outlets compete against frozen entrees in the "convenience" eating market, and so on.

This need-based perspective is essential if a manager wishes to avoid both overlooking threats and ignoring opportunities. This perspective is well described in Levitt's classic article (1960) that admonishes several industries for defining their businesses too narrowly. Railroads viewed themselves as providing rail-based rather than general transportation services and lost much of their business to trucks and airlines. Steel companies thought they were providing steel rather than general structural material. Some firms, on the other hand, do take a generic perspective in defining themselves and their competitors. For example, the world's largest business-to-business e-commerce network was GE Global Exchange Services. With over 100,000 trading partners and 1 billion transactions annually worth $1 trillion in goods and services, CEO Harvey Seegers viewed his competitors as the post office, telephone companies, and facsimile makers since they are also in the business of moving things from the physical to the digital world (Claburn, 2002). Brunswick, the maker of billiard tables, views itself as being in the furniture business, competing for fashionable products to fit in the home. As a result, it is developing new contemporary-styled tables that can be customized with felt of different colors (Fitch, 2003).

Benefits do not have to be defined at the product level. For example, in Japan, the large banks have new competition for consumer financial products from nonfinancial institutions with significant brand names that provide consumer confidence or extensive retail systems that supply convenience and availability (Dvorak, 2000). Examples of the former are Sony and BMW, which have both applied to Japanese regulators for permission to make consumer loans. An example of the retail availability benefit is Ito-Yokado, best known as the operator of the 7-Eleven convenience store chain.

A critical difference between generically defined competitors and either product form or product category competition is that the former is *outward* oriented while the latter two are *inward.* Product form and product category competitors are defined by products that look like those we are producing. Generic competitors are defined by looking outside the firm to the customers. After all, who really defines competition, the firm or the customer? It is the customer who determines what alternative products and services solve the problem at hand. Although in some cases there may be a limited number of ways to solve the same problem or provide the same benefit, in most instances focusing on the physical product alone ignores viable competitors.

Southwest Airlines has used this outward perspective on competition to build what is generally considered to be the most successful U.S. airline. The reasons for its success are well documented: it focuses on short-haul flights, it does not serve meals or offer in-flight films, but it does offer extraordinary value with fares often 60 percent below those of the competition, on-time flights, and airports with less congestion. When developing its concept, instead of focusing on rivals in the airline industry, Southwest realized that for short-haul destinations, surface transportation like cars and trains were substitutes for flying. By concentrating on the factors that led people to choose to drive versus fly and eliminating or reducing everything else, the company's value proposition was established (Kim and Mauborgne, 1999). While some airlines such as JetBlue and Song are challenging its domination in the low-price segment, Southwest is expected to fight strongly to maintain its position.

Procter & Gamble has also viewed an outward perspective on competition as key to the development of new products. In particular, the company reexamined the laundry detergent market to enter the home dry cleaning product business (Parker-Pope, 1998). Instead of looking at the $4 billion U.S. laundry detergent market, of which P&G held a 51 percent share, the company wanted to pursue the $10 billion that U.S. consumers spend annually to clean their clothes, including $6 billion for dry cleaning. They realized that the 50 percent share was just 20 percent of a much larger market. The company therefore introduced Dryel, a home dry-cleaning kit.

An even more general level of competition is *budget* competition. This is the broadest view of competition: It considers all products and services competing for the same customer dollar as forming a market. For example, a consumer who has $500 in discretionary disposable income could spend it on a vacation, a ring, a money market instrument, or a variety of other things. That this is the case can be seen in the advertisement shown in Figure 2.3 for De Beers diamonds. Clearly, the company realizes that the money spent on a diamond could be spent fixing up a kitchen, among a variety of other options. A purchasing manager may have a fixed budget for office equipment that includes copy machines, word processing software upgrades, or a new water cooler service. While this view of competition is

FIGURE 2.3   De Beers Advertisement

FIGURE 2.4   Defining Competition Using Customer Segments

Generic Competitors	Market Segments		
	Business Travelers	**Tourists**	**Students**
Airline	X	X	
Bus		X	X
Train		X	X
Automobile (own)		X	
Automobile (rent)		X	

conceptually useful, it is very difficult to implement strategically since it implies an enormous number of competitors.

Overlapping Market Segments

An additional and valuable way to conceptualize the definition of competitors is based on market segments. Consider the market for travel services shown in Figure 2.4. The modes of travel listed on the left are generic competitors in that they satisfy the benefits of providing transportation. The market segments across the top could be defined in many ways, depending on the benefit being analyzed. The generic competitors in the first column indicate how a customer would look at the travel problem. Consider the route between San Francisco and Los Angeles (a nine-hour drive or one-hour flight). For the business traveler, the major competitors would be airlines, primarily Southwest and United. For tourists, airlines, trains, car rental agencies, or their own cars would be substitutes if time is not critical. Students on a budget might consider buses and trains as competitors.

The Impact of Metamediaries

It should be noted that the growth of websites that perform multiple functions and offer a number of services has created a broad group of competitors. These sites, often called *metamediaries,* seek to bundle disparate services that fulfill a customer's needs for a particular transaction. For example, Figure 2.5 shows the home page from Autobytel.com. This company's most direct competitors are automobile retailers (product category competition). However, it can be seen that the site offers links to financing, insurance, warranties, maintenance, and other services bringing in competitors from other categories. This is of great concern to companies in those other categories that are more "vertically" positioned in that they can only handle one aspect of the transaction.

Product Strategy Implications

The four-level model of competition just described has significant implications for developing product strategy and for a product manager's marketing problems. A different set of tasks must be accomplished at each level of competition for a product to be successful in the market. Figure 2.6 shows these tasks in conjunction with the appropriate level of competition.

FIGURE 2.5   Autobytel.com Website

At each level of competition, part of the job of a marketing manager is fairly clear, and marketing managers are trained to handle it: Convince the customer that your company's version of the product, your brand, is better than others available. In other words, your most direct competitors are other brands of like product form. What differs at each level is how much additional marketing has to be done beyond touting your own brand's advantages. At the product form level, none is required. Clearly, when the competition is viewed as consisting only of other products with similar levels of features, marketing activities directly aimed at the similar competitors are all that is required (e.g., Toshiba is a better laptop computer than IBM). However,

FIGURE 2.6   Levels of Competition: Implications for Product Strategy

Competitive Level	Product Management Task
Product form	Convince customers that the brand is better than others in the product form
Product category	Convince customers that the product form is the best in the category
Generic	Convince customers that the product category is the best way to satisfy needs
Budget	Convince customers that the generic benefits are the most appropriate way to spend the discretionary budget

the problem becomes more complex as the competitor set widens. At the product category level, a marketing manager must also convince customers that the product form is best in the product category (e.g., tablets are better than notebook/laptop computers). At the generic competition level, a manager must also convince customers that the product category solution to the customer's problem (the benefit derived from the product category) is superior to the solution provided by other product categories (e.g., taking an airplane is superior to taking a train). This is critical when a totally new product category is introduced. For example, when Procter & Gamble introduced disposable diapers in the 1970s, the main marketing job was to convince mothers to switch from the generic competitors, cloth diapers and diaper services. Finally, it might also be necessary to convince customers that the generic benefit of the product is better than other ways to spend discretionary money (e.g., taking a cruise versus putting a down payment on a new car).

Consider the problem facing the marketing manager for a line of low-priced stereo components such as Pioneer. What competition does this manager face? First, competitors are fighting for the same segment of the stereo market (product form competitors), so the manager must show that Pioneer is superior to others competing in the low-priced segment. Second, there are other, higher-priced component manufacturers (product category competitors), and the Pioneer manager must communicate to customers the advantages of low-priced components over more expensive alternatives (e.g., Bang and Olufsen). Third, the manager must consider generic competitors. These could include all-in-one systems ("boom boxes") or lower-priced rack stereo systems as well as the manufacturers of other entertainment consumer durables such as TVs, video game systems, and DVD players (Sony, Nintendo, Panasonic, Sanyo). Customers must be convinced to buy stereos rather than these other products. Finally, alternative ways to spend the money could be relevant (budget competition). As a result, customers need to be convinced about the benefits of buying stereos instead of taking a vacation or buying stocks. While this latter problem may seem a little farfetched, it is undoubtedly true that stockbrokers, retail jewelers, travel agents, and many other businesspeople worry about customer alternatives for spending money.

It is also important to note that as one moves from product form toward budget competition, customer targets also begin to change. Product form competition suggests battling for exactly the same customers in terms of who they are and why they buy, although not necessarily where or when they buy: One soft-drink manufacturer (Coca-Cola) may concentrate on fountain sales and another (Pepsi) on grocery store sales. As the company moves toward budget competition, both who its customers are and why they buy begin to differ as the need to be satisfied becomes more general. Because the key to success in business is obtaining and keeping customers, the most crucial form of competition will generally be product form and category, in which competition occurs for the same customers. On the other hand, generic competition can destroy entire product categories when a major innovation occurs, and thus it too requires attention, especially for long-run planning.

Note that products thought of as substitutes, and therefore generic or budget competitors, may also be viewed as complements. For example, a customer might be trying to decide between purchasing word processing or spreadsheet software (budget competition). These potential competitors could be turned into allies through joint ventures or cobranding (e.g., Dreyer's Ice Cream and M&Ms) or bundling (Microsoft's Office suite of applications). Thus, this delineation of competitive levels defines *potential* competitors and not necessarily mortal foes.

Illustrations

The two illustrations introduced in Chapter 1 were energy bars and personal digital assistants (PDAs). Let's look at competitor definitions in light of the information provided in that chapter and some use of "managerial judgment."

Energy Bars

Figure 2.7 shows the competitive structure of the energy bar category. As can be seen, the narrowest definition of competition, product form, is at the center of the diagram and lists the main competitors in the energy bar product segment, including Odwalla. The next level out, product category competition, consists of the other bars that are positioned as either snacks or healthy food. The two circles combined comprise the snack bar "industry." The other two levels, healthy snacks and other snacks, would be generic competition because they fulfill some of the same needs as the energy bars. There is no budget competition shown here as it would consist

FIGURE 2.7 **Energy Bar Competition**

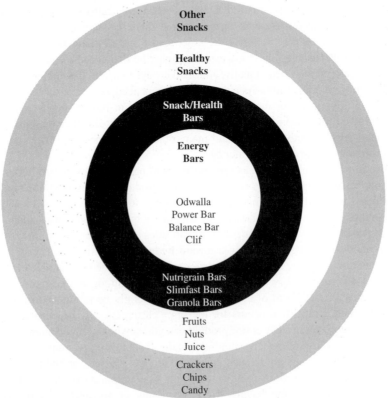

of any other product priced between $1 and $3 and is, therefore, not very useful for decision making.

Personal Digital Assistants

Figure 2.8 indicates the different levels of competition for the PDA category. The closest competitors were those PDAs that offered address/telephone/fax record keeping, calculators, financial calculations, and optional links to personal computers and modems via wireless communications (referred to as PIMs, or Personal Information Mangers). The major competitors to Handspring's Visor were products from Palm, Casio, and Compaq. These products were marketed as offering many of the functions needed by businesspeople away from the office at a moderate price. The product category consists of these plus lower-end PDAs with more limited communications capabilities, smaller screens, less software, and a lower price. One job of the Visor product manager, then, was to differentiate it from these lower-end models, primarily on the basis of price but perhaps also by indicating that a simpler product may be all that is needed, particularly if the user also has a notebook computer. The generic competition consists of two quite different kinds of products. First, as is the case today, notebook and subnotebook computers can provide all the benefits of PDAs at a larger size, a higher price, and slower access to the information. However, manual, paper-based solutions still exist. One can still use a Rolodex, a Day-Timer, or just paper files to obtain many of the benefits of the PDAs. Add a cellular phone and this combination matches the full-featured PDAs as well. There are many serious budget competitors. If we consider other business-related personal productivity items, we see that portable printers, home fax machines, and similar items compete with PDAs. Of course, other durable goods may also compete for the same dollar as well.

FIGURE 2.8   **PDA Competition**

Level of Competition	Definition	Competitors	Need Satisfied
Product form PDAs	Full-featured PDAs	Palm Pilot VII Compaq AERO Casioplus integrated communication	Personal information management
Product category	PIMs	Palm III Royal Casio PV-100	PIM only
Generic	Notebook/ subnotebook computers Paper-based solutions	IBM Toshiba Many others Rolodex Day Timer	Other solutions to the above
Budget	Business items costing $100–$1,000	Fax machines Personal copiers Cellular phones Furniture (e.g. Steelcase)	

FIGURE 2.9 Managerial Judgment of Competition

Markets/Customers	Product/Services	
	Same	Different
Same	A	B
Different	C	D

METHODS FOR DETERMINING COMPETITORS

The easiest way to define competition is to let someone else do it for you. For example, you can use the predefined categories provided by a commercial data service as the definition of the competitive set. A second example of an external definition of markets is the Standard Industrial Classification (SIC) code used by the U.S. government.[3] This system assigns products to two-digit major groups (e.g., 34, Fabricated Metal), three-digit groups (e.g., 342, Cutlery and Hand Tools), four-digit industries (e.g., 3423, Hand and Edge Tools), and five- or more digit representations of products (e.g., 34231,11 Pliers). Clearly, both of these external sources of information define competition based on physical product similarities (product form or category definitions). As a result, relying exclusively on these categorizations will overlook both generic and budget competitors.

Two alternative approaches to assessing the set of competitors operationalize the broader definition advocated in this chapter: managerial judgment and customer-based evaluation.

Managerial Judgment

Through experience, salesperson call reports, distributors, or other company sources, managers can often develop judgments about the sources of present and future competition. One way to structure the thought process is to use a tabular structure such as that shown in Figure 2.9 (a variant of Ansoff's [1965] well-known growth matrix). Box A represents product form competition, that is, those products or services that are basically the same and are pursuing the same customers. Box C represents product form competitors that target other customers.

The most interesting cell of Figure 2.9 is B. This cell represents potential future competitors that already have a franchise with our customers but do not offer the same product or service. In this case, a marketing manager might try to forecast which firms in B are likely to become more direct competitors. Examples of companies capitalizing on prior customer familiarity are numerous. In telecommunications, IBM had a considerable franchise with large business customers through its mainframe computer business. IBM easily moved to cell A through its investments

---

[3] Since 1997, the SIC code system has been replaced by the NAICS (North American Industrial Classification System), which updated the SIC industry categories. However, SIC data are still used worldwide.

in MCI and Rolm. In the orange juice category, Procter & Gamble had perhaps the best franchise of any consumer product manufacturer with both supermarkets and consumers, which it used to develop the Citrus Hill brand. Disney's purchase of Capital Cities/ABC is consistent with its entertainment franchise. Both Dell and Hewlett-Packard have started selling flat-panel TVs. This type of movement into new product areas is common; companies often try to leverage their brand equity in one category to grab sales in others that serve the same customers. Managers should assess the likelihood of such horizontal movements as well as their chances of success, although some moves, such as Dell's, will always be difficult to predict.

Cell D competitors are the most difficult to predict, as they currently sell different products to different customers. One example of the impact of such a competitor in consumer durables was Litton Industries' commercialization of microwave technology, which created a new competitor for General Electric in the kitchen appliance market.

Perhaps the least scientific but most useful way to see what a product or service might compete with is to imagine the item as a "prop" for a stand-up comedian. The comedian, unencumbered by convention (and sometimes good taste), can create many uses for a product, thereby identifying potential competition.

Technology substitution is particularly relevant for technological products. Judgments by engineers, marketing managers, and others may suggest other products or technologies that substitute for current ones. For example, in many telecommunications and computer networking applications, infrared or wireless communications are substituting for optical fiber, which in turn substituted for wire or "twisted pair," thus producing successive technological generations of competitors.

A study by Clark and Montgomery (1999) attempted to characterize how managers use judgment in identifying competitors. They found that three major factors are positively related to whether a company is perceived as a competitor:

- Size
- Success
- Threatening behavior

Interestingly, they also found that when using judgment alone, managers named relatively few competitors. Thus, due to their day-to-day experiences of competing with product form and category competitors, managers using judgment to define their competitive set run the risk of creating a set that is too small relative to the reality of market conditions.

Customer-Based Measures

Two types of customer data are commonly used to assess market structures: actual purchase or usage data and judgments (Day, Shocker, and Srivastava, 1979). The former are particularly useful for understanding product form and category competition; because it is difficult to understand what alternatives were considered when purchases were actually made, the usual assumption is that purchases are made within a narrow definition of competition. However, what customers have actually done does not necessarily indicate what they would have preferred to do in the past or are likely to do in the future. Judgmental data are needed to understand broader definitions of competition as well as to estimate how a new product affects the structure of competition.

Using Behavioral Data

A key source of purchase data used in consumer packaged goods applications is data collected from electronic scanners. Households enroll with a commercial firm, either A. C. Nielsen or Information Resources, Inc. (IRI). Before scanning in their purchases at the cash register, the cashier scans an identification code indicating that the purchases to follow are for a particular household. The brands and package sizes are coded by Universal Product Code (UPC, or bar codes). Alternatively, since many products have substantial purchase volume outside supermarkets (e.g., convenience stores, vending machines), A. C. Nielsen has developed an in-home scanning system called Homescan in which the panel member scans the UPC codes at home with an infrared "wand" and the data are dumped into a computer and downloaded via modem. While most of the data collected from consumers using these technologies are aggregated to estimate sales and market shares for brands, the household-level data are very useful for identifying patterns of repeat purchasing of brands and brand switching.

Figure 2.10 shows a common way to organize the data from scanners. The figure is a brand-switching matrix for a specific product category. Because most of these analyses concern predetermined product categories, patterns of competition within categories or subcategories (product form) but not across categories (generic) can be determined. This approach is usually best applied to frequently purchased goods or services. The numbers in the table represent purchase probabilities calculated across panel households from one purchase occasion (time t) to the next (time $t + 1$) for a set of brands, A through E. Probabilities of brand switching have been proposed as measures of customers' perceived similarities, and therefore substitutability, among brands (see, for example, Kalwani and Morrison, 1977, and Lehmann, 1972). High brand-switching probabilities suggest a high degree of competition.

The diagonal elements in Figure 2.10 represent the degree of brand loyalty; for example, 60 percent of the households buying brand A on one occasion repurchased it on the next purchase occasion. The off-diagonal elements represent brand-switching behavior; for example, 20 percent of the time purchases of brand A were followed by a purchase of B. The row numbers must sum to 1, as a household must buy one of the five brands.

While sophisticated methods are available for analyzing large brand-switching matrices, simple observation of Figure 2.10 indicates that there are clearly two main

FIGURE 2.10 **Brand-Switching Matrix**

		Time $t + 1$				
		A	B	C	D	E
	A	.6	.2	.2	0	0
Time t	B	.2	.3	.4	.1	0
	C	.2	.3	.5	0	0
	D	0	.1	.1	.5	.3
	E	.1	0	0	.4	.5

FIGURE 2.11 **Defining Competition with Brand Choice Data**

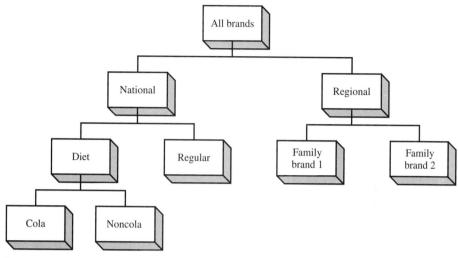

Source: Reprinted by permission from Vithela Rao and Darius Sabavala, "Inference of Hierarchical Choice Processes from Panel Data," in *Journal of Consumer Research,* June 1981, published by the University of Chicago Press. © 1981 by the University of Chicago.

groups of brands, A-B-C and D-E. In addition, within the A-B-C cluster, B and C seem to form another group. We could conclude that within the market for this product, there are two principal product forms and an even narrower set of two within one of the clusters.

An example of this kind of analysis on real consumer purchasing data for soft drinks appears in Figure 2.11 (Rao and Sabavala, 1981). These analyses typically create a treelike diagram with the branch structure indicating the competition implied by consumer purchasing patterns. As the figure indicates, the competition for a national brand is other national brands, while the major competition for a regional brand is the other regional or family brand. Within the national brand competition, the regular brands compete against one another, as do the diet brands. Finally, there is competition within national diet colas and national diet noncolas.

A problem with using purchase data to understand product form and category competition is that brand switches occur across complements as well as substitutes. Consumers might purchase complements when they want variety (McAlister and Lattin, 1985). For example, consider a consumer who views Coke and Pepsi as direct substitutes but sometimes likes a lemon-lime drink such as 7UP as a break from Coke/Pepsi. Now suppose a recording of purchases shows a purchase sequence of Coke–Coke–7UP–Coke. A researcher might analyze the brand switch from Coke to 7UP for that consumer and mistakenly infer it was due to substitutability reasons rather than to the desire for a change. If this were true for a large number of consumers, a marketing manager would believe that Coke and 7UP were competitors and might design his or her strategy with that in mind when the truth is that 7UP is not a competitive threat in the usual sense.

One problem with using purchase data is that the data are often at the household level. Observed switching between two brands could be due to different household members' preferences rather than to any substitutability reasons. For example, purchases of Coke and Pepsi could be for two different people or a true switch of brands by one individual. The difference is crucial.

Panel or sales data can be used to calculate cross-elasticities of demand, another basis for estimating patterns of competition. A cross-elasticity is the percentage change in one brand's sales compared to a percentage change in a marketing variable for another brand, such as price. If a cross-elasticity with respect to price is positive (a brand's sales decline when another brand's price drops), the two brands or products in question are considered to be competitive (Cooper, 1988).

The major problem with this approach is estimating the cross-elasticities: It is assumed there is no competitive reaction to the price cut and the market is static with respect to new entrants, product design, and so forth. In addition, a positive cross-elasticity does not guarantee cause and effect, that is, that the price decline (increase) of the brand in question actually caused the other brand's sales to decline (increase). And, as with measuring brand switching, the set of brands or products usually must be defined a priori.

In today's e-commerce environment, it is relatively easy for Internet-based companies to obtain site-switching data. Comscore Media Metrix, for example, tracks site navigation behavior (*clickstream* data) for a panel of Web surfers so an Internet retailer can determine from which sites a person has come and to which sites she or he is going after visiting or purchasing. These kinds of data are much more difficult to interpret, of course, as Web surfers can visit many sites in one session and skip around with low cost.

In summary, the estimates of competition using actual behavior are useful because they represent what consumers *actually* do, not what they *might* do, which surveys indicate. For the most part, however, without specially designed and expensive data collection, these estimates apply primarily to frequently purchased, nondurable goods. In addition, they tend to be most appropriate when a product class is defined a priori and when competition within product form or category is sought.

Using Customer Judgments

Several methods have been proposed for estimating competition from customer judgments. All are essentially paper-and-pencil exercises in which customers are surveyed in focus groups, shopping mall intercepts, or other environments. Although not based on actual customer behavior, they have the advantages of providing insight into potential future market structures, producing broader definitions of current structures, and being applicable to all types of products and services, including industrial products and consumer durables.

Judged overall similarity measures between pairs of products or brands, and it can be used to create geometric representations in multidimensional spaces called *perceptual maps*. The brands or products are represented by points in the space, while the dimensions represent the attributes customers use to make the similarity judgments. Brands located close to one another are judged to be similar and thus form a defined market.[4] If brands are the objects of the mapping exercise, only

---

[4] There are other methods for constructing perceptual maps besides similarity ratings, for example, factor and discriminant analysis of attribute ratings.

FIGURE 2.12   Defining Competition with Perceptual Mapping

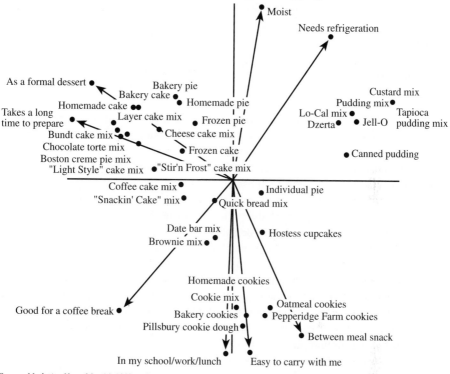

Source: *Marketing News,* May 14, 1982, p. 3.

product category or product form competition can be assessed. However, if a larger set of products is used, more interesting generic competition can be identified.

As an example, Figure 2.12 presents a perceptual map from the generic category of desserts. The analysis must begin with a prespecified set of the relevant alternatives, which can be developed through focus group research that identifies products satisfying a given need. The points not attached to the vectors represent the various products the focus group identified as filling the need for dessert. The vectors help determine attributes for defining the space, but are not relevant to the market competition issue. Information about the competitive sets is obtained by examining clusters of points. The upper-right quadrant would be very useful to, say, the brand manager for Jell-O. From the map, it is clear that Jell-O is perceived to be quite similar to custard, pudding, tapioca, Lo-Cal mix, and Dzerta, a mixture of gelatin and other products.

Similarity within consideration sets is an approach developed by Bourgeois, Haines, and Sommers (1979) that asks customers to take a large set of products and divide them into groups of items that can be substituted for one another, that is, items that would be considered together on a purchase occasion. The customers are then asked to judge the similarity of the products within each group. By accumulating similarity judgments across the customers, a perceptual map can be developed. Thus, this approach is somewhat similar to the preceding one, but it collects the similarity judgments after consideration sets have been formed. Other variants of this approach use verbal protocol data gathered as customers think aloud while considering a purchase decision.

The consideration set concept itself has been extensively explored (see, for example, Hauser and Wernerfelt, 1990, and Andrews and Srinivasan, 1995). When making a purchase decision, customers often simplify the process by reducing the number of available products and brands that can satisfy a need to a smaller set from which they make the ultimate decision. Clearly, the options in this smaller set closely compete against one another. However, the usefulness of the consideration set concept is limited by the sets' variability across customers and across distribution channels and by the fact that they are dynamic: Consideration sets change from one purchase occasion to another.

Product deletion is an interesting approach to defining competition based on customer reaction to product unavailability (Urban, Johnson, and Hauser, 1984). Products or brands in a set are presumed to be substitutes and consequently form a market if, when one of them is deleted from the choice set, customers are more likely to buy from the remaining products than from products outside the original set. For example, suppose a choice set of Internet websites for purchasing books is Amazon.com, BiggerBooks.com, Barnesandnoble.com, and others. If, when BiggerBooks.com is eliminated from the set, customers are more likely to choose Amazon or Barnesandnoble than any other site, the three brands are presumed to be competitors.

Although its authors describe product deletion as useful primarily to partition product form markets into submarkets, there is no reason the approach could not be used in a more general setting. For example, if milk is unavailable and orange juice and soft drinks are subsequently chosen more often than tea or coffee, then milk, juice, and soft drinks apparently compete at the generic level.

Substitution in use estimates degree of competitiveness through judged similarities of products in usage contexts (Stefflre, 1972; Ratneshwar and Shocker, 1991). First, customers list all possible uses and contexts (e.g., a party or one's own use) for a target product or brand. Next, either the original sample or a fresh sample of respondents list other products or brands that provide the same benefits or uses and rate their appropriateness for the different contexts or use occasions. This method clearly has the potential to produce a large number of generic competitors or even budget competitors.

As an illustration, suppose the target product of interest is a baseball game. A brief sketch of the analysis is as follows:

Target: Baseball game.

Uses: Sports event, entertainment.

Substitutes: Horse racing, movies, dinner at a restaurant, visiting a sports bar.

Thus, substitution in use can produce a fairly diverse set of competitors.

Summary

Figure 2.13 summarizes the methods for determining competition along two dimensions: (1) the usefulness of each method for determining competition at a certain level and (2) the kind of research data typically used to implement the method.

FIGURE 2.13   Methods versus Competition Levels and Information Required

Approach	Level of Competition				Typical Data Sources	
	Product Form	Product Category	Generic	Budget	Primary	Secondary
Existing definitions	X	X				X
Technology substitution	X	X	X		X	
Managerial judgment	X	X			X	X
Customer behavior based:						
Brand switching	X	X				X
Interpurchase times	X	X				X
Cross-elasticities	X	X	X			X
Customer evaluation based:						
Overall similarity	X	X	X		X	
Similarity of consideration sets	X	X	X	X	X	
Product deletion	X	X	X		X	
Substitution in use	X	X	X		X	

Note: An *X* indicates that either the method is useful for determining competition at that level or it employs data of a certain type.

With respect to the latter, information is divided into primary sources (data collected specifically to determine competitors) and secondary sources (data collected for some purpose other than to determine the structure of the market).

As Figure 2.13 indicates, all the methods are useful for determining product form competition. Managerial judgment and behavior-based customer data are useful mainly for developing product form and product category markets. Customer information that is judgment based, however, can also be used to assess generic competition. Since cross-elasticities, judged similarity, technology substitution, product deletion, and substitution in use either start with an a priori market definition (which could be very broad) or are usage based, they cannot really be used to define budget competition, that is, those products fighting for the same customer dollar. Since the consideration set approach has no such restrictions, it can be used to assess budget competition.

With respect to data requirements, judgment-based customer evaluations require primary data, while behavior-based methods can use secondary data. When applied to consumer packaged goods, behavior-based methods utilize commercially available scanner panel data. Consumer judgments might supplement purchase data with primary data, for example, from interviews focusing on motivations for brand switching. Managerial judgment can (and at least implicitly does) utilize both primary data (e.g., discussions with distributors) and secondary data (e.g., salesperson call reports).

COMPETITOR SELECTION

Examining competition at four levels makes intuitive sense, and the practical implications for a product manager are substantial. One implication already mentioned is that marketing strategy must be developed with an eye toward four different problems: (1) convincing customers in your market segment that your brand is best (product form competition); (2) convincing buyers that your product form is best (product category competition); (3) convincing buyers that your product category is best (generic competition); and, occasionally, (4) convincing buyers that the basic need your product fulfills is an important one. A marketing manager must decide what percentage of his or her budget to spend on each problem.

A second implication of the four levels of competition is that marketing managers must choose a selective competitor focus. A manager cannot focus either analysis or strategy on every product in the market perceived to be a competitor due to limited available resources. Choosing whom to compete against has major implications for both performance standards (e.g., determining share of what) and strategy (e.g., competitive advertising). For example, the Odwalla brand manager must select whether to compete against only other energy bars or against the broader snack bar category.

A marketing manager can decide which competitors to focus on by examining three factors: (1) the time horizon of the marketing plan being developed, (2) the stage of the product life cycle relevant for the product, and (3) the rate of change in the technological base of the product.

In the one-year operating marketing plan most common for product managers, competition generally is defined primarily on a product form basis and secondarily using other bases. Clearly, the brands that compete with the one in question on a day-to-day basis are in the product form or a subcategory. For these brands, the product manager must have intimate knowledge of the customers, the competitors, and the effects of environmental changes such as demographics. For example, in an annual planning cycle, Sanka's major competitors are primarily other decaffeinated instant coffees. What about other decaffeinated or regular coffees? The selection of other competitors in the product category (coffee) or generic group is a judgment call based on where the manager sees potential growth opportunities or whether a category or a generic competitor is attacking the product form. In this example, Sanka also competes more against other decaffeinated coffee brands than regular brands. As we mentioned earlier, competition such as soft drinks and juices is a serious issue for the category, and efforts to compete are funded by the coffee trade association. For longer-term plans, all four levels of competition are relevant, with special emphasis placed on the generic level to identify important competitive threats.

The stage of the product life cycle may be relevant to defining competition because the breadth of view of the industry varies over time. In the early growth stages of a product, particularly a new technology, competition must be broadly defined (generic competition) since a large part of the marketing task is to convince customers to substitute a new product for an existing one that was previously satisfying their needs. On the other hand, in mature markets, the focus should generally be on product form and category competitors to best assess whether or not to stay in a market.

Finally, where the rate of technological change is rapid, competition should be conceived as broadly as possible. This is characteristic of the communications field, in which such diverse products as word processors, fax machines, the Internet, home computers, cable TV, and satellites compete for certain services. Alternatively, narrow definitions are sufficient for fields in which new technical advances occur less frequently, as is the case with food products.

Given that the appropriate levels of competition have been selected, that is, that the "market" has been defined by the marketing manager, attention shifts to choosing relevant competitors. This assessment may require preparing a preliminary competitor analysis or at least updating the previous plan's competitor analysis. The factors determining which competitors are relevant relate to forecasts of competitors' likely strategies, which the competitor analysis should provide. However, the resources the competitors can bring to bear in the market are also critical. This focus on resources highlights a final perspective on competition called *enterprise competition.*

ENTERPRISE COMPETITION

Ultimately products and services do not compete against one another; companies do. The resources a company has to support the product are a key determinant of its ability to successfully implement a marketing strategy. Thus, while we have examined competition in this chapter from the perspective of a brand or product, it is important to note that enterprise competition (firm versus firm) involves a higher-level perspective in developing strategies.

For example, in the computer workstation market, the Hewlett-Packard product line competes against Sun, IBM, and Silicon Graphics, among others. However, not all competitors are created equal. When HP develops a marketing strategy against IBM, it competes not only in terms of product features and benefits communicated but also against IBM's resources: its financial support, sales force, and image. HP must develop different strategies to compete against IBM than those it uses to compete against Sun, which is many times smaller than IBM.

Figure 2.14 shows the diverse set of companies competing in the financial services industry. This could easily be expanded to include companies such as Fidelity, Vanguard, Citibank, and the like and products such as IRAs and annuities. As a traditional financial services company, American Express is used to competing against Merrill Lynch and Prudential in insurance, commercial lending, and securities. However, General Motors, General Electric, and Ford, typically thought of as industrial powers, also compete with American Express for consumer loans, credit/debit cards, commercial lending, and insurance. In addition, the "bricks and mortar" world of American Express is quite different from the Internet-only bank, NetBank. Thus, the American Express green card product manager competes against products with a very diverse set of corporate parents and some of the deepest pockets in the world.

It is often difficult to understand brand-level competition without understanding the broader context in which it occurs. For example, the Bic versus Cricket cigarette lighter battle may make little sense without recognizing the general competition between Bic and Gillette, which includes razors and pens as well as lighters. In addition, Kimberly Clark, a fierce competitor with Procter & Gamble (P&G) in the disposable diaper market, acquired Scott Paper with the intention of using the Scott brands (e.g., toilet tissue) to compete against P&G (Charmin) and therefore help dilute P&G's resources available to compete in the more lucrative diaper category.

FIGURE 2.14 Enterprise Competition in Financial Services

	FDIC-Insured Depository	Consumer Loans	Credit/Debit Cards	Mortgage Banking	Commercial Lending	Mutual Funds	Securities	Insurance
American Express	X	X	X			X	X	X
Ford		X	X	X	X			X
General Electric	X	X	X	X	X	X		X
General Motors		X	X	X	X			X
Merrill Lynch	X		X	X	X	X	X	X
Prudential	X	X	X	X	X	X	X	X
NetBank	X	X	X	X	X	X	X	X

Enterprise competition is often characterized by asymmetries in competitive perspectives. For example, Odwalla probably views PowerBar and Balance Bar as more serious competitors than Clif Bar because the former are owned by major companies (Nestlé and Kraft). Companies with large resources have to be monitored more carefully due to their abilities to disrupt the marketplace with large advertising and promotion campaigns. Since Clif Bar is independent, it is not as likely to pose large problems for Odwalla, at least in the short term. Conversely, Clif Bar certainly views the others as major competitors.

SUMMARY

In this chapter, we argued that the set of competitors that pose a threat to a product can be highly varied and can come from a variety of what have traditionally been referred to as industries. Therefore, a "market" or an "industry" is often dynamic and difficult to define; often the labels are used more for convenience than to accurately describe the underlying patterns of competition. We presented a framework to conceptualize competition and methods to help form ideas about the competitive set. Finally, we discussed approaches to selecting competitors by choosing the relevant levels and specific brands.

Essentially, we suggest that competitors are those companies whose products or services compete for the same customers either directly through offering similar products or services (product form or category competition), indirectly through satisfying similar basic needs (generic competition), or in terms of budget. The product manager in charge of an existing product in an established category would generally be most interested in product form or category competition, since those are the products that immediately threaten his or her "livelihood." However, for new product plans, a generic perspective is very important since the new product is substituting for another category satisfying similar customer needs.

References

Abell, Derek (1980) *Defining the Business.* Englewood Cliffs, NJ: Prentice-Hall.

Andrews, Rick L., and T. C. Srinivasan (1995) "Studying Consideration Effects in Empirical Choice Models Using Scanner Panel Data," *Journal of Marketing Research,* February, 30–41.

Ansoff, H. Igor (1965) *Corporate Strategy.* New York: McGraw-Hill.

Bourgeois, Jacques, George Haines, and Montrose Sommers (1979) "Defining an Industry," paper presented at the ORSA/TIMS Market Measurement Conference, Stanford University.

Claburn, Thomas (2002) "Inside Line," *Smartbusinessmag.com,* April, 28.

Clark, Bruce H., and David B. Montgomery (1999) "Managerial Identification of Competitors," *Journal of Marketing,* July, 67–83.

Cooper, Lee (1988) "Competitive Maps: The Structure Underlying Asymmetric Cross-Elasticities," *Management Science,* June, 707–23.

Day, George S., Allan D. Shocker, and Rajendra V. Srivastava (1979) "Customer-Oriented Approaches to Identifying Product Markets," *Journal of Marketing,* Fall, 8–19.

Dvorak, Phred (2000) "Japanese Banks Face New Competitors," *The Wall Street Journal,* May 17, A22.

Federman, Josef (2003) "In the Driver's Seat," *The New York Times,* May 19, R12.

Fitch, Stephane (2003) "Pocketing a New Market," *Forbes,* October 13, 125.

Hauser, John R., and Birger Wernerfelt (1990) "An Evaluation Cost Model of Consideration Sets," *Journal of Consumer Research,* March, 391–405.

Kalwani, Manohar, and Donald Morrison (1977) "A Parsimonious Description of the Hendry System," *Management Science,* January, 467–77.

Kim, W. Chan, and Renée Mauborgne (1999) "How Southwest Airlines Found a Route to Success," *Financial Times,* May 13, 20.

Lehmann, Donald R. (1972) "Judged Similarity and Brand-Switching Data as Similarity Measures," *Journal of Marketing Research,* August, 331–34.

Levitt, Theodore (1960) "Marketing Myopia," *Harvard Business Review,* July–August, 45–56.

McAlister, Leigh, and James Lattin (1985) "Using a Variety-Seeking Model to Identify Substitute and Complementary Relationships among Competing Products," *Journal of Marketing Research,* August, 330–39.

Parker-Pope, Tara (1998) "P&G Targets Textiles Tide Can't Clean," *The Wall Street Journal,* April 29, B1.

Rao, Vithala, and Darius Sabavala (1981) "Inference of Hierarchical Choice Processes from Panel Data," *Journal of Consumer Research,* June, 85–96.

Ratneshwar, S., and Allan D. Shocker (1991) "Substitution in Use and the Role of Usage Context in Product Category Structures," *Journal of Marketing Research,* August, 281–95.

Stefflre, Volney (1972) "Some Applications of Multidimensional Scaling to Social Science Problems," in *Multidimensional Scaling: Theory and Applications in the Behavioral Sciences,* Vol. III, A. K. Romney, R. N. Shepard, and S. B. Nerlove, eds. New York: Seminar Press.

Thomaselli, Rich (2003) "Travelocity Hands McKinney $30M Biz," *Advertising Age,* October 27, 6.

Urban, Glen, Philip Johnson, and John R. Hauser (1984) "Testing Competitive Market Structures," *Marketing Science,* Spring, 83–112.

Yip, George, and Jeffrey Williams (1986) "U.S. Retail Coffee Market (A)," Harvard Business School case #9-586-134.

Industry Analysis

Overview

For either new or existing products, managers must ask whether the category of interest is sufficiently attractive to warrant new or continued investment—by their company, current competitors, or potential new entrants. The product portfolio approach popularized by the Boston Consulting Group uses the market growth rate to indicate attractiveness. Other models utilize a two-dimensional strategic grid consisting of market attractiveness and business position (see Cravens, 1994).

The kind of analysis described in this chapter is often characterized as "category attractiveness" or "market" analysis. We focus on the product category, which defines the set of competitors against which one most often competes on a daily basis. While this may seem to be a narrow definition, particularly after the discussion in the preceding chapter, a manager can adapt the analysis presented in this chapter to the definition of product category or industry most appropriate for the circumstances.

An essential component of the marketing planning process is an analysis of a product's potential to achieve a desired level of return on the company's investment. An analysis of this type not only assesses financial opportunities but also provides ideas about how to compete better given structural characteristics of the category.

The characteristics of a product category rarely all point in the same direction. As a result, categories that some firms find attractive will be of little interest to others. For example, most food categories are characterized by low but steady sales volume growth. A growth rate of 4.5 percent in the frozen potato category would probably seem high to the Ore-Ida product manager but quite low to a Cisco Systems marketer. In the automobile market, most observers consider the luxury car segment (over $40,000) overpopulated with models from every major car manufacturer in the world. However, Ford chose to purchase Jaguar because of the considerable brand equity in the name and because Ford management believed the brand gave the company an instant entry into the luxury car field.

Besides the product manager for the manufacturer or service provider, another interested party to this analysis is the distribution channel. As noted in Chapter 1, more channel members, particularly retailers, are interested in category management, the profitable management of entire product categories. Clearly, retailers will give more space and/or selling time to those categories that are "attractive," which means faster

FIGURE 3.1 Category Attractiveness Summary

Aggregate category factors:
  Category size
  Category growth
  Stage in product life cycle
  Sales cyclicity
  Seasonality
  Profits
Category factors:
  Threat of new entrants
  Bargaining power of buyers
  Bargaining power of suppliers
  Current category rivalry
  Pressure from substitutes
  Category capacity
Environmental factors:
  Technological
  Political
  Economic
  Regulatory
  Social

inventory turnover, greater total profits, and less space for categories that are "unattractive." Thus, the kind of analysis described in this chapter is also relevant to (and probably also being performed by) the channel members in the distribution system.

In this chapter, we examine the important factors (summarized in Figure 3.1) in assessing the underlying attractiveness of a product category. The three main areas of inquiry include basic aggregate factors, category factors related to the major participants, and environmental factors. We also discuss sources of information for the attractiveness analysis components and apply the concepts to the energy bar and PDA categories.

AGGREGATE MARKET FACTORS

Six major market factors impact market attractiveness (Figure 3.2).

Category Size
Category size (measured in both units and monetary value) is an important piece of data about any market. It is clearly an important determinant of the likelihood that a product will generate revenues to support a given investment. In general, larger markets are better than smaller ones. Besides having more market potential, large categories usually offer more opportunities for segmentation than small ones

FIGURE 3.2 Attractiveness of Market Variables

	Attractiveness	
	High	Low
Market size	+	−
Market growth	+	−
Sales cyclicity	−	+
Sales seasonality	−	+
Profit level	+	−
Profit variability	−	+

(see Chapter 5). Therefore, both large firms and entrepreneurial organizations might find large markets attractive. Large markets, however, tend to draw competitors with considerable resources, thus making them unattractive for small firms. Witness the soft-drink category. Coca-Cola and PepsiCo spent $240 million in the first six months of 2003 on advertising alone supporting Coke, Diet Coke, Pepsi, and Diet Pepsi, and this did not include money spent on promotion (*Advertising Age,* 2003). Thus, absolute size by itself is not sufficient to warrant new or continuing investment.

Market Growth

As mentioned previously, market growth is a key market factor advocated by various planning models. Not only is current growth important, but growth projections over the horizon of the plan are also critical. Fast-growing categories are almost universally desired due to their abilities to support high margins and sustain profits in future years. However, like large categories, fast-growing ones also attract competitors. For example, while Procter & Gamble developed the U.S. market for disposable diapers, the high growth rate supported the entry of other firms such as Johnson & Johnson and Kimberly Clark. In technology-based markets, fast growth often means dramatic shifts in market shares and the virtual disappearance of rival products. In the Internet browser market, Netscape had 13 percent of the market and Mosaic had 60 percent in 1994. However, by 2002, Netscape had 8 percent of the market, Mosaic had disappeared, and Microsoft's Internet Explorer held 91 percent (Angwin and Sandberg, 2002). Thus, growth brings the prospects of increasing revenues but also dynamic market structures in terms of competitors.

Product Life Cycle

Category size and category growth are often portrayed simultaneously in the form of the product life cycle (see Figure 3.3). Usually presumed to be S-shaped, this curve breaks down product sales into four segments: introduction, growth, maturity, and decline. The introduction and growth phases are the early phases of the life

FIGURE 3.3 Category Attractiveness over the Product Life Cycle

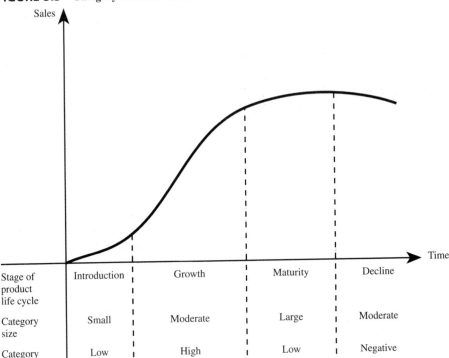

Stage of product life cycle	Introduction	Growth	Maturity	Decline
Category size	Small	Moderate	Large	Moderate
Category growth	Low	High	Low	Negative
Category attractiveness	Low	High	Low/high	Low

cycle when sales are growing rapidly, maturity represents a leveling off in sales, and the decline phase represents the end of the life cycle.

Figure 3.3 also presents a general assessment of the attractiveness of a category at each stage of the life cycle. In the introductory phase, both the growth rate and the size of the market are low, thus making it unattractive for most prospective participants, who would rather wait on the sidelines for a period of time. When market growth and sales start to take off, the market becomes more attractive. In the maturity phase, the assessment is unclear; while the growth rate is low, the market size could be at its peak. This is the classic pattern for soft drinks, fast food, and many other consumer packaged goods: large dollar volume with slow growth. Finally, the decline phase usually is so unattractive that most competitors flee the category.

However, the attractiveness of products in different phases of the life cycle is not always clear. While the introductory phase has low growth and sales volume, it can be attractive to be the pioneer from a long-run market share perspective (Kalyanaram, Robinson, and Urban 1995; Urban et al., 1986). Products in the growth phase are not ensured success—witness the failures of Osborne and Commodore in the early days of personal computers and the well-documented difficulties that even "big name" companies such as AT&T and Hewlett-Packard have had in the home segment of the personal computer market. Even products in the decline phase, e.g., the "last ice man," can be very profitable. Lansdale Semiconductor and Rochester Electronics were the last companies to manufacture the 8080 microprocessor introduced by Intel in 1974. Some companies in the toy, defense, and telecommunications industries make products or need spare parts that use these old chips.

Sales Cyclicity

Many categories experience substantial interyear variation in demand. Highly capital-intensive businesses such as automobiles, steel, and machine tools are often tied to general business conditions and therefore suffer through peaks and valleys of sales as gross domestic product (GDP) varies. Similarly, businesses tied to interest rates, such as real estate and other financial services, are susceptible to cycles. Products based on agricultural commodities are affected by yearly climactic conditions. This is clearly not an attractive characteristic of a category, as these sales swings affect profits, employment levels, and cash available for new product development. Many firms attempt to develop products and acquire other businesses to eliminate interyear sales cyclicity.

Seasonality

Seasonality—intrayear cycles in sales—is generally not viewed positively. For example, in the last few years, the toy industry has reduced its reliance on the Christmas period to generate most of its sales. Such seasonal business tends to generate price wars because there may be few other opportunities to make substantial sales. However, most products are seasonal to some extent. Some, such as cold remedies, lawn mowers, fuel oil, and ice cream, are very seasonal.

Profits

While profits vary across products or brands in a category, large interindustry differences also exist. For example, the average profit margins for footwear, personal care, and biotechnology were 5.7, 20.9, and 49.3 percent, respectively, in 2002.[1]

Differences in profitability across industries can be driven by a variety of underlying causes. These differences may be due to factors of production (e.g., labor versus capital intensity, raw materials), manufacturing technology, and competitive rivalry, to name a few. Suffice it to say that product categories that are chronically low in profitability are less attractive than those that offer higher returns.

A second aspect of profitability is that it varies over time. Variance in profitability is often used as a measure of industry risk. Semiconductors offer abnormally high returns when demand is good but concomitant poor returns when demand slumps. Food-related businesses, on the other hand, produce relatively steady, if unspectacular, profits. As is usually the case, marketing managers must

[1] *S&P Analysts' Handbook*, 2002 Annual Edition (New York: Standard & Poor's).

make a risk–return trade-off, evaluating the expected returns against the variability in those returns.

CATEGORY FACTORS

Although the aggregate factors just described are important indicators of the attractiveness of a product category, they do not provide information about underlying structural factors affecting the category. A classic model developed by Porter (1980) considers five factors in assessing the structure of industries:

The threat of new entrants.

The bargaining power of buyers.

The bargaining power of suppliers.

The amount of intracategory rivalry.

The threat of substitute products or services.

We adapt these factors to the category analysis and add a sixth factor, production or service capacity.

Threat of New Entrants

If the threat of new entrants into the product category is high, the attractiveness of the category is diminished. Except for the early stages of market development, when new entrants can help a market to expand, new entrants bring additional capacity and resources that usually heighten the competitiveness of the market and diminish profit margins. Even at early stages of market growth, the enthusiasm with which new entrants are greeted is tempered by who the competitor is. For example, while online investment companies like E*Trade publicly welcomed Charles Schwab's entry into the market, it is unlikely that they were as happy in private.

The barriers to entry erected by the existing competition are key to the likelihood that new competitors will enter the market. This sounds anticompetitive and illegal, but it is only definitely anticompetitive; making it difficult for new competitors through legal means is a common strategic weapon. Some of the potential barriers to entry follow.

Economies of Scale

An important barrier to entry in the automobile industry is the large plant size needed to operate efficiently, obtain quantity discounts on raw materials, and so on. Small manufacturers (e.g., Rolex) are normally content with serving the high-priced market segment. Economies of scale are obtainable in areas other than manufacturing. For example, in the hospital supply business, profit margins are better on larger orders because the costs of taking and fulfilling an order are largely fixed. Service costs are also subject to economies of scale because it costs about the same to set up a service center to service many customers or retailers as it does to service a few. Large advertisers usually get quantity discounts when buying blocks of media time on TV, radio, and other media.

Product Differentiation

Well-established brand names or company reputations can make it difficult for new competitors to enter. In the ready-to-eat breakfast cereal industry, the big four—Kellogg, Kraft/General Foods, General Mills, and Quaker Oats—have such long-established reputations that a new branded competitor would find it difficult to establish a brand franchise. The high barriers in the cereal industry were the subject of a lawsuit (ultimately unsuccessful) by the U.S. government.

Capital Requirements

Large amounts of capital may be necessary to establish manufacturing facilities, chain store locations, or marketing programs. It is easy to think of very capital-intensive industries, such as chemicals and aircraft, which require enormous amounts of money to set up plants. However, many categories are much more marketing intensive, through either advertising or distribution. For example, some mail-order computer companies buy their machines from other companies and spend most of their money on advertising, distribution, and service. Thus, capital barriers are clearly not confined to plant and equipment. The fast-food category has enormous fixed costs for marketing (advertising and promotion) and distribution.

Switching Costs

These are the costs of switching from one supplier to another. *Supplier* can be interpreted in a business-to-business sense or in an end-customer context. If switching costs are high, as they are in the mainframe computer and computer software businesses, it is difficult to convert a competitor's existing customers. Federal Express has given its business customers software that enables them to monitor the status of their own packages in the FedEx system. This creates a barrier to potential new entrants as well as making it difficult for competitors to get FedEx customers to switch package delivery firms. It is more difficult to build in switching costs into consumer products, particularly supermarket items, as consumers can simply change brands the next time they shop. However, a notable exception is Gillette, which tries to sell the notion of a shaving "system" and thus promotes the use of its blades with its razors. Another example is home video game manufacturers such as Sony and Nintendo, which have security devices in their game cartridges and proprietary hardware that allow only games made by the company or its licensees to be used with each system.

In the information technology arena, building such barriers to switching is often referred to as *lock-in* (Shapiro and Varian, 1999). Loyalty programs are good examples of building switching costs from lock-in. If you are a member of United Airlines' Mileage Plus program, you tend to choose United when possible in order to increase the accumulated mileage in your account.

Distribution

New products can find it difficult to obtain shelf space. Coca-Cola and PepsiCo have created so many varieties of their basic colas that branded rivals such as 7Up have found it more difficult to gain shelf space, particularly since private labels have made significant inroads into the soft-drink category. Supermarkets, drugstores, and other chain retailers often charge *slotting allowances,* payments from manufacturers for placing their goods on shelves. This practice obviously creates a barrier to entry, particularly for smaller firms that find it difficult to pay the fees.

The willingness of the competitors in the category to vigorously retaliate against newcomers can also act as a barrier. When small Minnetonka, Inc., innovated with a pump for hand soap, both Colgate-Palmolive and Procter & Gamble immediately copied the package and outspent Minnetonka in promotion. That story has been repeated in the toothpaste category.

Barriers change over time. When Xerox's patent on its basic copying process expired, the number of competitors in the copier market expanded dramatically. Likewise, when a prescription drug's patent protection ends, a generic with a much lower price is invariably introduced.

It is important not only that marketing managers note the likelihood of a new entrant based on the above factors, but also that they assess the ability of a product to heighten entry barriers. Again, although raising barriers to entry has a negative connotation, particularly to a company's lawyers, there are legal means of inhibiting competition in a product category. Thus, a manager could ask: Is there anything I can do to make it more difficult for a new entrant or even a current competitor to compete against me? The answers are related to the factors noted above. For example, if threat of entry is easy (a negative for the category), then (1) differentiate more; (2) raise the stakes (capital) required to compete effectively; (3) build in switching costs, thus making it harder for customers to switch brands; (4) lock up distribution and/or supply to the extent it is legal; or (5) if appropriate, signal your intention to strongly retaliate. Successful managers commonly attempt most of these tactics. Note that brand extensions occupy shelf space, and many companies spend money to limit brand switching through database marketing and loyalty programs, that is, tracking individual customer buying habits and offering promotions via direct mail or telemarketing.

Bargaining Power of Buyers

Buyers are people or organizations that receive finished goods or services from the organizations in the category being analyzed. Buyers can be distributors, original equipment manufacturers (OEMs), or end customers. Suppliers are institutions that supply the category of concern with factors of production such as labor, capital, raw materials, and machinery.

High buyer bargaining power is negatively related to industry attractiveness. In such circumstances, buyers can force down prices and play competitors off against one another for benefits such as service. Some conditions that occur when buyer bargaining power is high include the following:

1. *When the product bought is a large percentage of the buyer's costs.* Historically, the automobile industry (the buyer) had little buying power over the steel industry (the industry of concern) because steel has been so important to car manufacturing. This power, however, is increasing as car manufacturers replace steel with plastics and reduce the number of suppliers they use to gain price concessions and productivity improvements.

2. *When the product bought is undifferentiated.* If the selling firms in a category of concern view what they sell as a commodity, buyers will have a great deal of power. Good examples of this include the leverage held by customers of commodity chemicals or bulk semiconductors. In such situations, buyers view the offerings as indistinguishable and bear down on price.

3. *When the buyers earn low profits.* Ailing industries such as farm equipment can generally extract better terms from supplier industries than can healthy industries.

4. *When the buyer threatens to backward integrate.* Among other pressures felt by semiconductor manufacturers is the constant threat by computer companies to make their own chips. IBM's purchase of part of Intel is such an example. Consumers also backward integrate, as the growth of do-it-yourself hardware and furniture stores indicates.

5. *When the buyer has full information.* Consumers can exert more power in retail stores if they are fully aware of competitive offerings. For example, car dealers are more willing to negotiate on price when a buyer demonstrates he or she has collected dealer cost information from a source such as *Consumer Reports* or Edmunds.com.

6. *When substitutes exist for the seller's product or service.* Although this is a separate category factor, described below, it also clearly affects buyer power.

In general, consumers wield their buyer power only on an individual and generally limited basis. This is not true in industrial businesses in which customers such as the U.S. government can wield large amounts of power. However, if consumers can be organized as a group, they become a more important customer and thus exert more power than would otherwise be the case. For example, the large population of retired consumers are powerfully linked through the American Association of Retired Persons (AARP). Similarly, buying cooperatives have increased power. For example, major U.S. hospitals have banded together to demand better terms of purchasing routine supplies such as tongue depressors, bandages, etc.

Again, the firm's general objective is to decrease buyer power. This is accomplished, for example, by increasing product differentiation (e.g., making your product an essential component), helping customers become more profitable through services such as technical assistance or manufacturing-related consulting, and building in switching costs.

Bargaining Power of Suppliers

This assessment is really the mirror image of the buyer power analysis. High supplier power is clearly not an attractive situation because it allows suppliers to dictate price and other terms, such as delivery dates, to the buying category. Supplier bargaining power is generally higher under the following circumstances:

1. *Suppliers are highly concentrated, that is, dominated by a few firms.* Organizations in need of supercomputers face strong suppliers because very few exist worldwide (IBM, Cray, NEC, and a few others).

2. *There is no substitute for the product supplied.* The supercomputer falls in this category, although this power is diminishing with the increased computing speed offered by workstations. The power of the Organization of Petroleum Exporting Countries (OPEC) diminished as many industries converted plants to use oil and coal, and recently increased as demand has grown.

3. *The supplier has differentiated its product or built in switching costs.* AK Steel Inc. increased its power with the automobile industry by offering General Motors a delayed payment plan, a guarantee of no work stoppages, a demonstration of how cheaper steel could be substituted in certain areas, and extra service such as supplying steel already prepared with adhesives for some applications.

4. *Supply is limited.* Clearly when capacity and output are limited, buyers have little opportunity to extract special terms.

Managers can reduce supplier power by, for example, looking for new sources of supply and substitute materials.

Category Rivalry

Product categories characterized by intense competition among the major participants are not as attractive as those in which the rivalry is more sedate. A high degree of rivalry can result in escalated marketing expenditures, price wars, employee raids, and related activities. Such actions can exceed what is considered "normal" market competition and can result in decreased welfare for both consumers and competitors.[2]

Several examples highlight the negative aspects of rivalry. In the cell phone category, four of the top six service providers (Verizon, Cingular, AT&T, and Sprint) spent over $1.5 billion on advertising in the first half of 2003. What did this accomplish? The four companies have customer "churn" (loss) rates of 1.9, 2.8, 2.7, and 2.7 percent *monthly.* Compaq (prior to its acquisition by Hewlett-Packard) and Dell were well known to be bitter rivals in the personal computer industry; situated 200 miles apart in Texas, they stole each other's employees, traded vicious attacks in the press, and hired focus groups to find holes in the rival's strategies (Pope, 1993). Other well-known intense rivals are Oracle and Siebel in the software industry, chipmakers Intel and AMD, amusement park operators Six Flags and Disney, and giant Japanese trading companies Matsushita and Sony in consumer electronics.

These are some of the major characteristics of categories exhibiting intensive rivalries:

1. *Many or balanced competitors.* The fast-food, automobile, and personal computer industries each have several large, well-endowed competitors. At one time, the commercial aircraft manufacturing industry had one strong company, Boeing, and two weaker companies, McDonnell Douglas and Airbus. With Boeing's acquisition of McDonnell Douglas and Airbus's string of successes in landing customers, the two are now quite even and bitter competitors.

---

[2] *New York Times,* November 24, 2003, p. C4.

2. *Slow growth.* The relevant issue here, of course, is that in mature markets, growth can come only from a competitor.

3. *High fixed costs.* In such categories, there is intense pressure to keep operations running at full capacity to lower average unit costs. For this reason, capital-intensive industries such as paper and chemicals are highly competitive.

4. *Lack of product differentiation.* When little differentiation exists, products and services look like commodities to customers and price warfare erupts.

5. *Personal rivalries.* In some industries, personal rivalries develop around strong personalities who exhibit strong competitive instincts. Sun's Scott McNealey and Microsoft's Bill Gates frequently snipe at each other in speeches and articles. Oracle and Siebel are competitors in the customer relationship management (CRM) category. Even though he used to work for Oracle, Tom Siebel and Larry Ellison (Oracle's CEO) bring corporate competitiveness into the personal arena.

In general, it is difficult for any single product manager to have a major impact on category rivalry.

Pressure from Substitutes

Categories making products or delivering services for which there are a large number of substitutes are less attractive than those that deliver a relatively proprietary product, one that uniquely fills a customer need or solves a problem. Since almost all categories suffer from the availability of substitutes (recall the discussion from Chapter 2), this may not be a determinant of an unattractive product category. However, some of the highest rates of return are earned in categories in which the range of substitutes is small. For example, the broadcast media industry, which had few substitutes (although that is changing rapidly), earned much higher margins (nearly 30 percent) than coal (under 10 percent), which definitely has available alternatives.

Determining the degree to which substitutes exist relates to the definition of the category. However, as noted in Chapter 1, some products, such as soft drinks, clearly have more generic competitors, whereas others, such as farm tractors, find their main competition within the category.

Capacity

Chronic overcapacity is not a positive sign for long-term profitability. When a category is operating at capacity, its costs stay low and its bargaining power with buyers is normally high. Thus, a key indicator of the health of a category is whether there is a consistent tendency toward operating at or under capacity. For example, during recessions, consumer spending on travel services is low, resulting in overcapacity at many worldwide resorts. This leads to low bargaining power with buyers, who can bargain down rates on cruises and other vacations.

Figure 3.4 summarizes the category analysis. For an actual marketing plan, each of the major categories in the figure should be expanded to include the factors discussed in this chapter. In addition, the implications of the analysis should be stated,

FIGURE 3.4   **Impact of Category Factors on Attractiveness**

	High	Low
Threat of new entrants	−	+
Power of buyers	−	+
Power of suppliers	−	+
Rivalry	−	+
Pressure from substitutes	−	+
Unused capacity	−	+

not just whether or not the category is attractive. Since, as a marketing manager, you are usually in the category whether you like it or not, the important output of the category analysis is what the manager learns about how to better compete in the product category.

ENVIRONMENTAL ANALYSIS

The *environment* encompasses those factors outside the control of both the firm and its industry, or, stated another way, the external factors unrelated to the product's customers and competitors that affect marketing strategies. The vulnerability of a product category to changes in the environment is an unattractive characteristic, but virtually all product managers must deal with it. As mentioned earlier in the chapter, if a category's sales are tied to the domestic economic situation, cyclicity can result. Alternatively, categories that are well positioned to take advantage of environmental changes may prosper, as can managers who view these changes as opportunities to gain competitive advantage.

Environmental factors fall into five groups: technological, political, economic, regulatory, and social. These factors should be examined to assess category attractiveness and to determine if any forecasted changes dictate changes in strategy.

Technological Factors

Figure 3.5 displays a model of the technological environment that is useful for conceptualizing sources of technological change in an industry (adapted from Thomas, 1974, for a product category). The "technology" and "impetus" dimensions are self-explanatory. The "process" dimension draws a distinction between the development of a new product (invention), the introduction of the product (innovation), and the spread of the product through the population (diffusion).

The two key dimensions used to assess a category's attractiveness are technology and process. Major changes are occurring in the energy, materials, transportation, information, and genetic (bioengineering) areas. With respect to information, for example, electronic scanning systems installed at supermarket cash registers enable retailers to closely monitor sales of different items for both inventory and shelf space allocation decisions. Bioengineering research is being used to both improve crop yields and find cures for various diseases such as cancer.

FIGURE 3.5 Typology of Technical Developments

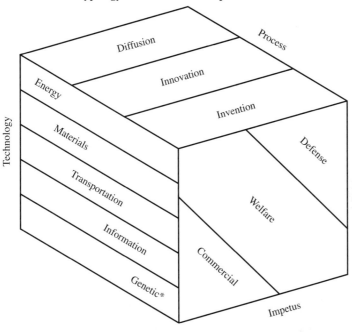

*Includes agronomic and biomedical developments.
Source: Philip S. Thomas, "Environmental Analysis for Corporate Planning," *Business Horizons* 17 (October 1974), p. 27.

Product categories that are weaker on the technology dimension are particularly vulnerable to competition both from new products and from foreign competitors that have made the necessary investment. For example, in the 1980s most major U.S. steel firms used blast furnace technology developed in the 1800s. Foreign steel firms and domestic companies that invested in modern manufacturing technology have been highly successful in the past decade. On the positive side, U.S. strength has been computer software. Thus, an attractive product category is one that is well positioned to take advantage of technological changes that may be necessary to remain competitive against new, substitute technologies.

There is, however, a point beyond which technology can create a backlash, particularly among consumers. This has been referred to by John Naisbitt (1984) as "high tech versus high touch." For example, automatic teller machines have depersonalized banking to the point where some consumers yearn for the human contact afforded by tellers. Several years ago, Citibank in New York proposed to allow only its wealthiest customers to make transactions through personal contact; other customers would have been forced to use machines. Consumers protested so vehemently that Citibank scrapped the idea. Although frequently touted as a wave of the future, home banking through personal computers has never really caught on with consumers in a big way. Similarly, although grocery shopping through the Web grew significantly due to the efforts of companies like Freshdirect, Peapod, and some other small companies, it still accounts for less than 1 percent of the $400 billion U.S. retail grocery market (Lee, 2003).

Attractive product categories are strong in invention, innovation, or diffusion of new products or services. Most technologically based companies must continually innovate because the life cycles for their products are extremely short. In contrast, success in frequently purchased packaged goods, while often continuously upgraded in various ways (e.g., packaging, flavor), is determined more by the quality of the marketing programs such as promotion, advertising, etc.

Political Factors

A second environmental factor relates to the category's sensitivity to political factors. These are particularly relevant for products with substantial foreign markets. Figure 3.6 conceptualizes the sources of political risk, the groups that generate political risk, and political problems in operating the business (Robock, 1971).

FIGURE 3.6   **Conceptualizing Political Risks**

Sources of Political Risk	Groups through Which Political Risk Can Be Generated	Effects on International Business Operations
Competing political philosophies (nationalism, socialism, communism)	Government in power and its operating agencies	Confiscation: loss of assets without compensation
Social unrest and disorder	Parliamentary opposition groups	Expropriation with compensation: loss of freedom to operate
Vested interests of local business groups	Nonparliamentary opposition groups (Algerian "FLN," guerrilla movements working within or outside country)	Operational restrictions: market shares, product characteristics, employment policies, locally shared ownership, and so on
Recent and impending political independence		
Armed conflicts and internal rebellions for political power	Nonorganized common interest groups: students, workers, peasants, minorities, and so on	
New international alliances		Loss of transfer freedom: financial (dividends, interest payments, goods, personnel, or ownership rights, for example)
	Foreign governments or intergovernmental agencies such as the EEC	
	Foreign governments willing to enter into armed conflict or to support internal rebellion	Breaches or unilateral revisions in contracts and agreements
		Discrimination such as taxes or compulsory subcontractings
		Damage to property or personnel from riots, insurrections, revolutions, and wars

Source: Stefan H. Robock, "Political Risk: Identification and Assessment," *Columbia Journal of World Business,* July–August 1971, p. 7.

For example, many multinational companies are either actively marketing or considering marketing products in China and other countries experiencing economic reform, such as Vietnam, Cambodia, and even Iraq in the post-Saddam era. Following Figure 3.6, the sources of political risk are competing political philosophies (the risk that communism or some form of autocracy hostile to market reforms could return) and possible social unrest and disorder. The results of these risks could be a halt to conducting business, damage to property, and personal risk to employees.

Such analysis aids in evaluating geographically defined market segments for the line. If a sufficient percentage of a product's sales came from risky foreign markets, the product could in fact look unattractive relative to others.

Domestic U.S. political risk is generally not as great, but it is still important. Domestic risk is usually related to which political party is in power. Republicans tend to favor free market economies. Therefore, products hard hit by foreign competition (e.g., shoes, commodity semiconductors, automobiles) would probably receive no relief through quotas or increased tariffs. With Democrats, defense spending has historically been a target, and hence the fortunes of defense-related products are at risk. However, these political risks are dynamic. With the lowering of world tensions following the demise of the Soviet Union and the Eastern European communist bloc, defense spending declined. However, after the events of September 11, 2001, industries supplying defense and security-related products have done very well.

Economic Factors

Almost all capital goods industries (machine tools, farm equipment, mainframe computers) are sensitive to *interest rate fluctuations,* since their high costs to buyers are often financed at short-term interest rates. Consumer durables such as homes, cars, and stereos are also sensitive to interest rates, although consumer credit card rates do not react as much to changes in the prime lending rate as do commercial rates. Inflation rates, of course, are tied to interest rate fluctuations.

The financial impact of having foreign markets or producing in other countries can vary widely over time depending on *currency exchange rates.*

Since service businesses often hire relatively unskilled labor at low wage rates, they are highly dependent on *employment conditions.* When employment rates are high, for example, fast-food employees are hard to find and it is necessary to pay them more because higher-paying jobs are available. Demand and supply of labor for each industry must be considered as well. The supply of engineers is cyclical. When supply is down, many firms in technically related businesses suffer from a shortage of skilled labor.

Products such as automobiles and other consumer durables that have broad customer bases are often sensitive to *fluctuations in GDP growth.* When the country is in a recession, the sales of these products decline.

Regulatory Factors

Government and other agencies have an impact on category attractiveness through regulations. Some product categories have become less attractive over time because of recent laws that restrict managers' abilities to market or that raise the overall cost of doing business. Government regulations, for example, restrict the media the tobacco industry can use for advertising. Pharmaceutical companies and many companies that make medical products are subject to stringent testing requirements that can change over time. Alternatively, government intervention can help some product categories. The U.S. government's restrictions on Japanese auto exports is an example, as is the subsidy given to certain agricultural commodities.

A good example of the impact of regulation on a pharmaceutical product is Genentech's tPA, an anticlotting drug. The company was so confident that the drug would succeed that it invested a considerable amount of money in manufacturing equipment, employees, premarketing, and product inventory. However, the Food and Drug Administration rejected the drug in May 1987, and within a week Genentech's market value dropped by nearly $1 billion.

It is not possible to generalize about the sources of regulatory impact because each product category is affected by different regulatory bodies. As a result, this part of the analysis must be highly category specific.

Social Factors

Trends in demographics, lifestyles, attitudes, and personal values among the general population are of particular concern for consumer product manufacturers and services. First, new products have been developed to fit into today's lifestyles. The growth of the size of the section in many supermarkets devoted to freshly prepared entrees is a direct result of the increase in dual-career and busy households with a need for convenience and easy preparation. Second, new features have been added to existing products. Upper-income consumers can have global positioning system (GPS) mapping systems in their cars and telephones with which they can surf the Web and snap digital pictures. Finally, promotion has changed. The aging "baby boomer" (reportedly similar in age to the clearly youthful authors) is commonplace today in television ads, as is the mysterious "Generation X" (young adults) consumer and "Gen Y" youths.

What is not as generally recognized is the importance of understanding trends in lifestyles and demographics for business-to-business products. Because the demand for such products is often derived demand, that is, ultimately generated by consumers, changes in the source of that demand can clearly affect demand for an industrial product. For example, the chemical manufacturer making polymers used in paints is affected by the amount of money consumers spend in fixing up houses and in new construction. For companies that provide business-to-business products, the key question to ask in assessing attractiveness is whether the *customers* of the product being considered are in the "right" industries. Unsurprisingly, firms supplying the "hot" categories tend to do well, and those that are heavily tied to declining consumer products do not.

For consumer products, a key question is whether the product category under consideration is well positioned to take advantage of current trends. Some products are "hot" because they appeal to the large and increasingly affluent baby boomer group; these include furniture and electronic appliances, upscale fast-food chains, clothing, and financial and travel services. Other products have been developed for consumers at the older end of the baby boom generation (those now reaching their late-50s). For example, a large part of the market for the Audi TT, Porsche Boxster, BMW Z3/4, and other sports cars introduced in the late 1990s through the early 2000s are

FIGURE 3.7 Projected Change in U.S. Population 1995–2005

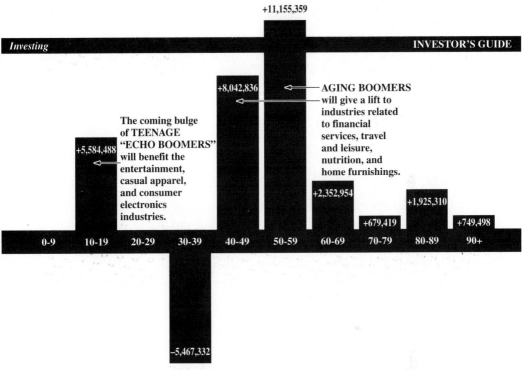

Source: "Betting on the Boomers," by Erick Schonfeld, *Fortune,* December 2, 1995. © 1995 TIME INC. REPRINTED BY PERMISSION.

people over 40 who wish to reduce their psychological age. Products having trouble, on the other hand, include coffee, cigarettes, and brown alcohol (except for high-end scotch whiskey), which are being buffeted by demographic and taste trends.

Because of the rise of the Internet globally, many pundits forecast that the 21st century will be the age of the customer. The shift of power from the seller to the customer is facilitated by both the increase in the information that customers have available to them and the lowering of shopping costs, which makes it easier for customers to compare options in terms of features and price. It has been said that customers can pretty much have what they want when they want it and at the price they wish to pay (Apparently this doesn't apply to the authors).

At least in the early part of the 21st century, the major demographic changes in the United States that will underlie consumer demand are the following (Miller, 1999):

- The aging of the baby-boom generation (those born between 1945 and 1964); Figure 3.7 shows the change in the U.S. population over the years 1995–2005. Witness the growth in the 40- to 59-year-old age bracket. Clearly, this has tremendous implications for products and services targeting more mature consumers.
- The increasing importance of children as consumers; see Figure 3.8 for one writer's conceptualization of how today's children, or N-Geners (for the net generation),

FIGURE 3.8   **The 10 Themes of N-Gen Culture**

The Net Generation: Youth between 4 and 20 who are computer and Internet literate.

1. *Fierce independence:* A strong sense of independence and autonomy.
2. *Emotional and intellectual openness:* When N-Geners go online, they expose themselves.
3. *Inclusion:* A global orientation in their search for information, activity, and communication.
4. *Free expression and strong view:* The Internet has exposed them to a much greater range of ideas, opinions, and arguments than they would have experienced without it.
5. *Innovation:* A constant search for ways to do things better.
6. *Preoccupation with maturity:* N-Geners insist that they are more mature than adults expect.
7. *Investigation:* A strong ethos of curiosity, investigation, and the empowerment to change things.
8. *Immediacy:* The children of the digital age expect things to happen fast, because in their world, things *do* happen fast.
9. *Sensitivity to corporate interest:* They believe that too many perspectives are being left out of the broadcast images and they believe corporate agendas play a role in this shortfall.
10. *Authentication and trust:* Because of the anonymity, accessibility, diversity, and ubiquity of the Internet, N-Geners must continually authenticate what they see or hear on the Web.

Source: Don Tapscott, *Growing Up Digital* (New York: McGraw Hill, 1998).

can be characterized. It is undoubtedly the case that children growing up in today's technology-charged society will be different consumers when they reach their prime spending years than their parents.

- A growing gap between society's haves and have-nots. Figure 3.9 shows that despite overall increased prosperity, the differences between the wealthier U.S. households and the poorer is increasing, particularly comparing the top 10 percent to the bottom. On a net worth basis, the differences are even greater. The net worth of families in the top 10 percent jumped 69 percent, to $833,600, in 2001 from $492,400 in 1998. By contrast, the net worth of families in the lowest fifth of income earners rose only 24 percent, to $7,900 (Andrews, 2003).
- An increasingly diverse population; by 2025, non-Hispanic whites will comprise 62.4 percent of the U.S. population, down from 72.5 percent in 1998.

Given this as a backdrop, some key forces driving the era of the consumer are the following:

1. *The shrinking day.* More time spent working and committing to family-related activities means less time doing things consumers do not want to do, like housework and cooking. This latter phenomenon is manifested in the growth of the share of food purchases in restaurants versus supermarkets. As can be seen in Figure 3.10, the share of purchases in restaurants passed the supermarket share in 1992 and the gap is widening. What consumers increasingly value in terms of products and services is time and convenience.

FIGURE 3.9 U.S. Income Inequality

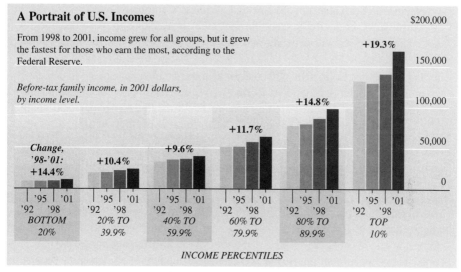

A Portrait of U.S. Incomes $200,000

From 1998 to 2001, income grew for all groups, but it grew the fastest for those who earn the most, according to the Federal Reserve.

Before-tax family income, in 2001 dollars, by income level.

+19.3%

150,000

100,000

+14.8%

+11.7%

50,000

Change, '98-'01: +10.4% +9.6%
+14.4%

0

'95 '01 | '95 '01 | '95 '01 | '95 '01 | '95 '01 | '95 '01
'92 '98 | '92 '98 | '92 '98 | '92 '98 | '92 '98 | '92 '98
BOTTOM 20% | *20% TO 39.9%* | *40% TO 59.9%* | *60% TO 79.9%* | *80% TO 89.9%* | *TOP 10%*

INCOME PERCENTILES

Source: "Economic Inequality Grew in 90's Boom, Fed Reports," *New York Times,* January 23, 2003, p. C1.

2. *Connectedness.* It is predicted that the Web will be where people turn to for a sense of community—between buyers and sellers, information suppliers and consumers, friends and family. While it is perhaps premature to say that all of this exists today (2004), clearly the trends point in that direction. It is commonplace for college students to chat with their friends for hours using an Instant Messenger service, and even for family members in the same house to communicate with each other.

3. *Body versus soul.* Some forecast that the new consumers will increasingly stay home to shop, meditate, and pamper their bodies but that they will also expect more in terms of entertainment (e.g., big screen plasma TVs). An example of this trend is what has been termed the "entertainmentization" of retailing where stores stage events, show videos on big screens, and attempt to add entertainment to

FIGURE 3.10 Share of Food Purchases

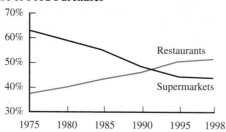

70%
60%
Restaurants
50%
40% Supermarkets
30%
1975 1980 1985 1990 1995 1998

Source: *Nation's Restaurant News,* 1999.

everyday shopping experiences. The shrinking day also leads to consumers placing higher value on the spiritual. Witness Campbell Soup's motto: "M'm! M'm! Good for the Body. Good for the Soul." Investments in personal fitness will remain strong as will expenditures on expensive junk food (e.g., super-premium ice cream).

4. *Individualism.* Consistent with the trend toward individualism is an increase in products and services tailored to small groups, called *mass customization*. From Nike's custom-designed running shoes to Dell's made-to-order personal computers, customers want products built for them (or at least, they want the impression that they are). This trend toward the individual has also led to a dramatic growth in the small office, home office (SOHO) market to about 4 million workers who now claim their main offices in their homes. Accompanying mass customized products are marketing programs tailored to individuals, or *1–1 marketing.*

Any attempt to project these kinds of trends is fraught with difficulties, of course; the landscape is littered with forecasts that have gone awry (see, for example, Schnaars's 1989 book describing a number of such erroneous forecasts). In addition, many books continue to be produced that attempt such forecasts (books by Popcorn and Marigold, 1998, and Wacker, Taylor, and Means, 2000, are examples). However, the fundamental demographic and socioeconomic factors that underlie the forecasts provide incontrovertible evidence that change will occur. It is essential that managers think about the impact of these changes on their businesses.

ILLUSTRATIONS

Energy Bars

Figure 3.11 summarizes a category attractiveness analysis for the energy snack bar category. Sources of information for this and the PDA illustration are listed in Chapter 1 in Figures 1.10 and 1.13. The aggregate market factors overall are very positive. The total market size is not that large but it has a significant growth rate, and the profit margins are very high. A particularly positive factor is that the product is not seasonal due to the year-round use of exercise (i.e. running, skiing, gym workouts). The category factors are not so positive. Since it is a food product that is relatively easy to make, the threat of entrants is quite high, particularly from companies already in the food business. Switching costs are low and differentiation is difficult. There are also many substitutes and a considerable amount of competition. The environmental factors are generally positive, particularly the social factors which have helped to grow the category.

The purpose of this analysis is to enable the marketing manager to focus on aspects that expose weaknesses of the category and the brand. These are, of course, those factors with minus signs next to them. While the energy bar category has some significant positive factors (e.g., growth), there are some problems that product managers have to deal with. Obviously, key issues are in the areas of product differentiation and barriers to entry. Building strong brand names is one activity that accomplishes both objectives. This could also happen as the large companies

FIGURE 3.11 Energy Bars: Category Attractiveness Summary

Factors	Analysis	Assessment Market Attractiveness
Aggregate Market		
Category size	• $504 million energy bars in 2001. • Energy bar category contains four primary brands, plus their sub-brands and over a hundred smaller players.	++
Category growth	• Average annual growth rate of 57% between 1997 and 2001. • U.S. energy bar category sales forecasted at $750 million in 2003 for a continued expected growth of 22%. • Industry reports suggest current annual growth for the energy bar market at 25%–30%. • Category expanding: new competitors are entering, existing brands are expanding with new products and flavors, market penetration and usage occasion is increasing.	++ ++
Product life cycle	• Both the category and Odwalla Bars specifically are both securely in early stages of the growth phase.	++
Sales cyclicity	• While energy bars are premium-priced for their convenience and nutrient level, the base dollar point of $1–$3 per bar is low such that they are not directly impacted by GDP variations.	+
Seasonality	• Year-round sales. • Category overall may experience a slight sales increase in the spring and summer months during "race season" and as users are engaged in more outdoor activities and desire quick, portable energy.	++
Profits	• As most major competitors are within the product portfolios of larger consumer goods companies, it is difficult to benchmark profitability within the energy bar category specifically. Nevertheless, the recent acquisition of the leading competitors reflects an expectation for strong profit potential. • Increased category competitiveness may lead to lower pricing and profits.	+
Category		
Threat of new entrants/exits	• Strong potential for new competitors given that the category is profitable, fairly easy to enter, and increasingly relevant to consumers. • Further, with the "big three" brands strongly in place (PowerBar, Clif (including Luna), and Balance), it is most likely that small competitors will enter through the natural foods channel, creating more direct competition with Odwalla bars.	−

continued

FIGURE 3.11   **Energy Bars: Category Attractiveness Summary**—*continued*

Factors	Analysis	Assessment Market Attractiveness
Category (contd.)		
Economies of scale	• Competitors within the broader category of snack bars would likely experience economies of scale with a relatively easy entry into the energy bar market.	−
Product differentiation	• Within the mainstream energy bars, differentiation is largely through brand, taste, and flavor variety. With the exception of targeted nutrition products like protein- or carbohydrate-specific products, nutritional levels are largely at parity.	−
Capital requirements	• Capital requirements are relatively low, increasing the threat of new entrants.	−
Switching costs	• Switching costs are very low, opening the door to potential competitors.	−
Distribution	• As there are no specialty requirements for distribution (refrigeration, etc.), it would be very easy for any of the "center of the store" consumer food companies to enter the category and add on to their existing distribution structure. This is particularly true for companies that have an established relationship with the category buyer. • Shelf life	−
Bargaining power of buyers	• Lots of competitors with relatively similar options distinguished by brand and taste keeps retailer power strong.	−
Bargaining power of suppliers	• As the suppliers of raw inputs for energy bars are largely agricultural, the commodity nature of agriculture keeps prices and supplier power low. While still relatively low, supplier power will be higher for nutrient supplement suppliers.	+
Pressure from substitutes	• Considerable. • Fresh fruit, cereal bars, smoothies, candy bars, etc. are all suitable portable substitutes for the mainstream energy bar consumer. True athletes are most likely to substitute with higher nutrient level energy bars.	−
Category capacity	• Appears to be high given current scenario of more than 100 manufacturers and many more products. But, still, it is too early to determine true capacity.	+
Current category rivalry	• Very high. Differentiation largely by taste and flavor variety, and by targeting unique market segments.	−

FIGURE 3.11   Energy Bars: Category Attractiveness Summary—*continued*

Factors	Analysis	Assessment Market Attractiveness
Environmental		
Technological	• Technology could play a significant role with respect to manufacturing efficiencies and taste profiles.	+
Economic	• While premium priced, energy bars have so far seemed to fare the recession well. Still, however, if economic conditions persist, consumers may opt for less expensive alternatives like fresh fruit or non-energy snack bars.	+
Political/ regulatory	• The energy bar category is regulated by the FDA as are other food products. There are not to our knowledge, however, additional regulations directed toward the energy bar category.	0
Social	• As lives get busier and mealtimes shrink, energy bars will continue to be an acceptable meal replacement.	+ +

involved with the category (Nestlé, Kraft, and Kellog's) raise their advertising and promotion spending and put more money into distribution. This raises the barriers to entry from a financial perspective and makes it more difficult for the smaller, independent brands to compete.

Personal Digital Assistants

Figure 3.12 shows a category attractiveness analysis for PDAs (recall that this is circa 1999). The aggregate market factors showed a market that was in the growth stage of the product life cycle. The factors here were all positive. The Palm Pilot created a market out of one thought dead by many observers. The market size, growth, and profitability of this category were all very positive factors that led to increased competition. With little cyclicity or seasonality, it is easy to see why. The category factors were a mixed bag. On the plus side, the bargaining power of buyers was low due to strong brand names (Palm, Casio) and switching costs to changing brands due to different interfaces, file formats, and the like. Supplier components were relatively standard but on occasion, semiconductor supplies become tight. On the downside, the rivalry between brands was becoming intense and there was increasing price competition. Perhaps more importantly, there were significant substitutes on the horizon in the form of wireless cellular phones that could perform many functions (which we see today). Of course, the Day-Timers, old standard, are still very popular. The environmental factors were mixed. Further deregulation of the telecommunications industry will help the high-end PDAs due to their extensive communications capabilities. The main plus for the product category from this set of factors was that it was right in step with the way work is changing: More work out of the office and on the road increases the need for quick, convenient ways to take notes and keep records of phone numbers and appointments. The main negative factor was technology.

FIGURE 3.12 Category Attractiveness Analysis: Personal Digital Assistants

Factor		Attractiveness
Aggregate Market Factors:		
Market size	$2.3 billion	+
Market growth	30%–40%	+
Product life cycle	Growth	+
Profits	Good	+/0
Sales cyclicity	None	+
Sales seasonality	None	+
Category factors:		
Threat of new entrants	Moderate; R&D required, distribution	0
Bargaining power of buyers	Low; high switching costs	+
Bargaining power of suppliers	Moderate; PCs use similar components	0
Category rivalry	Intense	−
Pressure from substitutes	High	−
Category capacity	Not a problem for now	+
Environmental factors:		
Technological	Very sensitive	−
Political/regulatory	Telecommunications deregulation	+
Economic	Relatively inexpensive	+
Social	More work done on the road	+

Continued miniaturizing of components and product innovation could make the PDA category obsolete if the functions were transferred to phones, watches, or "wearable" computers such as those that have come out of MIT's Media Lab. While the basic customer benefits provided will not change, the form factor certainly could.

Again, the objective is to seek out the negatives in this analysis and try to develop programs to turn them around. In this case, the main negatives, category rivalry, pressure from substitutes, and sensitivity to technological change, are difficult to handle. Perhaps the main message was that Handspring should not have been wedded to its existing form factor (i.e., the handheld PDA) but should have leveraged its brand into new forms as the technology evolved. This, of course, happened with the revolutionary Treo.

SUMMARY

As we went through the three major groups of factors for assessing category attractiveness, we stressed the importance of qualitative assessment: indicating whether the factor had a positive or negative (or possibly neutral) impact on product management in that category of analysis. Clearly, certain factors have the potential to affect some products in a category more than others. For example, a product with a strong brand name is better able than one without strong brand identification to create a barrier to entry as a potential limit to brand switching. Thus, the purpose of this analysis is to develop a general perspective on the effects of the major factors on a firm competing in the category.

References

Advertising Age (2003) October 13, 26.

Andrews, Edmund L. (2003) "Economic Inequality Grew in the 90's Boom, Fed Reports," *The New York Times,* January 23, C1.

Angwin, Julia, and Jared Sandberg (2002) "Netscape Goes One More Round," *The Wall Street Journal,* January 24, B1.

Cravens, David W. (1994) *Strategic Marketing,* 4th ed. Burr Ridge, IL: Richard D. Irwin, Chap. 2.

Kalyanaram, Gurumurthy, William T. Robinson, and Glen L. Urban (1995) "Order of Market Entry: Established Empirical Generalizations, Emerging Empirical Generalizations, and Future Research," *Marketing Science,* Part 2 of 2, G212–21.

Lee, Louis (2003) "Online Grocers: Finally Delivering the Lettuce," *Business Week,* April 28, 67.

Miller, Annetta (1999) "The Millennial Mind-Set," *American Demographics,* January, 60–65.

Naisbitt, John (1984) *Megatrends: Ten New Directions for Transforming Our Lives.* New York: Warner Books.

Petersen, Laurie (1992) "Pepsi Buys the Month of April, But Will It Sell?" *Marketing Week,* February 24, 9.

Popcorn, Faith, and Lys Marigold (1998) *Clicking: 17 Trends That Drive Your Business—And Your Life.* New York: Harperbusiness.

Pope, Kyle (1993) "For Compaq and Dell, Accent Is on Personal in the Computer Wars," *The Wall Street Journal,* July 2, A1.

Porter, Michael E. (1980) *Competitive Strategy.* New York: The Free Press.

Robock, Stefan H. (1971) "Political Risk: Identification and Assessment," *Columbia Journal of World Business,* July–August, 7.

Schnaars, Steven P. (1989) *Megamistakes.* New York: The Free Press.

Shapiro, Carl, and Hal R. Varian (1999) *Information Rules.* Boston: Harvard Business School Press.

Thomas, Philip (1974) "Environmental Analysis for Corporate Planning," *Business Horizons,* 17, October, 27.

Urban, Glen L., Theresa Carter, Steven Gaskin, and Zofia Mucha (1986) "Market Share Rewards to Pioneering Brands: An Empirical Analysis and Strategic Implications," *Management Science,* June, 645–59.

Wacker, Watts, Jim Taylor, and Howard B. Means (2000) *The Visionary's Handbook: Nine Paradoxes That Will Shape the Future of Your Business,* New York: Harperbusiness.

Competitor Analysis

Overview

Consider the following scenario (Green, 1998). A dozen students descend on Disney's Paradise Island in Orlando, Florida. They have been assigned to interact with strangers and extract secrets from them. One student targets a Philadelphia landscaper. Within minutes, she has discovered that he makes $1,500 per week, has lost his savings in a divorce settlement, and owns a house worth $150,000. Another student finds from an Arkansas businessman that he keeps at least $1,000 in his checking account. While the reader might think that this is an "unofficial" school for thieves and scam artists, it is actually a course sponsored by the Centre for Operational Business Intelligence. Their teachers are former counterintelligence agents experienced in uncovering secret information and training others to do the same. The students have been sponsored by companies to help their employers gather competitive intelligence.

The collection of competitor intelligence is of course not limited to domestic companies or ethical behavior. Consider this quote from a 50-year veteran of Japan's corporate industrial "spy wars" on how he obtains information from corporate employees (Fulford, 1995): "We follow our targets to their favorite bars, make friends with them and find out what their weak spots are. If they don't have any, we make them." These examples highlight the often negative view many have of competitive analysis. Here we take a different approach and emphasize that useful competitor analysis does not require illegal or unethical activities.

Global competition, technological change, and economic downturns have intensified competitionable pressures. In slow-growth markets, sales growth must come from the competitors. With shorter product life cycles, managers must recoup investments in a shorter period of time, which makes errors of judgment about competitive difficult to overcome. Technology available to managers makes collecting and disseminating information within the organization easier as well as quicker. Finally, given the generally high level of turbulence managers face from increased foreign competition, dramatically changing technology and rates of innovation, large shifts in interest rates and stock valuations (both up and down), and changing customer tastes, it is more important than ever to keep abreast of changes in all factors exogenous to the firm, including competition. As Figure 4.1 suggests, the manager of competitor intelligence has become an important figure in many multinational corporations.

76

FIGURE 4.1   Advertisement for Competitor Intelligence Manager

International Competitive Intelligence Manager

McGraw-Hill Higher Education – Sales/Marketing Division

McGraw-Hill/Irwin has an opening for an International Competitive Intelligence Manager in our Sales & Marketing Division. Through online learning and multimedia tools McGraw-Hill Higher Education, Professional and International group, is a leading global provider of educational materials and professional information.

Tasks:

- Collect, process and report competitive data and intelligence.
- Coordinate, improve and develop information systems in our Sales & Marketing Division.
- Supply analyses of competitors for the numerous divisions in Higher Education.

The Manager will be part of the Sales & Marketing Information team and will report to the V.P of Sales & Marketing Information. The office location is in Hightstown, New Jersey.

Qualifications:

- Bachelor's Degree and at least three years of International Marketing/Sales, preferably in a business-to-business market.
- Experience in international competitive intelligence and college textbook publishing.
- Effective communication and interpersonal skills.
- Ability to set priorities; to plan, organize and control workflow; and analyze the situations and the marketing environment.
- Thorough understanding of information systems, information technology and the role of systems in processing and communicating competitive data and intelligence.

We offer a challenging career in an exciting international environment with good opportunities for advancement.

For further information, please contact the Human Resource Director for Higher Education Margaret Hanover at 609-789-5221 or by e-mail marg_hanover@McGraw-Hill.com

Please send your application with attention to Human Resource Director-MHHE, 148 Princeton/Hightstown Road, Hightstown, NJ 08520-1450

McGraw-Hill Higher Education
A Division of The McGraw-Hill Companies

McGraw-Hill Higher Education is a world leader in educational and professional information in a variety of formats including web-publications, technology and textbooks. Headquartered in Hightstown, NJ. More information can be obtained by visiting our website at www.McGraw-Hill.com

In fact, given the number of marketing books with the term *warfare* in the title (see, for example, Ries and Trout, 1985), the recent history of marketing strategy has been as oriented toward competitors as the 1960s were toward the customer. The traditional view of the marketing concept is a focus on the needs and wants of the customer. Since the 1980s, however, it has become increasingly clear that meeting customer needs is not enough for success. What is critical to a product's success is meeting customer needs *better* than a competitor can, often at a lower cost. This implies an equally strong focus on understanding competitors' marketing strategies and capabilities.

Many companies have, of course, discovered the importance of competitor analysis. Here are some examples[1]:

- Microsoft deployed a team of engineers and marketers specifically to track Linux, the fast-growing, free operating system that is becoming more popular. The team has attempted to convince potential corporate users that Linux is not a real competitor to Windows.

- Frontier Airlines competes head-to-head with United on many routes in the western United States. To try to anticipate United's moves, Frontier hired a former United planning executive as its planning director to get "inside" United's corporate head. For example, instead of swamping a market with flights, Frontier learned that if it flew only twice a day to a city, United was not likely to increase its capacity there.

- Every week, Tom Sternburg, founder and CEO of Staples, the office supply superstore, drops by one of his stores and a competitor's. He focuses mainly on what the competitor is doing well rather than simply criticizing the competitor for its weaknesses. He looks at customer service, store visibility, displays, and how easy the prices are to read.

- Palm Computing has a chief competitive officer whose job is to predict competitors' likely future strategies. His main job is to follow Microsoft and its Windows CE operating system. His methods include talking with customers, sales staff, and suppliers.

An annual survey of the best American players in the intelligence game found the following rank ordering (Green, 1998):

1. Microsoft
2. Motorola
3. IBM
4. Procter & Gamble
5. General Electric, Hewlett-Packard (tied)
6. Coca-Cola, Intel (tied)

[1] Sources for these examples are Lee Gomes (1999), "Upstart Linux Draws a Microsoft Attack Team," *The Wall Street Journal,* May 21, p. B1; Stephanie Gruner (1998), "Spies Like Us," *Inc.;* Scott McCartney (1999), "Upstart's Tactics Allow It to Fly in Friendly Skies of a Big Rival," *The Wall Street Journal,* June 29, p. B1; Todd Wasserman (2000), "Spy or Spinmeister?" *Marketing Computers,* May, pp. 53–58.

It would be a mistake to assume that competitor intelligence gathering is only for large companies. An example illustrates that small companies can profit from such activity as well (*The Wall Street Journal,* 1989). The CEO of a small company turned a discussion with a customer into a problem for a competitor. The company, an importer of lamps and office furniture, had recently faced increased competition. The CEO learned from a retailer that one of the company's competitors had just raised the prices of some expensive lamps. The executive quickly relayed the information to the firm's salespeople, who used the knowledge to win new business. Given the amount of information that is available on the Internet for free and for anyone who searches, there is no reason that a small company cannot be almost as sophisticated as a large one in understanding its competitors.

It is a fact that competitors, both large and small, constantly provide information to the marketplace, what economists refer to as *signals* (see, for example, Schelling, 1960). Signals can be of two varieties. *Costly* signals are actual actions taken by a competitor such as the construction of a new plant, the introduction of a new product, a change in price, and so forth. The other variety is communications through the media, with customers, and with other marketplace actors. These have been referred to as *cheap talk* signals as they are costless, nonbinding, nonverifiable communications.[2] An example of this kind of signal is the marketing manager who announces in an interview that she intends to match a competitor's price if it is lowered. The job of a marketing manager is to collect both kinds of information and be wary about cheap talk signals that may be less than truthful.

Why don't all firms have a formal reporting system designed to collect and analyze information about competitors? After all, in some companies (e.g., Japanese firms), managers are trained to make competitive intelligence gathering everyone's business. Yet the Conference Board estimates that fewer than 5 percent of U.S. companies have sophisticated intelligence systems.

Overconfidence about a product's continued success can reduce willingness to collect competitor information. An impressive list of companies (General Motors, Coca-Cola, McDonald's) that were somewhat overconfident at one time can be produced, along with a list of competitors that were ignored until they made significant inroads into the markets (Toyota, Pepsi, Burger King). A second reason for insensitivity to competition is uncertainty about where to collect the necessary information and how to analyze it. This excuse grows weaker all the time as consultants specializing in competitive intelligence gathering, articles and books containing tips on where to collect information, and computerized databases containing articles about companies proliferate, and as the Web is increasingly and easily used for obtaining information. A final reason for not collecting competitive intelligence is an ethical consideration: the fear that either illegal methods or otherwise "dirty tricks" have to be used to obtain such information. Many examples of such approaches to collecting information exist, and some of

[2] Actually, they are not entirely costless. Some companies such as Apple have been sued by stockholders for not delivering on new products that the company has announced.

these are mentioned later in the chapter. However, information can almost always be obtained ethically.

At the very minimum, firms should view methods for collecting information about competitors from a defensive perspective, that is, how they can prevent information about themselves from landing in the laps of important competitors. John Sculley, the former CEO of Apple, became so alarmed at the number of leaks of important secrets that he had a six-minute video made for new employees warning them about the implications of "loose lips" (Zachary, 1989). This is becoming increasingly problematic for companies as improved technology for "eavesdropping" and decreased employee loyalty from corporate downsizings increase competitors' ability to obtain corporate secrets. A 1995 survey of Fortune 1000 companies showed that about 75 percent believe theft or attempted theft by computer of customer information, trade secrets, and new product plans increased over the previous five years (Geyelin, 1995).

To analyze competitors, a commitment to developing a competitive strategy that includes a willingness to expend resources on collecting data is necessary. However, the data themselves are usually not the major problem product managers face. There are many sources of competitive intelligence. What is often lacking is a structure to guide the collection and analysis of the data, that is, a clear idea of what questions the data should address.

Figure 4.2 shows the competitor analysis model used in this chapter. At the top of the figure, the key inputs to the model are, of course, data. The first part of this chapter describes data sources available for competitor analysis. It may seem to make more sense to first identify the questions to be answered, but the data collection process for understanding competitor behavior is somewhat unstructured, and information is continually being received and processed. It is thus useful to first understand the major sources of information and then apply them to the important questions that must be addressed. The two kinds of data described are *secondary* data, or data that have already been collected by someone else for some other purpose (i.e., "library" data), and *primary* data, or information derived from studies specially designed to answer a particular set of questions.

The data analysis portion of the process is the second major area of this chapter and is represented by the three questions in Figure 4.2. These cover six major areas of interest:

Who are the major competitors?

How do the competing products/services stack up against each other?

What are the objectives of the major competitor products?

What is the current strategy being employed to achieve the objectives?

Who has the competitive edge?

What are they likely to do in the future?

We addressed the first question in Chapter 2. Even though an attribute advantage (e.g., faster processing speed) does not necessarily translate into product success, a matrix featuring the attributes of the competing products/services is a useful

FIGURE 4.2 **Competitor Analysis System**

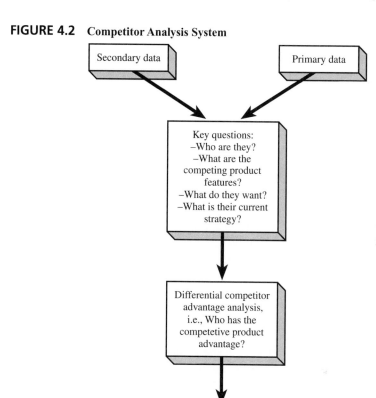

exercise simply to compare the offerings. The next two parts of the analysis assess the current objectives and strategy of the competing products. Differential competitor advantage analysis assesses the strengths and weaknesses of competing products based on information about the competitors' capabilities along a set of dimensions. An important output of this analysis assesses key strengths and weaknesses. The final element of the competitor analysis could be called the "bottom line." The purpose of examining the competitors is to be able to forecast what they are likely to do over the next planning cycle so we can then incorporate that forecast into our own strategies. Taken together, the issues shown in Figure 4.2 comprise a fairly complete picture of the activities of competing products.

A caveat to this chapter is that an intensive analysis of competition cannot substitute for a customer focus. In the end, it is generally better for a manager to satisfy customer needs and ignore competition than do the reverse. Placing too much importance on keeping up with competitors can result in inadequately monitoring shifts in customer tastes. One benefit of the systematic approach to marketing planning advocated in this book is that it does not favor or ignore either customers or competitors.

SOURCES OF INFORMATION

Secondary Sources of Information

As with marketing research in general, product managers should always begin a competitor analysis with a search of secondary sources of information. Secondary sources are generally less expensive and easier to obtain than primary data and often cover most of the important questions we need to ask about competitors. Figure 4.3 identifies popular secondary sources companies can use. An exhaustive listing of all secondary sources of information is beyond the scope of this book; however, many good listings of these sources exist (see, for example, Lehmann, Gupta, and Steckel, 1998; Patzer, 1995). Many of these sources are also useful for tracking foreign companies doing business in the United States or other markets. Fortunately, with the explosive growth of the Internet, many of these sources are available from your desktop, rendering obsolete the former term for secondary sources of information, "library" sources.

Internal Sources

Good information about competing products probably already exists within the company or division. Data can be found in past marketing plans, special studies commissioned by strategic planning groups, or simply in someone's office. As noted at the beginning of the chapter, some companies establish competitor hot lines or databases that can be accessed easily.

Local Newspapers

An excellent inexpensive source of information about competitors is local newspapers. For example, if a key competitor's product is manufactured in a small town, subscribing to the local newspaper is an excellent way to keep tabs on hirings and other changes. A U.S. medical supply manufacturer was shocked when a Japanese competitor significantly increased output at a new plant in Kentucky. The U.S. company had to reduce prices to maintain market share. What is interesting is that many

FIGURE 4.3 **Secondary Sources of Competitor Information**

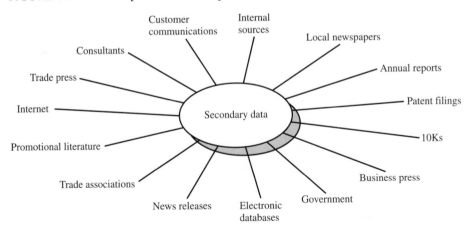

details about the new plant—cost, number of employees, the products to be produced—were reported in the *Lexington Herald-Leader* in 1987, three years before the plant opened (Teitelbaum, 1992).

Annual Reports

Much of the information in an annual report is for public relations value, and the discussion is at the corporate, not product, level. However, careful analysis of annual reports can produce some interesting insights even at the product level, particularly by examining the product areas the report does *not* mention. Often one can get useful information about areas of corporate emphasis from the message from the chairman or the text. Annual reports sometimes mention locations of manufacturing facilities and the names of key corporate decision makers. Although the financial information is aggregate, some data on cost of goods sold can be useful. These reports are, of course, available only for publicly held companies. For private companies, Dun & Bradstreet publishes its famous D&B reports, which estimate the financial performance of those firms.

10K Statements

Another reporting requirement for publicly held corporations is the 10K statement. Often this is more useful than the annual report because it is broken down by line of business and does not have the "gloss" of the annual report.

One clear implication of these two sources of information is that a cheap way to keep up with the corporate parent of a competitor is to become a shareholder (preferably a small one!). Shareholders receive the annual reports and 10Ks as well as admission to the annual shareholder meetings, which can be another useful resource.

Financial documents, including annual reports and 10Ks, are also available at most business libraries and stockbrokerage offices, where other useful financial documents such as new business prospectuses can be found.

Patent/Trademark Filings

Within the last decade, commercially available data networks such as CompuServe have made patent filings available. Obviously, patents give some notion of the manufacturing process and technology underlying the product. However, companies have been known to apply for patents on mistakes or on products that they have no intention to market. A company called MicroPatent (see Figure 4.4) permits the downloading of patents and technical diagrams via its Web-based service.

General Business Publications

Excellent sources of information about products and companies are general business publications such as *Business Week, Fortune, Forbes,* and *The Wall Street Journal.* One might wonder why companies are often willing to disclose what should be proprietary information concerning, for example, future marketing strategies. Some potential audiences are investors, employees, and perhaps even competitors who might be the target for strategic warnings. To get information from these publications, a company can subscribe to clipping services and electronic databases or clip appropriate articles themselves.

FIGURE 4.4 **Micropatent**

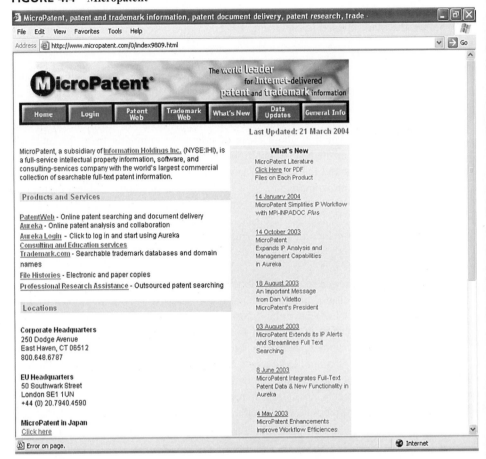

Source: MicroPatent's PatentWeb Services, *http://www.micropatent.com/o/patentweb9809.html,* March 31, 2000.

News Releases

Companies usually retain public relations firms to release information to the press concerning new products, senior management appointments, and the like. These releases often show up in newspapers and trade publications, but it is possible to get on a direct distribution list.

Promotional Literature

Sales brochures (often referred to as *collateral material*) or other promotional literature focusing on a competing product or product line are extraordinarily valuable. Sales literature is a rich source of information concerning the product's strategy, since it usually has details about how the product is being positioned and differentiated versus those of competitors (including your product), product attribute and performance data, key phone numbers, and even personnel to contact.

Trade Press

These periodicals narrowly focus on a particular industry or product category. Representing this class of literature is *Women's Wear Daily* for the retail clothing trade, *Billboard* for the record and video industry, *Rubber Age* and *Chemical Week* for their respective industries, and *Test and Measurement World* for semiconductor testing equipment. This class of publications is obviously a rich source of information concerning new product announcements, personnel shifts, advertisements for products, and industry or category data on sales and market shares. Somewhat broader are "new economy" magazines such as *Wired* and *Business 2.0* which followed companies with a technology orientation. Some "e"-zines such as *Colloquy* deliver information about new loyalty/frequency programs. It is safe to say that virtually every product category and business sector has its own set of publications.

Consultants

Competitor analysis is a fertile area for consulting services. Many of these firms sell industry reports to different companies. They usually develop these reports from secondary sources and thus sell a service that substitutes for the firm's own efforts. One type of company services all industries. For example, New York–based FIND/SVP offers a variety of industry research reports through its website, *www.findsvp.com.* In 2004, the company offered a 234-page report, "Chinese Markets for Baby Care Products," for $3,500. The report covers consumption trends, primary competitors, distribution channels, and consumer behavior. The website, *www.marketresearch.com,* brokers competitor analysis reports from a number of different companies. (See Figure 4.5).

Employee Communications

Companies often publish internal newsletters targeted toward employees. These newsletters may report on new vendors, new employees, and so forth.

Trade Associations

Most companies are members of trade associations (a listing of such associations is available in business libraries). These associations are usually formed for public relations or lobbying purposes, but they also often perform market research for the member firms. While usually focused on customers, this research may also provide some information about market shares, price levels, and so on.

Government Sources

The U.S. government collects a considerable amount of information about industries. However, as noted in Chapter 2, the data are usually at the NAIC (North American Industrial Classification) level and therefore are not very useful for understanding specific product competitors. More useful information is collected by agencies such as the Federal Communications Commission, the Food and Drug Administration, and state agencies. For example, if a regulated company submits a request for a rate increase, competitors can obtain cost information from the filing since the request is public information.

FIGURE 4.5 Market Research

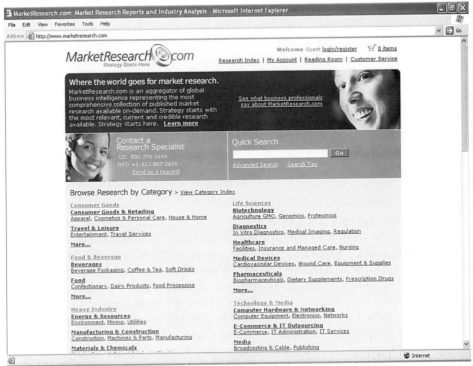

Source: Market Research.com, *http://www.marketresearch.com/*. Copyright © 2000, All Rights Reserved, Market Research, Inc.

Electronic Data Services

The Web has a number of sites that are of particular interest for this kind of analysis. Some of them offer free information and others are subscription based:

- Hoover's Online: Income statement and balance sheet numbers for public companies.
- Dun & Bradstreet's Online Access: Short reports on 10 million U.S. companies, many of them privately held.
- NewDirectory's 24-Hour Newsstand: Links to the websites of more than 14,000 English newspapers, business journals, magazines, and computer publications around the world.
- American Demographics: Provides demographic data as well as a directory of marketing consultants.
- Competitive Intelligence Guide (*www.fuld.com*): Sleuthing tips along with an "Internet Intelligence Index."

The biggest of all of these services is DIALOG, which offers access to such databases as Port Import Export Reporting Service (PIERS), the *Financial Times,* Moody's, and press releases by more than 10,000 U.S. corporations.

A number of specialized Web-based services exist that perform a variety of competitive intelligence activities. Here is a sampling:

- Strategy Software (*www.strategy-software.com*) takes the data you have collected about competitors and organizes it into reports.
- C4U is a download that scans the Web for any changes in a predefined set of sites and reports the changes.
- AdRelevance offers a Web advertising tracking service that, among a number of services, can help you determine whether a competitor is increasing/changing its advertising.
- Company Sleuth has an e-mail alert system that notifies you via e-mail if information about a new SEC filing, new release, patent, and so on from a competitor has been published on the Internet.

A convenient way to search through the Web is with a search engine such as Google. The user can type a company name, such as "Sony," and (eventually) reach Sony's home page and other pages linked to Sony. At Hewlett-Packard's page (*www.hp.com*), a browser can find product information and news about HP (see Figure 4.6). Information seekers can determine HP's resellers, the extent of technical support, and a large amount of other data.

FIGURE 4.6 **Hewlett-Packard Website**

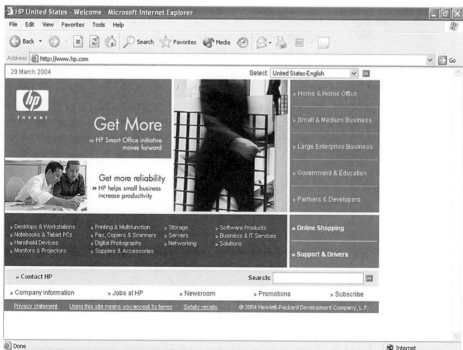

Source: ©1994–2004 Hewlett Packard Company.

Primary Sources of Information

Figure 4.7 lists the most important primary sources of information about competitors. Many of these are also sources of secondary information, depending on when the information was originally collected.

Sales Force/Customers

One of the most underutilized sources of information in companies is the sales force. Salespeople are trained to sell, but how many are trained to be part of a competitor intelligence force? Since they interact with customers on a regular basis, salespeople are in an excellent position to find out about recent competitor sales pitches, pricing, and many other dimensions. Depending on the product, salespeople are often in a position to collect information merely by being trained observers. Xerox salespeople, for example, are trained to note competitor copiers. Forward-looking companies use information from salespeople for quick updates on competition. With notebook computers, salespeople can make their calls, fill out call reports electronically, and send the information back to the local office or headquarters via modem. For competitor tracking, the call report should have a section related to noting anything new or different picked up during the call.

Of course, the salespeople must get the information from customers. Every attempt by suppliers and vendors to cultivate a potential customer involves the transmission of information. Unfortunately, customers may be reluctant to give away such information, believing it means playing "dirty tricks" on the competition. To aid in overcoming this reluctance, the data collection can be positioned as giving the vendor an opportunity to provide better service or products to the customer; that is, the salesperson can clearly show that the customer will benefit by passing along the information. Usually the data can be obtained from public sources anyway; it is just quicker for the vendor to obtain it from the customer (Yovovich, 1995).

FIGURE 4.7   **Primary Sources of Competitor Information**

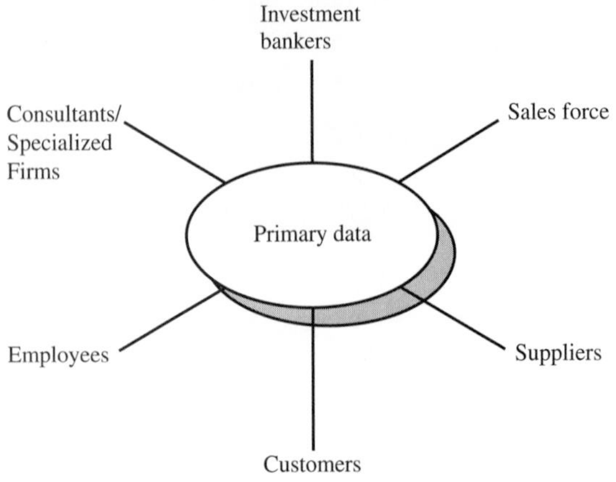

Employees

Generalizing from the use of salespeople to collect competitor intelligence, much can be learned about competition from observation in the marketplace by any company employee. If the product category in question is sold in the supermarket, an employee can easily observe changes in price, packaging, and shelf display.

Suppliers

Often competitors' suppliers are willing to give information about shipments to impress potential buyers. Imprints on packaging cartons can provide useful information because they often disclose the name and address of the carton's maker. Following up with the carton manufacturer may lead to estimates of sales volume.

Consultants/Specialized Firms

Consultants can often be used to develop special-purpose reports, as opposed to the off-the-shelf variety referred to under secondary sources. For example, tns media intelligence/cmr is one of the leading firms developing reports on media spending by brand.

Investment Bankers

Investment bank reports are excellent sources of both secondary and primary data on competitors, particularly if a bank wishes to gain the firm as a new client. Analysts employed by the investment banks develop detailed analyses of the prospects of different firms and products in an industry. While their perspective is financial performance, much of the information is useful to marketers.

Other Sources

Help-Wanted Ads

Often help-wanted ads contain valuable information, such as job requirements and salary levels. Other information is available as well; sometimes the purpose of the ad is to fill positions opened by an expansion of business or a new plant opening. Although many ads disclose only a box number for a reply, many provide information about the organization paying for the ad. This can be done online as well, through searches of help-wanted ads from Monster (*www.monster.com*), craig's list (*www.craigslist.com*) and other similar sources.

Trade Shows

Company representatives often attempt to obtain information at the booths of competitors. This is becoming more difficult, however, as companies increasingly try to screen the people to whom they provide information to avoid revealing too much to competitors. In addition, spying is now so common at trade shows that hot new products are usually displayed only in hotel suites open to major customers, joint venture partners, and industry reporters who agree not to disclose information until product release dates. This is particularly true at large trade shows such as Comdex, the computer industry trade show, where industry players like Michael Dell, founder of Dell Computer Corporation, roam through the aisles trying to pick up information quickly before they are recognized. Even if some information is gained, however, about as much is lost from your own company, so usually the net gain is small.

Plant Tours

This is a rapidly disappearing phenomenon, largely because companies are becoming skittish about giving away valuable information. The most popular tourist destination in Battle Creek, Michigan was Kellogg's cereal plant until the company stopped giving tours several years ago, citing competitor information gathering as the reason. Gerber stopped its Fremont, Michigan plant tours in 1990 after spotting sales representatives from competitor firms taking the tour. Although there are some exceptions, most tours today are like the amusement park–like tour at Hershey Foods' facility in Hershey, Pennsylvania, which offer little to be learned about how the products are really made.[3]

Reverse Engineering

A common way to analyze a competitor's product is to purchase it and take it apart. This is referred to as *reverse engineering* in high-technology industries and sometimes as *benchmarking* in service markets.[4] In general, it is wise to become a customer of a competitor by, for example, purchasing a computer or software, opening a small bank account, etc. One important reason to do so is to estimate the competitor's costs of manufacturing or assembly. Another objective is to assess the product's strengths and weaknesses. Companies such as Emerson Electric, General Motors, and Xerox perform this kind of analysis routinely. For example, in the late 1970s, Xerox benchmarked Canon's copiers and tried to beat each component of the latter's machines on cost and quality. In designing the Lexus, Toyota bought competitors' cars, including four Mercedes, a Jaguar XJ6, and two BMWs, put them through performance tests, and then took them apart (Main, 1992).

Monitoring Test Markets

Some companies test market products in limited areas of the country or the world to better understand decisions about pricing, advertising, and distribution. While this is often useful, test markets can be fertile grounds for competitors to get an early view of the product and how it will eventually be marketed after rollout to the larger market.

Hiring Key Employees

This practice obviously provides a considerable amount of information. However, new employees may not legally transmit what are considered to be trade secrets to new employers. Trade secrets can have a narrow interpretation, however, that does not cover marketing strategies or complete plans. Some companies attempt to hinder

---

[3] A good article on how to analyze the data obtained from a plant tour is David M. Upton and Stephen E. Macadam (1997), "Why (and How) to Take a Plant Tour," *Harvard Business Review,* May–June, pp. 97–106.

[4] The term *benchmarking* is also used more generally to refer to the tracking and analysis of any process such as manufacturing, billing, customer service, and so on, in both competing and noncompeting organizations.

employees, particularly senior managers, from jumping to a competitor by including a special non-compete clause in the employment contract. At Hewlett-Packard, new employees are asked to sign nondisclosure agreements and attend a training program, complete with video, that defines how HP interprets "trade secrets" (Guthrie, 1993).

Ethically Questionable Sources

Our purpose in describing some of the unethical approaches to collecting competitor information is not to encourage readers to use them but to point out that such activities do occur. As mentioned earlier in the chapter, a key reason to learn about the various approaches to collecting information about competitors is to become more defensive minded. Of course, it is virtually impossible to completely defend against lying and cheating. However, on a hopeful note, these approaches rarely uncover something an ethical approach cannot; there are usually several ways to collect a key piece of information.

Aerial Reconnaissance

It is illegal in the United States for a company to hire an airplane or a helicopter to take aerial photographs of a competitor's facilities as they are being constructed, because this action is interpreted as trespassing. Procter & Gamble won a lawsuit against Keebler for spying on a new soft-cookie-making facility being constructed in Tennessee in 1984. Companies can, apparently legally, purchase photographs taken from satellites: Sweden and France are partners in a satellite joint venture that sets aside a limited percentage of the transponder time for commercial purposes (usually map making and municipal planning). In 1994, Lockheed Missiles & Space Company, a subsidiary of Lockheed Corporation, received the first license from the U.S. government to sell spy-quality satellite pictures for commercial use. Lockheed has the technology to photograph a car from 400 miles in space.

Buying/Stealing Trash

It is not illegal to take a company's trash after it leaves the firm's facility. However, companies have been known to either bribe employees or otherwise obtain access to discarded documents. Recently, Avon admitted it had hired private detectives to run through rival Mary Kay's trash to attempt to defend against a takeover attempt by the latter. The maneuver was not illegal because Mary Kay's dumpster was in a public parking lot (Zellner and Hager, 1991). In a highly publicized 2000 incident, Oracle hired a firm to sift through the trash of the Independent Institute, a think tank Oracle accused of having a tie to Microsoft after it ran a high-profile ad criticizing the U.S. government's antitrust case against the software company. Even the highly-regarded Procter & Gamble has been involved with "dumpster diving"; in 2001, it was found guilty of stealing Unilever's trash. Simple defensive mechanisms include shredders and incinerators. Unfortunately, in today's online world, "trash" also means electronic mail that was thought to be discarded when it actually was not.

Bribing Printers

Some companies attempt to obtain predistribution copies of catalogs and other material.

Running Phony Want Ads

Not all help-wanted ads are for actual positions. Some companies run ads in an attempt to get disgruntled employees from competitors to apply. These applicants then can be probed for information.

Snooping on Airplanes

The continuous process of squeezing more seats into airplanes and the proliferation of laptops provide ample opportunity for business travelers to collect information from screens. Some flights are notoriously packed with executives from particular industries; for example, the flights from San Jose to Austin are generally filled with computer industry people.

One executive was creative in deterring such activity. On a flight from San Francisco, he detected a pair of eyes intently looking at his computer screen. Having experienced this before, with a few keystrokes he opened a file called READTHIS.doc which produced a single sentence on the screen: "If you can read this, you ought to be ashamed of yourself." The passenger in the next seat retreated (De Lisser, 1999).

The ethics of various data collection methods is a continuum from methods that are clearly illegal (stealing a competitor's marketing plans) to obviously legal (reading an article in a trade magazine). Today there is more pressure than ever to uncover information about competitors. The Society of Competitive Intelligence Professionals, now numbering over 7,000 members, has established an ethical code that requires members to comply with the law, identify themselves when seeking information about competitors, and respect requests for confidentiality. However, those bent on violating legal and ethical standards do not tend to join such societies. It is therefore incumbent on companies to develop policy statements that clearly define the standards expected from employees in this area of competitor intelligence gathering and to strongly enforce them.[5]

ANALYZING PRODUCT FEATURES

Although product features do not always translate into benefits sought by customers, a very useful graphic is to simply chart the differences between the main products or services offered in the category. The basic structure of the analysis is shown in Figure 4.8. A useful complement to the features matrix is a set of importance weights (see Chapter 5) or at least some indicator of the relative importance of the different features. Taking the basic feature information together with the relative importance weights gives you a very good idea of the strengths and weakness of your product relative to the competition.

---

[5] For further reading on the ethical aspects of competitor analysis, see U. Srinivasa Rangan and Michael E. Porter, "Ethical Dimensions of Competitive Analysis," *Harvard Business School* case study number 9-792-088, 1992.

FIGURE 4.8 Product Features Matrix

Features	Competitor A Brand $1 \ldots K_A$	Competitor B . . . Brand $1 \ldots K_B$
F_1		
F_2		
.		
.		
.		
F_n		

ASSESSING COMPETITORS' CURRENT OBJECTIVES

A critical step in a competitor analysis is to assess what the current objectives are for the major competitor products. An assessment of current objectives provides valuable information concerning the intended aggressiveness of the competitors in the market in the future. It also provides a context for assessing the capabilities of competitors; that is, does firm marketing brand A have the resources to successfully pursue such an objective?

When discussing objectives, it is important to define them precisely, for many different types of objectives exist. In the context of marketing planning, three basic business objectives can be identified. A *growth* objective usually implies increasing unit sales or market share, with profit conditions being secondary. The *hold* objective could also be termed a *consolidation* objective. A hold scenario might be logical for a brand that is losing market share in that a reasonable first step in reversing its fortunes is to stop the slide. Finally, a *harvest* objective, also referred to as *milking,* describes a situation in which profit is paramount relative to market share. In other words, at the product level, objectives are typically stated in terms of either market share or profits. At the corporate level, return on investment or other, more aggregate, statistics becomes more relevant.

Determination of Competitor Objectives

While the objective determines, to a great extent, what strategies will be pursued and hence what actions will be taken in the marketplace, usually it does not take a substantial amount of research to uncover it. What is required is sensitivity to competitors' actions through observation, salesperson call reports, and the other resources mentioned in the previous section of this chapter. For example, in 1998, Boeing announced in a major business publication that it was going to emphasize profits over market share—good news for Airbus (Browder, 1998).

Let us consider two major options outlined above: the growth versus harvest choice. If a competitor's brand is being pushed to improve its market position at the expense of short-term profits, some of the following are likely to occur: a cut in price, increased advertising expenditures, increased promotional activity to both consumers and distributors, or increased distribution expenses.

In other words, a product manager who is trying to expand a brand's market share will spend money on market-related activities and/or reducing price. Such actions can be easily monitored by brand managers, advertising account representatives, and other parties with access to information about the rival brand's actions.

Brands being harvested would be marketed in the opposite way. An increase in a competitor's price, decreases in marketing budgets, and so on can be interpreted as a retreat (perhaps only temporary) from active and aggressive competition in the market. While it is difficult to precisely estimate the size of the share loss expected, it is not difficult to establish the direction of the impact, which is still important competitor information.

Two other factors are relevant to the assessment of competitors' objectives. First, the product objectives of a firm with a foreign-based parent are often affected by the country of origin. In many cases, such firms have financial backing from a government or major banks and are not as concerned with short-term losses as they are with establishing a viable market position or obtaining foreign currency. Although at one time Japanese firms were the ones usually referred to in this context, other countries, such as Korea and Singapore, are also homes to firms that are strongly interested in building market share in the United States. Thus, depending on the competitor, cues concerning the competitor brand's objectives can be obtained from the geographical home of the parent firm. A second relevant factor is whether the ownership of the competitor firm is private, public, or government. Since private firms do not have to account to stock analysts, long-term profits may be more important than showing consistent positive quarterly returns. On the other hand, if a family depends on a firm it controls for current income, profits may be more important than market share. Finally, government-controlled firms may have objectives such as maintaining employment, providing service, or currency exchange.

An interesting variant of the impact of private ownership on objectives occurs if the privatization resulted from a leveraged buyout (LBO). In these cases, even though the company is private, it is often more interested in profits and cash flow to pay down debt than it is in plowing money into market share gains. An excellent example is the well-publicized LBO by Kohlberg Kravis Roberts & Company (KKR) of RJR Nabisco in 1988. Because of the large load of debt the firm took on, many of RJR's brands became vulnerable to competitors that took advantage of the opportunity to go for market share gains. These included Philip Morris in tobacco products because RJR was reluctant to enter the low-price cigarette category, and competitors in snack foods, which took advantage of large cuts in advertising and promotion expenditures for Ritz crackers and Planters products. As of 1995, RJR was free of KKR, and began to attempt to regain the market share lost to Philip Morris, particularly for its flagship Winston brand (Teinowitz, 1995). A similar result often occurs as a result of mergers (Lorge, 1999).

A less apparent level of objectives can be deduced from a firm's operating philosophy and procedures. For example, a firm that seeks to minimize capital investment will be slow to respond to a competitor that makes a heavy capital outlay (for example, Emery Air Freight when Federal Express bought its own airplanes in the mid-1970s). Similarly, firms that compensate sales staffs with commissions based on a percentage of sales indicate that volume rather than profitability is a key objective. In fact, the key performance measure by which employees are judged has a distinct influence on a firm's performance.

Estimates of the objectives pursued by competitors provide important information for the development of strategy. Certainly a brand that is aggressive in its pursuit of market share must be viewed as a different type of competitor than one that is attempting primarily to maximize profits. The latter would clearly be more vulnerable to an attack on its customers, whereas a confrontation with the former brand might be avoided. In other words, a study of the brands' objectives provides a first-level analysis of the competitor brand's likely strategy.

This type of analysis has been profitably applied. During the late 1970s, Coca-Cola was concerned primarily with holding market share and improving profits. PepsiCo, on the other hand, viewed its rival's drowsiness as an opportunity and became more aggressive, gaining share points and improving its position versus Coca-Cola in store sales. Miller Brewing's successful attack on Budweiser during the 1970s was prompted by a similar observation.

ASSESSING COMPETITORS' CURRENT STRATEGIES

The second stage in competitor analysis is to determine how competitors are attempting to achieve their objectives. This question is addressed by examining their past and current marketing strategies.

MARKETING STRATEGY

Many authors have attempted to define the concept of strategy. At the product level, a marketing strategy can be thought of in terms of three major components: target market selection, core strategy (i.e., positioning and differential advantage), and implementation (i.e., supporting marketing mix). These components are described in more detail in Chapter 7; we will briefly discuss them here in the context of understanding a competitor's product strategy.

The first major component is the description of the market segment(s) to which competing brands are being marketed. Market segments can be described in various ways, as shown in Chapter 5 (Figures 5.5 and 5.6). Since few brands are truly mass marketed, that is, marketed equally to all potential customers, the key is to determine which group(s) each competitor has targeted. This helps to avoid segments in which there may be intense competition and to determine under- or nontargeted segments that may represent opportunities.

The second strategy component is what is called the *core strategy*. This is the basis on which the rival is competing, that is, its key claimed differential advantage(s). Differential advantage is a critical component of strategy because it usually forms the basic selling proposition around which a brand's communications are formed. It is also called the brand's *positioning* or *value proposition.*

Marketing managers essentially have a choice between two types of differential advantage: advantage based on price/cost or on product features. In other words, products are usually positioned on price or quality dimensions, although some marketers choose a "value" positioning with midrange price and quality. Concentration on price often follows the classic approach developed by the Boston Consulting Group in the 1970s, which advocates taking advantage of the experience curve that assumes costs are driven down with increases in cumulative production volume, thus allowing the firm manager to cut prices and maintain margins over time. The quality differential advantage is superiority on some other product dimension (real or psychological) such as service, packaging, or delivery terms. Necessary conditions for such a core strategy to be successful are that customers value the characteristics claimed as advantages and that the differential can be maintained for a significant period of time without being copied.

An important characteristic of quality differential advantages is that they can be perceived, rather than actual, differences. For example, IBM's core strategy since its inception has been service based. This advantage can be supported by hard data (e.g., number of field service representatives, mean response time, and so on). On the other hand, Reebok's claimed differential advantage during its "U B U" campaign was related to individuality. Such positioning is clearly outside the domain of physical product differences, but it can still be effective in differentiating Reebok from Nike. Physical product differences are often stressed in industrial, durable, or new frequently purchased product strategies. Companies producing mature frequently purchased products that are physically similar or "commodities" often emphasize perceptual differences.

Comparing Value Chains

Porter (1985) developed a concept called the *value chain* that can be used to compare a brand or company's strengths and weakness against another. The basic value chain is shown in Figure 4.9. An important point made by the value chain is that differentiation can be obtained through efforts of the whole corporation, not just through marketing. One way to differentiate is through *inbound logistics,* that is,

FIGURE 4.9 **Value Chain**

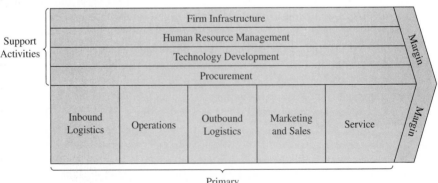

Source: Michael Porter, *Competitive Advantage* (New York: Free Press, 1980), p. 37.

through the selection of the highest-quality raw materials and other inputs including technology. A reason that Steinway has consistently built the best pianos in the world is through the use of the best wood that can be found. For years, the supercomputer company Cray had a significant technological edge on other companies. A second way to gain competitive advantages is through *operations* advantages. One of the ways that McDonald's has been the fast food market leader throughout the world is by significant investments in training programs that produce consistency in service and product quality. *Outbound logistics* provides a third basis for differentiation. This can be through speedy and on-time delivery such as the Federal Express promise and fulfillment of the promise during its earlier days of being there "absolutely and positively overnight." A company called Premier Industrial Corporation distributes nuts and bolts, seemingly a commodity, but differentiates itself from competition (and has higher margins) by agreeing to ship in any quantity desired by the customer. *Marketing and sales* also serve to differentiate. The IBM sales force has historically been a major advantage to the company in terms of its ability to satisfy customer needs better than competitors. Finally, *service* can be an important differentiator, as the retailer Nordstrom has found. The product manager can use the value chain concept to check at each step of the process if and how a competitor is gaining competitive advantage in the category.

Marketing Mix

The final strategy component of competitors that must be assessed is the supporting marketing mix. The mix provides insight into the basic strategy of the competitor and specific tactical decisions. These decisions are what customers actually see in the marketplace; neither are they exposed to nor do they particularly care about a product's marketing strategy. However, customers are exposed to price, advertising, and other marketing mix elements. The areas to consider and some questions to address follow.[6]

Pricing

Pricing is a highly visible element of a competitor's marketing mix; therefore, it raises several questions. For example, if a brand's differential advantage is price based, is the list price uniform in all markets? If the strategy is quality based, what is the price differential claimed? Are discounts being offered? What is the pattern of price changes over time? In general, any price-related information pertaining to the implementation of strategy is relevant.

Promotion

With respect to sales management, what kinds of selling approaches are being employed? Are the salespeople aggressive in obtaining new accounts? What are their commission rates? In terms of advertising, what media are being used? What creative activities? Are competitors referred to either directly or indirectly? Sales promotion activities—for example, which types and how often—are also important.

---

[6] For a more complete description of the components of a marketing strategy, see Russell S. Winer, *Marketing Management,* 2nd ed. (Upper Saddle River: Prentice-Hall, 2004).

Distribution

Have the channels of distribution shifted? Is the brand being emphasized in certain channels? Is the manufacturer of the competing product changing the entire system, for example, by opening its own retail outlets or putting more emphasis on direct marketing?

Product/Service Capabilities

A major determinant of a company's capabilities, at least in the short run, is the physical makeup of its product or service, which in general is less easily changed than, say, price or advertising. A product filled with expensive parts is unlikely to be positioned as a low-end product. Similarly, physical properties (e.g., stability under high temperatures) go a long way toward dictating target market uses and hence strategy. Many engineering plastics categories are segmented on the basis of physical properties, for example, DuPont's Delrin versus Celanese's Celcon. Different applications can be dominated by a different company's offerings. Therefore, a comparison of the competitive product offerings, the physical product or service, and how it is presented and sold should be performed.

How to Assess Competitors' Strategies

Recall that the two key elements of a strategy are the segments it appeals to and the core strategy. For industrial products, both can be easily determined by examining three sources of information: product sales literature, the company's own sales force, and trade advertising. The former provides information about the core strategy because brochures usually detail the points of difference the competitor wants to emphasize. Even if the sales literature does not present a product features chart, it should indicate the brand's major strengths. Physical brochures are not often needed today; most industrial firms' websites provide a wealth of technical and positioning information that helps to determine the core strategy. A firm's own sales force can provide some data concerning targeted companies or industries, much of it resulting from informal contacts, trade show discussions, and the like. Finally, trade advertising is useful because it reveals the segments being targeted and the differential advantage being touted. One can determine the differential advantage directly from the ad copy and the target segments at least partially by the publication (location) in which the ad appears.

For consumer goods or other products targeted toward a large audience, simply tracking competitors' ads, either yourself or by using one of the services such as those mentioned earlier in this chapter, provides most of the necessary information. Television ads can be examined for their messages (differential advantage) and for the programs in which they appear (target segment[s]). TV advertising is quite useful for determining the core strategy because the nature of the medium prohibits communicating all but the most important messages. Similarly, print advertising can provide equivalent information, but with greater elaboration of the core strategy.

For example, consider the copy for a print ad in *Forbes* for Rolex watches, shown in Figure 4.10. From data obtained from Mediamark Research's *Magazine Total Audiences Report, Spring 2003,* we know that 73.8 percent of the readers are 18 to

FIGURE 4.10 Detecting a Competitor's Strategy

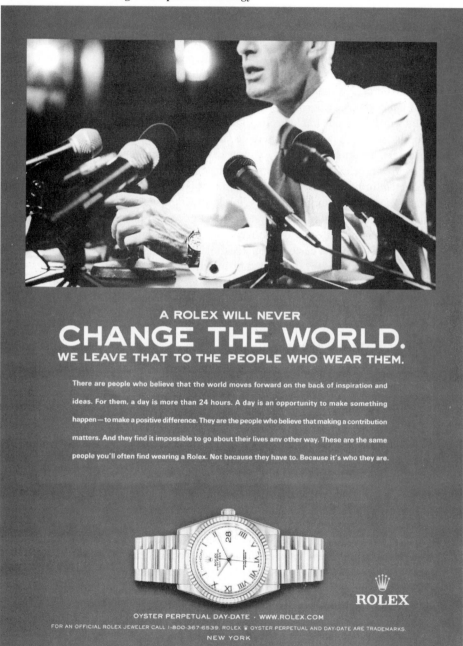

Source: *Forbes,* January 12, 2004, p. 17.

49 years old, 38.8 percent have household income over $75,000, and 83.3 percent either attended or graduated from college (among many other variables measured by Mediamark Research). It is probably not a surprise that readers are businesspeople with high incomes. Looking at the copy itself, the ad copy says nothing about the physical characteristics of the watch, only the people who wear them: people in (or who aspire to) leadership positions. Note that there is no explicit mention of the competition. Of course another key factor is the price of the ad; these data are obtainable from publications such as *Marketer's Guide to Media.*

Information about implementing current strategies is also easily found. Pricing information can be obtained from basic market observation: Distributors, salespeople, customers, advertising agencies, or even a firm's own employees acting as customers on their own behalf can be the sources of pricing data. Promotion, distribution, and product information can be obtained from similar sources. In other words, as in determining competitors' objectives, it takes market sensitivity rather than sophisticated management information systems to assess much of the competitive activity.

One apparent but often overlooked source of information mentioned earlier in this chapter is being a customer or stockholder of competitors. Both customers and stockholders get special mailings and information that make strategy assessment easier. Furthermore, personal use of competitors' products often gives one a feeling for them that does not come through even the best-prepared research. Thus, policies that forbid or discourage the use of competitive products are usually foolish.

Technology Strategy

An important task is to assess the technological strategies of the major competitors. This can be done using the following framework of six criteria (Maidique and Patch, 1978):

1. Technology selection or specialization.
2. Level of competence.
3. Sources of capability: internal versus external.
4. R&D investment level.
5. Competitive timing: initiate versus respond.
6. R&D organization and policies.

These decisions generally lead to four basic strategies, each of which has different requirements for success, listed in Figure 4.11. Consider the blank audiocassette market in the early 1970s. This was the early stage of the product life cycle, with no major competitors. Gillette's Safety Razor Division was considering entering this market, as was Memorex, a manufacturer of computer tape and related products. Gillette had competitive advantages over Memorex in marketing and finance, but it was decidedly at a disadvantage in terms of R&D, manufacturing, and the apparent match of its skills and image to the cassette category in the minds of customers. The end result was a success for Memorex and a failure for Gillette in test marketing.

At this point in the analysis, it is often useful to summarize the products of the major competitors. Figure 4.12 provides a general format that is useful for both summarizing the results and for communicating them.

FIGURE 4.11 Typical Functional Requirements of Alternative Technological Strategies

	R&D	Manufacturing	Marketing	Finance	Organization	Timing
First to market	State-of-the-art R&D	Pilot and medium-scale manufacturing	Stimulating primary demand	Access to risk capital	Flexibility over efficiency; encourage risk taking	Early-entry inaugurates the product life cycle
Second to market	Flexible, responsive, and advanced R&D capability	Agility in setting up manufacturing medium scale	Differentiating the product; stimulating secondary demand	Rapid commitment of medium to large quantities of capital	Flexibility and efficiency	Entry early in growth stage
Late to market or cost minimization	Skill in process development and cost-effective production	Efficiency and automation for large-scale production	Minimizing selling and distribution costs	Access to capital in large amounts	Efficiency and hierarchical control; procedures rigidly enforced	Entry during late growth or early maturity
Market segmentation	Ability in applications, custom engineering, and advanced product design	Flexibility on short to medium runs	Identifying and reaching favorable segments	Access to capital in medium or large amounts	Flexibility and control required in serving different customers' requirements	Entry during growth stage

might assume the trend will continue, that is, suppose that the only relevant information is the historical pattern of past strategies. For example, if the brand has a track record of positioning with a high-quality, high-price program, one could extrapolate into the future and assume the trend will continue. Similarly, if a brand has been appealing to increasingly mature consumers, a manager might assume it will continue to do so. An alternative way for the forecaster to proceed is to try to establish a cause-and-effect relationship between the resource variables and the strategy, in other words, to link changes in resources or abilities to the strategies to be pursued.

Some examples will help clarify this approach. Several years ago, Merrill Lynch spent heavily to bring in managers with packaged goods experience to develop the markets for its financial services. Competitors (Dean Witter, E. F. Hutton) could forecast that this would result in an emphasis on market segmentation (pursuing high-potential customers) and increased spending on marketing-related activities such as advertising. Similarly, Bethlehem Steel invested billions of dollars to upgrade its flat-rolled steel facilities. Competitors could forecast that this investment in highly efficient capacity would improve Bethlehem's ability to simultaneously cut price and protect margins. A third approach to strategy forecasting does not explicitly employ historical data but rather makes use of data in a different way. Corning Glass's highly profitable Corning Ware line was coming off patent. At the same time, it was well known that several companies (Libby-Owens-Ford, Anchor Hocking) were looking at that business. Corning was interested in finding out how a competitor would enter to preempt the entry strategy. To forecast the probable entry strategy, it asked senior managers to role-play (i.e., simulate) a competitor and determine how, if they were managing the entry, they would attack Corning Ware. This exercise provided useful defensive information for Corning.

Thus, a third approach to forecasting competitors' possible actions is to simulate them. One can take the existing data already collected, have different managers play the roles of the product managers for the competitors, and develop competitor action scenarios. SmithKline Beecham (now GlaxoSmithKline), the pharmaceutical company, did exactly that when Tagamet (an antiulcer drug), then the largest-selling prescription drug in the world, was coming off patent. In this case, it knew who the competitor was going to be: Glaxo Holdings. SmithKline prepared its salespeople for Glaxo's anticipated promotion of its drug, Zantac, in terms of differential advantage (fewer doses needed per day) and for counteracting arguments against Tagamet. Although Zantac eventually replaced Tagamet as the category leader, SmithKline believed the simulation helped dampen the impact of Zantac. Another company using the simulation approach is Intel, which has a full-time group within the company that develops strategies that competitors may follow. To complete the Merrill Lynch–Schwab story started above, Schwab managers concluded that their company stood for "full service" on the Internet the way Merrill stood for that strategy in the offline world. Thus, to be proactive, Schwab increased the amount of guidance its employees offered customers and provided more high-quality research on the Schwab site (Kirsner, 1999).

In general, there has been little systematic study of how to predict competitor moves. Using the airline industry as a case history, some recent research has studied how competitors react to a competitive move (Chen, Smith, and Grimm, 1992). The main empirical findings were:

The greater the competitive impact, the greater the number of responses made.

The greater the intensity of the move, the greater the number of counteractions.

The greater the implementation requirement, the smaller the number of responses.

The more tactical the move, the greater the competitive response.

An approach similar to simulation uses economic game theory. While game theory is theoretically elegant, it is limited in its ability to model real-world situations involving large numbers of competitors and many possible moves. However, the basic principles can be shown in the illustration highlighted by Figure 4.16 (Clark, 1998; Moore and Urbany, 1994). Suppose "our" firm ("we") is thinking about lowering its price on a product. In the time period of the price cut (first period), we would expect customers to compare our new, lower price to the competitor's ("their") price and that this would increase our unit sales and perhaps profits (depending upon the price elasticity of demand). However, where most managers fail is that they do not anticipate the competitor's reaction in the second or next period after our price cut. If they cut their price as well, the customer response will be more complicated but it will probably result in lower sales and profits for us. If we anticipate that the competitor will lower price, it does not make much sense for us to do so in the first period since the resulting "equilibrium" will be the same

FIGURE 4.16 **A Competitive Conjecture Process**

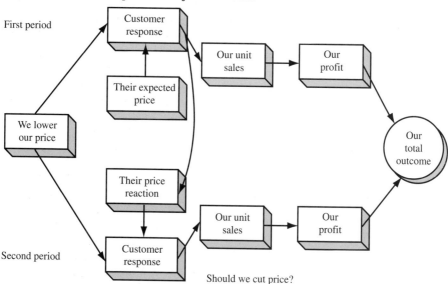

Source: Adapted from Marian C. Moore and Joel E. Urbany, "Blinders, Fuzzy Lenses, and the Wrong Shoes, Pitfalls in Competitive Conjecture," *Marketing Letters,* July 1994.

FIGURE 4.19 Energy Bar: Current and Future Strategy Matrix

	Clif Bar Inc.	PowerBar Inc.	Balance Bar Inc.	Kashi Co.
Objectives	Grow market share and volume.	Grow market share and volume.	Grow market share and volume.	Grow revenue and distribution.
Current strategies	Product innovation.	Product introductions in new segments, increased advertising spend.	Products launching and expanding in multiple segments of category.	Product line extensions (new flavors) and distribution focus.
Expected future strategies	Focus on product innovation and grassroots marketing.	Focus on product development, increased advertising, and promotions.	Focus on product line and brand extensions to fill category.	Focus on expanding distribution to gain shelf space nationally in grocery, drug, and mass channels.

Clif Bar: This is the most customer-oriented brand as its managers do the best job of interacting with customers and listening and responding to their needs. It is perceived by consumers to be the most innovative and creative of the major brands.

Kashi: Kashi is a natural cereal and convenience foods company. The company's products are made with a blend of sesame and seven whole grains. The brand is strongly associated with grain and fiber.

Expected Future Strategies

PowerBar: This brand is likely to continue to be more aggressive in targeting mainstream markets and thus continue to launch more brand extensions. The brand's managers will also invest heavily in advertising and promotions.

Balance Bar: With the assistance of Kraft's resources, the brand will continue to introduce more extensions.

Clif Bar: Like the others, the emphasis for this brand will be on extensions. Its goal is to remain ahead of both Balance Bar and PowerBar.

Kashi: This brand will focus on new flavors and expand distribution to gain shelf space in grocery, drug, and mass channels.

Personal Digital Assistants

In this category, there are many competitors and product features. A sampling of the features matrix is shown in Figure 4.20 (again, circa 1999). The analysis will focus on the offerings from Handspring's two major competitors, representing different operating system platforms, Palm (Palm OS) and Casio (PocketPC/Windows CE).

Brand Objectives

Since the PDA was in the growth stage of the life cycle, all of the products were trying to gain volume to bring down costs and establish market positions. This

FIGURE 4.20 PDA Product Features Matrix

	Visor	Visor Deluxe	Palm III	Palm IIIe	Palm Pilot PE	PV-100	PV-200	Cassiopoeia E-100	Cassiopoeia E-11
Price suggested retail price	$179 ($149++)	$249	$216	$205	$235	$123	$100	$499	$276
Physical Properties									
Form	Pad	Pad	Pad	Pad	Pad	Pad	Pad	Pad	Pad
Size	4.8 × 3.0 × 0.7	4.8 × 3.0 × 0.7	4.7 × 3.6 × 0.7	4.7 × 3.2 × 0.7	4.6 × 3.2 × 0.7	4.9 × 3.2 × 0.6	4.9 × 3.2 × 0.6	5.1 × 3.3 × .8	4.9 × 3.3 × 0.8
Weight, oz	5.4	5.4	6.4	5.8, 6.0 with battery	5.1		4.8	9	6.7
Memory and Processor Speed									
RAM, processor speed	2 MB	8 MB	2 MB, 16 MHz	2 MB	1 MB, 16 MHz	1 MB	2 MB	16 MB, 131 MHz	8 MB, 100 MHz
Expandable RAM	No	No	No	No	No	No	No	Yes	No
Display									
Diagonal screen size	3 in	3 in	4.1	4.1 in	4.1 in	4 in	4 in	3.9 in	3.9 in
Resolution			160 × 160		160 × 160	128 × 128	128 × 128	240 × 320	240 × 320
Color (if no, gray shades)	No	No, 16 shades	No, 4 shades	No	No, 4 shades	No, 4 shades	No, 4 shades	Yes	No, 4 shades
Touch screen	Yes	Yes	Yes	Yes	Yes	Yes	Yes	Yes	Yes
Backlight	Yes	Yes	Yes	Yes	Yes	Yes	Yes	Yes	Yes
Other									
Interfaces									
Total # of serial ports	0	0	1	1	1	1	1	1	1
Number of type II PC cards	0	0	0	0	0	0	0	0	1
IR port	Yes	Yes	Yes	yes	0	0	0	Yes	Yes
Other ports	USB, Spring-board Slot	USB, Spring-board Slot							

resulted in a price drop of the major competitors (e.g., Palm) following the usual early skimming approach to grab those who need to be the first with the latest technology (at the highest price).

Brand Strategies

Palm: This company decreased price on the low-end models (Palm III) and introduced higher-end models (Palm V) with advanced features and color screens. The strategy was clear: Offer different product options for different target segments. Of particular interest to Palm was the nonbusiness user, that is, an expansion into the "average" or home user segment.

Casio: Differentiating on the basis of the operating system was not working as, despite Microsoft's feelings to the contrary, users did not see the advantages of PocketPC/Windows CE over Palm's operating system. Therefore, Casio attempted to differentiate on the basis of product features and not price.

Differential Competitor Advantage Analysis

Figure 4.21 shows a competitive capabilities matrix. The main implications are the following:

Palm:

Strengths: Market leader, cash availability, large number of software developers, large and strong community of users, strong brand equity.

Weaknesses: Lost key managers to Handspring, uncertainty from the spin-off from 3Com.

Casio:

Strengths: Economies of scale in production, creativity, good brand name (though weaker than Palm in this category).

Weaknesses: Dilution of resources into 61 different businesses run by the corporation.

Expected Future Strategies

Palm:

Continued licensing of its operating system and establishment of the Palm OS as the industry standard. If the Palm III does not work with the low-end, nonbusiness market, they will probably develop a new product just for this market. Possible venture into non-PDA products and applications that use the Palm OS (e.g., home Web appliances).

Casio:

Continue to develop its head-to-head rivalry with Palm and build a brand around advanced and creative product innovation. Unlike Palm, Casio was already a known brand with the consumer market. Thus, like Palm, they will probably introduce a product into this segment soon.

FIGURE 4.21 Comparison of Competitor Resources: PDAs

Company's Ability to . . .	Palm Pilot	Casio (Windows CE Platform)	Handspring
1. Conceive and design (technical and human resources, funding, etc.)	Loss of talent (many original Palm founders have left) may negatively impact its ability to create new products.	Casio is a Japanese company and given the way Japanese companies normally operate, we assume it has plenty of resources, both human and capital.	• Handspring has a great ability to conceive and design products since its founders created the Palm Pilot. They have a lot of experience, vision, and creativity. • Due to the founders' success, they have a lot of funding available to them since investors are confident with their ability to succeed. • Again, due to the founders' prior success and high-profile careers, Handspring has attracted the best talent to work here.
2. Produce (physical and human resources)	Palm relies on contract manufacturers to produce its products. Given the volume produced by Palm, its leadership position, and the abundance of electronic contract manufacturers, Palm probably has no problem with production.	Great economies of scale. Plants worldwide.	• Depends on contract manufacturers to make the PDAs. Upside: many contract manufacturers so there is flexibility and we make what we need. Downside: depends on someone else so cannot entirely control quality and also in times when demand is great, may not demand what we want. Also have lower bargaining power relative to Palm due to smaller production volumes. • Handspring has good contacts with manufacturers since founders previously transacted with them. • Handspring depends on the module producers to make the modules. But again, due to the abundance of consumer electronic manufacturers, the production of modules will not be difficult or too risky.
3. Market (sales force, distribution, service/sales policies, advertising, human resources, funding)	Palm is the leader and has been in the industry for several years. As such, it will have very good and strong relations with retailers. Retailers know that Palm sells and they will give Palm a relatively higher portion of the shelf space.	Strong marketing experience of electronics products to the channels.	• Because of start-up status, Handspring has limited overworked resources. Limited in how many PDAs they can sell and distribute over year 2000. • Need to market the most strategically attractive segments since we are resource constrained (human and financial). • Limited sales force. • New and not very strong relationships with distribution channels, so may be harder to get Handspring in the door. • Internet is a good resource.
4. Finance (debt, liquidity, cash flow, budget system, etc.)	Hard to separate from 3Com. Presumed to have growing sales with a 70+% market share.	Decreasing growth in sales and losses in FY99.	Financially, limited to how much they can spend so can't be as aggressive as would like. For example, cannot target every segment in full force. Must focus on the most strategically attractive segment and will not be able to target all over the next year.

SUMMARY

Competitive analysis is an important component of strategy development. Many approaches have been followed and this chapter provides a framework (Figures 4.8, 4.13, 4.14, and 4.15) that integrates several of these. Like most other analyses, however, the key ingredient is not clever devices, unethical behavior, or elegant presentation. Rather, the quality of competitor analysis depends heavily on the effort devoted to it.

References

Bittar, Christine (2001) "Balancing Act: P&G Shuffles Brands, People," *Brandweek,* March 26, 8.

Browder, Seanna (1998) "Course Change at Boeing," *Business Week,* July 27, 34.

Chen, Ming-Jer, Ken G. Smith, and Curtis M. Grimm (1992) "Action Characteristics as Predictors of Competitive Responses," *Management Science,* March, 439–55.

Clark, Bruce H. (1998) "Managing Competitive Interactions," *Marketing Management,* Fall/Winter, 9–20.

De Lisser, Eleena (1999) "Hearing and Seeing Business Travel Blab and Laptop Lapses," *The Wall Street Journal,* November 8, A1.

Fulford, Benjamin (1995) "Spy Biz Thrives on Sex, Lies, Audiotapes," *The Nikkei Weekly,* December 23, 1995, p. 1.

Geyelin, Milo (1995) "Why Many Businesses Can't Keep Their Secrets," *The Wall Street Journal,* November 20, B1.

Green, William (1998) "I Spy," *Forbes,* April 20, 90–96.

Guthrie, Julian (1993) "Brain Drain," *San Francisco Focus,* October, 24.

Kirsner, Scott (1999) "Charles Schwab & Company," *Wired,* November, 135–44.

Lehmann, Donald R., Sunil Gupta, and Joel H. Steckel (1998) *Marketing Research.* Reading, MA: Addison-Wesley.

Lorge, Sarah (1999) "Attacking at a Moment of Weakness," *Sales & Marketing Management,* April, 13.

Maidique, Modesto A., and Peter Patch (1978) "Corporate Strategy and Technological Policy," unpublished working paper, Harvard Business School.

Main, Jeremy (1992) "How to Steal the Best Ideas Around," *Fortune,* October 19, 102–6.

Moore, Marian C., and Joel E. Urbany (1994) "Blinders, Fuzzy Lenses, and the Wrong Shoes: Pitfalls in Competitive Conjecture," *Marketing Letters,* July, 247–58.

Patzer, Gordon L. (1995) *Using Secondary Data in Marketing Research: United States and Worldwide.* Westport, CT: Quorum Books.

Porter, Michael E. (1985) *Competitive Advantage.* New York: The Free Press.

Ries, Al and Jack Trout (1985) *Marketing Warfare.* New York: McGraw-Hill.

San Francisco Chronicle (1995) "MCI Details Assault on the Baby Bells," March 7, D-2.

Schelling, Thomas C. (1960) *The Strategy of Conflict.* Cambridge, MA: Harvard University Press.

Teinowitz, Ira (1995) "Marketing, Ad Woes Choking RJR Brands," *Advertising Age,* June 26, 3.

Teitelbaum, Richard S. (1992) "The New Race for Intelligence," *Fortune,* November 2, 104–7.

The Wall Street Journal (1989) "'Competitor Intelligence': A New Grapevine," April 12, B2.

Yovovich, B. G. (1995) "Customers Can Offer Competitive Insights," *Business Marketing,* March, 13.

Zachary, Pascal (1989) "At Apple Computer Proper Office Attire Includes a Muzzle," *The Wall Street Journal,* October 6, A1.

Zellner, Wendy and Bruce Hager (1991) "Dumpster Raids? That's Not Very Ladylike, Avon," *Business Week,* April 1, 32.

Customer Analysis

Overview

Since businesses run on revenue and revenue comes from customers, it is critical to understand them. It is thus no accident that this is the longest chapter. Customers, not products, are the ultimate source of operating income. Companies increasingly at least espouse being customer-centric and a large and increasing number have created the position of customer insights managers or the equivalent to assemble and disseminate the customers' "voice" throughout the organization. Further, increased emphasis is being placed on customer "touch points," places where the customer comes in contact with the company or its products and services. How these encounters turn out determines in large measure future sales and the success (or failure) of a product. However, before deciding how to satisfy or even delight customers, you first need to identify them: who they are, where they are, what they want, etc. This chapter provides some guidance on how to approach this critical task.

By *customer* we mean not only current customers of a given product but also both customers of competitors and current noncustomers of the product category (i.e., potential customers). The term *customer* also refers both to immediate customers (i.e., supermarkets and discount stores and critically Wal-Mart for consumer product companies such as P&G and manufacturers for component manufacturers such as Intel) and to final customers (i.e., individuals and businesses). Similarly, while many firms have recently made huge ($100 million) investments in customer relationship management (CRM) systems that emphasize IT (information technology), few feel the investment has paid off. Hence, our focus here is on understanding customers rather than data collection and warehousing.

In this chapter, we do three things. First, we suggest an approach to systematically analyzing customers. Figure 5.1 suggests that product managers need to answer eight questions. Who are the customers for this product or service? What are customers buying and how do they use it? (Customers buy benefits rather than simply product features or characteristics.) Where do customers buy products? When are purchase decisions made? How do customers make purchase decisions? Why do customers choose a particular product? In other words, how do they value one option over another? How do they respond to marketing programs such as advertising and promotions? And finally, will they buy it again? Second, we introduce the concept of long-term value of customers. This is an essential concept

120

FIGURE 5.1 What We Need to Know about Current and Potential Customers

Who buys and uses the product
What customers buy and how they use it
Where customers buy
When customers buy
How customers choose
Why they prefer a product
How they respond to marketing programs
Will they buy it (again)?

which guides the amount of effort to direct to specific customers. Finally, we discuss market segmentation, that is, how to efficiently and effectively group customers to simplify strategic and tactical thinking and decisions.

WHAT WE NEED TO KNOW ABOUT CUSTOMERS
Who Buys and Uses the Products
Buyers versus Users

For most industrial goods and many consumer products, the *who* must be broken into several different entities within the organization or household, including the following:

1. Initiator (who identifies the need for product).
2. Influencer (who has informational or preference input to the decision).
3. Decider (who makes the final decision through budget authorization).
4. Purchaser (who makes the actual purchase).
5. User.

The identities of the above individuals can differ widely. For example, in an industrial market, the end user may be an engineer who is concerned mainly with technical features, whereas the purchasing agent emphasizes cost and reliability of delivery. One reason for the success of Federal Express was its ability to take the decision on how to send overnight packages away from the shipping clerk by making the user the purchaser. Similarly, adults often purchase cereal, toys, or fast-food meals even though the user of the product is a child. Products targeted toward gift givers (e.g., silverware as a wedding gift) also highlight the difference between the buyer and the user.

This distinction between buyer, user, and other purchase influencers is particularly important for industrial products. The mark of a top salesperson is the ability to identify the different people involved in making a decision, understand the relative power over the purchase each person holds, and learn what they value. For example, in selling word processing software to a law firm, the needs of the secretaries (ease of use, support, readable screen) differ from those of the office manager (high productivity, no bugs in the software, good service) and from the person

FIGURE 5.2 Buying Roles and Needs/Benefits Sought

Needs/Benefits Sought	Buying Roles				
	Initiator(s)	Influencer(s)	Decider(s)	Purchaser(s)	User(s)
A					
B					
C					
D					

approving the purchase (low cost, reliable delivery). Figure 5.2 provides a template for this kind of analysis.

Descriptive Variables: Consumer Products

The most obvious and popular basis for describing consumers is their general characteristics (Figure 5.3). The key categories are:

1. *Demographic.* The most commonly used demographics are age, sex, geographic location, and stage in the life cycle. These characteristics have the advantage of being relatively easy to ascertain. Unfortunately, in many cases segments based on demographics are not clearly differentiated in their behavior toward the product.

2. *Socioeconomic.* Socioeconomic variables include income and such related variables as education, occupation, and social class, with income and education generally being more useful. As in the case of demographics, the relationship between these variables and purchase behavior can be weak.

3. *Personality.* Given the relatively limited predictive power of demographic and socioeconomic variables, the fact that many marketing people are trained in psychology, and the natural desire to find a general basis for profiling consumers that will be useful across many situations, it is not surprising that marketers have attempted to use personality traits as a basis for segmentation. Unfortunately, general personality variables have proven even less useful than demographic or socioeconomic variables in predicting purchasing behavior.

4. *Psychographics and values.* Psychographics represent an evolution from general personality variables to attitudes and behaviors more closely related to consumption of goods and services. Also known as lifestyle variables, psychographics generally fall into three categories: activities (cooking, sports, traveling, etc.), interests (e.g., art, music), and opinions. They are thus, not surprisingly, often referred to as AIO variables. These have been widely used as bases for segmentation and for the creation of advertising themes. Many researchers have used the VALS (Values and Lifestyles) typology and its updated version, VALS2, (see Figure 5.4) developed by SRI International, as a basis for defining segments.

FIGURE 5.3 Major Segmentation Variables for Consumer Markets

Variable	Typical Breakdown
Geographic	
Region	Pacific, Mountain, West North Central, West South Central, East North Central, East South Central, South Atlantic, Middle Atlantic, New England
City or metro size	Under 5,000; 5,000–20,000; 20,000–50,000; 50,000–100,000; 100,000–250,000; 250,000–500,000; 500,000–1,000,000; 1,000,000–4,000,000; 4,000,000 or over
Density	Urban, suburban, rural
Climate	Northern, southern
Demographic	
Age	Under 6, 6–11, 12–19, 20–34, 35–49, 50–64, 65+
Gender	Male, female
Family size	1–2, 3–4, 5+
Family life cycle	Young, single; young, married, no children; young, married, youngest child under 6; young, married, youngest child 6 or over; older, married, with children; older, married, no children under 18; older, single; other
Income	Under $10,000; $10,000–$15,000; $15,000–$20,000; $20,000–$30,000; $30,000–$50,000; $50,000–$100,000; $100,000 and over
Occupation	Professional and technical; managers, officials, and proprietors; clerical, sales; craftspeople, foremen; operatives; farmers; retired; students; homemakers; unemployed
Education	Grade school or less; some high school; high school graduate; some college; college graduate
Religion	Catholic, Protestant, Jewish, Muslim, Hindu, other
Race	White, black, Asian
Nationality	American, British, French, German, Italian, Japanese
Psychographic	
Social class	Lower lowers, upper lowers, working class, middle class, upper middles, lower uppers, upper uppers
Lifestyle	Straights, swingers, longhairs
Personality	Compulsive, gregarious, authoritarian, ambitious
Behavioral	
Occasions	Regular occasion, special occasion
Benefits	Quality, service, economy, speed
User status	Nonuser, ex-user, potential user, first-time user, regular user
Usage rate	Light user, medium user, heavy user
Loyalty status	None, medium, strong, absolute
Readiness stage	Unaware, aware, informed, interested, desirous, intending to buy
Attitude toward product	Enthusiastic, positive, indifferent, negative, hostile

Source: Philip Kotler, *Marketing Management*, 8th ed., 1994, p. 271. Adapted with permission of Prentice Hall, Inc. Upper Saddle, NJ.

FIGURE 5.4 Lifestyle Typologies

VALS	VALS2	GLOBALSCAN
Inner-directed consumers	Principle-oriented consumers	Strivers
Societally conscious	Fulfilleds	
Experientials	Believers	Achievers
I-am-me consumers		
Outer-directed consumers	Status-oriented consumers	Pressured
Achievers	Achievers	
Emulators	Strivers	Adapters
Belongers		
Need-driven consumers	Action-oriented consumers	Traditionals
Sustainers	Experiencers	
Survivors	Makers	
	Strugglers	

Figure 5.4 also shows a lifestyle typology, GLOBALSCAN, which was developed by the advertising agency Backer Spielvogel Bates Worldwide based on a survey of 15,000 adults in 14 countries.

Another typology, the List of Values (LOV) Scale (Kahle, Beatty, and Homer, 1986), delineates nine basic values:

1. Self-respect.
2. Security.
3. Warm relationship with others.
4. Sense of accomplishment.
5. Self-fulfillment.
6. Sense of belonging.
7. Respect from others.
8. Fun and enjoyment.
9. Excitement.

These typologies are often related to purchasing patterns and afford the product manager the opportunity to match potential buyers with the appropriate media and message to communicate with them (Corfman, Lehmann, and Narayanan, 1991).

Descriptive Variables: Industrial Products

The same type of variables used to describe consumers can also be used to describe organizations (see Figure 5.5 for a list of some popular variables). For industrial-product customers, the traditional focus has been on firm characteristics such as size (e.g., number of beds in a hospital), industry, and location; that is, the demographic variables appropriate for describing companies. However, a variety of other kinds of variables can be used, such as operating variables (e.g., customer technology), purchasing approaches (e.g., centralized versus decentralized), situational factors (e.g., order size, physician specialty), and "personal" characteristics (e.g., attitude toward risk).

FIGURE 5.5 Major Segmentation Variables for Business Markets

Demographic
- *Industry:* Which industries should we focus on?
- *Company size:* What size companies should we focus on?
- *Location:* What geographical areas should we focus on?

Operating Variables
- *Technology:* What customer technologies should we focus on?
- *User/nonuser status:* Should we focus on heavy, medium, light users or nonusers?
- *Customer capabilities:* Should we focus on customers needing many or few services?

Purchasing Approaches
- *Purchasing-function organization:* Should we focus on companies with highly centralized or decentralized purchasing organizations?
- *Power structure:* Should we focus on companies that are engineering dominated, financially dominated, etc.?
- *Nature of existing relationships:* Should we focus on companies with which we have strong relationships or simply go after the most desirable companies?
- *General purchase policies.* Should we focus on companies that prefer leasing? Service contracts? Systems purchases? Sealed bidding?
- *Purchasing criteria:* Should we focus on companies that are seeking quality? Service? Price?

Situational Factors
- *Urgency:* Should we focus on companies that need quick and sudden delivery or service?
- *Specific application:* Should we focus on certain applications of our product rather than all applications?
- *Size of order:* Should we focus on large or small orders?

Personal Characteristics
- *Buyer–seller similarity:* Should we focus on companies whose people and values are similar to ours?
- *Attitudes toward risk:* Should we focus on risk-taking or risk avoiding-customers?
- *Loyalty:* Should we focus on companies that show high loyalty to their suppliers?

Source: Philip Kolter, *Marketing Management,* 8th ed., 1994, p. 278. Adapted with permission of Prentice Hall, Inc. Upper Saddle River, NJ.

Concepts of personality and psychographics can also be applied to organizations. Although it may be unusual to think of a firm as having a personality, one important segmentation variable in technologically oriented industries is innovativeness. The innovators, organizations that adopt new technologies earlier than others in their industry, are often referred to as "lead users." Lead users have two characteristics: (1) they face general needs before the bulk of the industry does, and (2) they can benefit significantly by obtaining an early solution to those needs (Urban and von Hippel, 1988). These are obviously valuable customers, as they not only provide early sales and spread (hopefully) favorable word of mouth information, but also help the company make necessary product modifications and improvements.

Many of the same variables used to segment markets for consumer and industrial goods are used to segment markets internationally. Figure 5.6 lists key segmentation variables used in direct marketing campaigns in Europe.

FIGURE 5.6 Key Segmentation Variables Used in Direct Marketing Campaigns in Europe

	Belgium	Denmark	France	Germany	Greece	Ireland	Italy	Netherlands	Portugal	Spain	UK
Most commonly used consumer segmentation criteria	Social class Nielsen zones Geographic Database	Demographic from census Database	Sociodemo-graphic Database	Age Profession Income Family status Lifestyle	Urban/rural Profession Database	Age Income Profession Family status Database	Age Sex Profession Housing types	Age Sex Geographic Lifestyle Database	Income Urban/rural Education Political bias Database	Age Sex Education Urban/rural Geographic proximity Database	Age Sex Profession Lifestyle Database
Most commonly used business segmentation criteria	SIC* Size VAT	SIC Size Turnover Decision	SIC Size Turnover	SIC Turnover Size	Size Turnover SIC	Size Turnover Location Liquidity	SIC Size Turnover Number of telephone lines	Size/SIC Turnover Branches Credit rating Decision makers	Size SIC	Size Turnover	SIC Size

*SIC: Standard Industrial Classification.
Source: *Marketing Director International,* 1991.

What Customers Buy and How They Use It

The most obvious answer to the "what" question revolves around the identity of the items or services purchased (including brand, purchase amounts, and benefits and features chosen). Any marketing manager who doesn't have such basic data is generally not long employed.

Benefits

The firm produces features but customers purchase benefits. Recognizing this distinction is a problem in technology-driven companies that tend to focus on the development of new technologies and complex products without adequate concern about whether the benefits the technology provides solve customers' problems better than the old products do. Focusing on benefits is also important in understanding the competitive set. The old story about the drill manufacturer that recognized it was selling holes, not drills, not only indicates that benefits are more important than the physical product but also helps to define the competition based on the benefit (referred to in Chapter 2 as *generic competition*). Thus, a key problem facing a marketing manager is to understand what benefits different customer groups or market segments are seeking. As Figure 5.2 shows, the needs or benefits sought can vary with the buying role in the decision-making unit as well as by customer segment.

For example, consider a Cadillac Seville. The following distinction can be drawn between features and benefits:

Feature	Benefit
300-horsepower engine	The ability to pull away quickly from potentially dangerous situations. With the increased traffic, you'll feel much safer in this car.
Northstar engine	Will not need a tuneup for the first 100,000 miles. You'll enjoy a smooth-running engine with fewer trips to the dealer for service.
Adjustable seats	Controls allow you to make easy adjustments to your seating position so you'll stay fit, alert, and comfortable throughout your trip.
ABS brakes	Your wheels won't lock up and skid. This means you have an extra margin of safety.

This kind of description appeals both to the features-hungry customer and to the customer who needs the features translated into terms he or she can understand.

Purchase Pattern (Product Assortment)

As mentioned in Chapter 1, there is increased use of customer databases for target marketing and customer retention programs. Database marketers often use three criteria for evaluating and segmenting customers in their databases:

1. *Recency:* How recently has the customer bought from you?
2. *Frequency:* How many different products does the customer buy, and what are the time intervals?
3. *Monetary value:* What is the value of the customer's purchases in terms of profits?

The RFM approach is used to rate each customer in the database on a scale, perhaps by multiplying the three criteria and then rank ordering customers in terms of attractiveness. When prospecting for new customers, top-ranked customers can be profiled using the descriptors noted earlier, and then potential customers can be matched against these descriptors.

The ultimate customer profile is based on their lifetime value. Decisions about customer acquisition and retention (i.e., will they buy it again?) as well as the level of effort to direct toward each customer depend on the future net revenues expected from them. While measures such as size, wealth, and past purchases provide crude estimates of worth, the value of a customer is the discounted sum of future net revenue of the customer. The net revenue depends on the amount and type of transactions (i.e., volume and margin) as well as the cost to service (retain) the customer.

On a direct-cost basis, not all customers are profitable. Often small accounts do not generate sufficient revenue to cover the cost of servicing them, although the cost of dealing with large accounts often makes them unprofitable as well. In fact, some companies estimate that 80 to 90 percent of their customers are nonprofitable, leading to such contested practices as "slamming" (transferring accounts to other companies without their consent). Credit card holders who pay off their balances on time, cable subscribers in remote areas, and "high service" customers who heavily use toll-free numbers are common examples of unprofitable customers.

On the other hand, customers who are unprofitable in the short run may be very profitable in the long run. While the cost of acquiring a customer (solicitation plus special deals) is typically greater than first-year profits for life insurance, magazine subscriptions, and many other businesses, lower long-run maintenance costs (due to high repeat rates) lead to strong positive returns in subsequent years. Calculating the value of a customer is straightforward, although heavily influenced by assumption (see Appendix A).

A useful way of quickly summarizing potential customers is to describe where they are (and plan to be) in terms of relating to the product. Potential customers fall on a continuum from unaware to enthusiastic advocates. The stages include:

1. Unaware
2. Aware
3. Accepting (i.e., willing to use the product)
4. Attracted (i.e., have a positive attitude toward the product)
5. Active (i.e., buy and/or plan to buy the product)
6. Advocates (i.e., not only buy but actively encourage others to do so)

Delineating which, and how many, customers fall in each stage provides an important basis for strategy formulation (e.g., how much unmet potential is there?).

Product Assortment

Another useful piece of information related to the "what" question involves the number of different brands purchased by customers in the segments (i.e., what else). For many frequently purchased consumer goods, panel or similar data are available that provide purchase histories for individual consumers (e.g., brands purchased were A, A, A, B, A, A, C, A, A, A), which when aggregated produce switching tables such as Figure 2.10. For industrial products, it is useful to understand how many different vendors a customer employs and the assortment of models, quality levels, and the like from which the customer chooses. For example customers may also use Emery, DHL, UPS, the U.S. Postal Service, fax, and e-mail.

Share of Wallet is another key characteristic of customers. Knowing what fraction of spending is on your particular product has clear implications for strategy. (Hint: It is hard to get more than 100 percent.)

Use

How customers use a product is fairly straightforward, including when, where (e.g., at home or in the office), how, and with what else they use it. In essence this gets at the key concept of product experience. For example, cranberry sauce is widely used at Thanksgiving in the United States out of a sense of tradition and to provide color to the meal, which is very different from for nutritional value or to fill up.

Arm & Hammer found out about putting a box in the refrigerator and using baking soda to deodorize drains from customer suggestions. Often customers find uses for a product that the company never dreamed of. Interestingly, the way a product is used may or may not be related to why customers originally bought it.

Where Customers Buy

Where customers make purchase decisions is a critical input into decisions about the channels of distribution. Many managers think of channels as being fixed and traditional, but customers migrate to other channels as their information needs and other market conditions change.

Take, for example, the home stereo market. During the 1960s, consumers started replacing consoles (the turntable, tuner, and amplifier housed in what looks like a piece of furniture) with stereo components. The locus of purchase was mainly small stereo stores and some mail-order firms. In the 1990s most of these purchases occurred in electronics superstores such as Best Buy. Recently the Internet has emerged as an important source of both product information and purchases.

Why did this happen? First, consumers' need for information diminished over time. The component system is no longer a novelty; most people are not buying their first system but upgrading an old one. Media such as *Consumer Reports* provide excellent information on features and quality. Thus, whereas customers relied on salespeople for technical information and product comparisons in the 1960s, Best Buy merely indicates what is on sale and whether it is in stock. In addition, more products are available, which has brought down margins. Large-volume retailers (e.g., Best Buy, Wal-Mart) typically dominate in such an environment.

A similar picture emerged in personal computers. The small computer retailers gave way to large hardware and software superstores such as CompUSA, specialized software discounters such as Egghead, mail-order firms such as Dell and Gateway 2000, and eventually Internet sites. The phenomenon of moving from specialty retailer to discounter is often repeated and predictable.

When Customers Buy

A relevant dimension to understanding customers is the timing issue. When they buy encompasses time of year, time of month, and even time of day. Fast-food operators, for example, segment by "daypart," that is, breakfast, lunch, dinner, and snacking times. *When* also includes when customers buy in terms of sales or price breaks and rebates, on the assumption that those who buy because of a special deal (i.e., deal-prone consumers) may be different than those who pay full price.

Some sales variation is predictable due to the nature of the product. Snowblower sales to end users are most likely to be highest during winter or in late fall; sales to channels occur earlier. Capital equipment sales are often made near the end of a fiscal year to spend money that may not be there next year. However, as noted in Chapter 3, highly seasonal categories are less attractive due to the pressures placed on manufacturing, personnel, and cash flow. Thus, competitors in such categories look for ways to even out demand as much as possible. For example, cold remedies are marketed well before the major cold seasons to get households to stock up and lock out competing brands.

How Customers Choose

One major focus is on how customers collect (or are exposed to) information about products (e.g., advertisements, in-store personnel, brochures, magazines, or, increasingly, the Internet). In addition to defining information sources, the process used to make decisions is relevant. Often the decision process is emotional, holistic, automatic, and/or spontaneous. (Responses to the question "How did you choose it?" include "I just wanted it," "It was in stock," "The old one broke/ran out," or "I just grabbed something.") Knowing the manner in which choice is made is relevant to strategy decisions even when the decision process is not very deliberate. Frequently, however, the process is, or can be, described as "rational." For this type of decision, customers essentially compare alternatives on features via a multiattribute model.

Consideration

Being in the consideration set (akin to an approved supplier list for business-to-business purchases) is critical. Understanding who is willing to use the product (finds it acceptable) goes a long way toward forecasting sales and formulating strategy.

The Multiattribute Model

The process of how customers make decisions has been extensively studied (Wilkie, 1990). In addition, comprehensive models have been developed that focus on consumer decision processes (Howard, 1989), information processing (Bettman, 1979), and organizational buying behavior (Johnston and Lewin, 1996). While it is impossible to provide a comprehensive discussion here of how customers make choices, the multiattribute model offers a concise and practical conceptualization of customer decision making that is useful in both consumer and industrial contexts. The multiattribute model of decision making is composed of four parts. First, the products or alternatives in a product category are assumed to be collections of attributes. Attributes can be defined in terms of physical characteristics or, as described earlier, benefits sought. Second, each customer is assumed to have a perception about how much of each attribute the alternatives in a product category contain. Third, each customer is assumed to place an importance value, or weight, on obtaining each attribute when making a choice in the category. Finally, customers are assumed to combine the attribute and importance weight information using some process, or *rule,* to develop their most preferred option in the product category. We therefore address four questions:

1. Which attributes do customers use to define a product?
2. What are the perceptions of the products on the attributes?
3. What are the importance weights?
4. What decision rule is used to combine the information?

Attributes Identifying the set of relevant attributes is not easy; using managerial judgment alone can seriously misestimate the number and types of attributes used in making decisions. One way to collect information is through focus group research. Participants in the focus group are first selected from the relevant segment(s). The moderator of the focus group then elicits from the set of respondents what characteristics or benefits the customers want to see in a product.

A second approach is through survey-based methods, using open-ended and/or fixed-response questions. For example, to determine the set of attributes for a notebook computer, the product manager could ask the respondent to list (open-ended) or check off (closed-ended) those used in making a decision.

Perceptions Once the attributes have been identified, the next step is to determine customers' perceptions of the amount of each attribute possessed by each brand or product option in the category. This is often done by direct questioning. Suppose that weight is a key attribute of a notebook computer. Then the following question could be asked: "On a 1 to 7 scale where 1 is the lightest and 7 is the heaviest, how heavy is the _____ brand of laptop computer?" This question would be asked for the brands or models of interest to the product manager (often restricted to those the customer is familiar with or willing to consider buying). Similar questions would be used for other attributes.

An indirect approach to determining perceptions uses a marketing research methodology called *multidimensional scaling* (also referred to as *perceptual mapping*). This method provides a spatial representation of the brands in a product category based on customers' perceptions of similarity (or dissimilarity) among products. The characteristics used to differentiate customers' perceptions of the brands are inferred from their relative locations in the product space. The perceptions of the characteristics are inferred from their positions along the axes in the space (see Figure 2.12 for an example). Suppose a bank manager is interested in understanding customers' perceptions of the five retail (consumer) banks in a city. One approach is to take all the possible pairs of the five banks (10) and ask respondents to rate on some scale—say, 1 to 10, with 10 being the most similar—how similar each pair is. A computer program (e.g., SAS) would then be used to locate the banks in a multidimensional space such that the number of dimensions was as small as possible but that the implied perceptual distances

FIGURE 5.7 **Bank Perceptual Map**

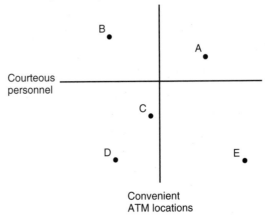

between the banks were replicated. Figure 5.7 shows a representative output of such a program.

Each bank is represented by a point in the two-dimensional space. The distances between the points closely replicate the information given by the respondents. For example, banks B and E are the farthest apart in the space. This means that those two banks were perceived to be the most dissimilar. The labels on the two axes (the attributes) can be determined by two methods: judgmentally based on the manager's knowledge of the market, or estimated based on other information collected from the respondents. The map leads to two major implications. First, the two key characteristics used by bank customers in this city are the courtesy of the personnel and the convenience of the locations of the automated teller machines (ATMs). Second, the perceived performance of the banks on those attributes differs. Bank E is perceived to have the surliest personnel, and bank D has the most convenient ATM locations. Thus, perceptual mapping can give useful information about both the characteristics being used in assessing perceived similarities and dissimilarities among products and the perceptions of the products on those characteristics. While not generally thought of as a substitute for direct questioning, which has largely supplanted it in practice, it can provide useful supplemental information.

Importance Weights   Like product attribute ratings, attribute importance weights can be assessed through direct questioning. Returning to the notebook computer example, a sample question could be the following: "On a 1-to-7 scale with 7 being very important, how important is weight in your purchase decision?" The same question would then be asked on the other attributes, such as speed of the microprocessor, screen viewing characteristics, and so on. The respondent could also be asked to rank order the attributes in terms of importance.

An alternative approach uses *conjoint analysis* (Green and Wind, 1975). This method permits a marketing manager to infer the importance of different product attributes from customer rank orderings of alternative product bundles of attributes.

FIGURE 5.8 Conjoint Analysis: Notebook Computers

Three attributes of laptop computers:
  Weight (3 pounds or 5 pounds)
  Battery life (2 hours or 4 hours)
  Brand name (HP, Dell)
Task: Rank order the following combinations of these characteristics from 1 = Most
  preferred to 8 = Least preferred

Combination	Rank
3 pounds, 2 hours, HP	4
5 pounds, 4 hours, Dell	5
5 pounds, 2 hours, HP	8
3 pounds, 4 hours, HP	3
3 pounds, 2 hours, Dell	2
5 pounds, 4 hours, HP	7
5 pounds, 2 hours, Dell	6
3 pounds, 4 hours, Dell	1

As an example, assume there are three important attributes in a notebook/sub-notebook computer purchase decision: weight, battery life, and brand. Assume also that each characteristic can have two different levels or values, as shown in Figure 5.8. The respondent's task is to rate on some scale or rank order the eight combinations from most to least preferred.

In Figure 5.8, a hypothetical response to the rank ordering task gives a 1 to the most preferred combination and an 8 to the least preferred. One combination (three pounds, four hours, and a Dell) clearly dominates, and another (five pounds, two hours, and a Hewlett Packard) is clearly the least preferred. However, trade-offs must be made for the combinations of attributes between those two options. In this case, the average ranking for the three-pound options is 2.5 ($[1 + 2 + 3 + 4]/4$); for the five-pound options, 6.5; for the four-hour options, 4.0; for the two-hour options, 5.0; for the Dell, 3.5; and for HP, 5.5. Looking at the differences in the average ranks, the most important characteristic to this respondent is weight (difference = 4.0), followed by the brand name (2.0) and finally battery life (1.0). While the actual analysis and design of conjoint studies are more complicated than this, the basic ideas are the same.

An example of how importance weights can vary by market segment is shown in Figure 5.9. There is a dramatic difference in the rankings of the attributes when comparing personal computer attributes/benefits among home users, information systems (IS) professionals, and managers. Note also how price, commonly thought to be the most important attribute, was way down the list for IS professionals and not even on the lists for the home users and managers.

Combining the Information The most common way to combine attribute information is to use a *compensatory* rule, which simply multiplies each attribute importance weight by the attribute value and sums these terms for each person and product, as

FIGURE 5.9 Importance Weight Variation by Segment

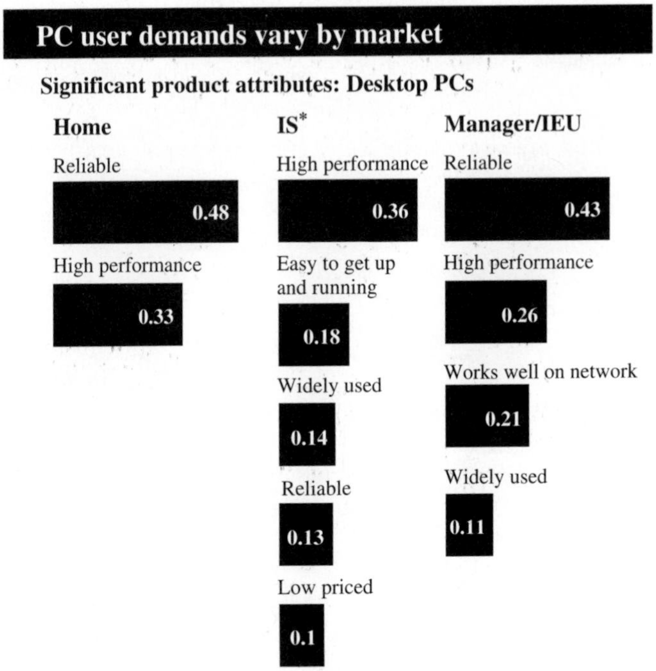

PC user demands vary by market

Significant product attributes: Desktop PCs

Home	IS*	Manager/IEU
Reliable	High performance	Reliable
0.48	0.36	0.43
High performance	Easy to get up and running	High performance
0.33	0.18	0.26
	Widely used	Works well on network
	0.14	0.21
	Reliable	Widely used
	0.13	0.11
	Low priced	
	0.1	

*Information Systems Professionals

Source: *Brandweek,* December 5, 1994, p. 21. © 1994 ASM Communications, Inc. Used with permission.

in Figure 5.10. The product of importance weight times rating is simply summed down each column of the table to get a score for each segment. A separate score is constructed for each competing brand.

A compensatory rule such as the multiattribute model implies that all attributes are considered and that weakness in one can be compensated for (hence the name) by strength in another. Of course other rules may be in effect, many of which are easier for the purchaser to implement.[1] For example, a *lexicographic* rule first compares all products on the most important characteristic alone and eliminates those which are not at the top. A *conjunctive* rule assumes the customer sets minimum cutoffs on each dimension and rejects a product if it has any characteristic below the cutoff.

Customers as Problem Solvers

Customers can be described in terms of the difficulty of the problem they are attempting to solve (Howard, 1989). In extensive problem-solving (EPS) situations, customers are concerned mainly with understanding how the product works, what it competes with, and how they would use it. EPS is generally found among first-time

---

[1] Of course, there are other explanations, such as a dominated brand being a more effective marketer in terms of distribution. Many of the brands rated highly by *Consumer Reports* do not have the highest market shares in their categories.

FIGURE 5.10 **Multiattribute Decision Making: Compensatory Rule**

	Segment 1	Segment 2	Segment 3
Attribute A	Weight $\times$ Rating $=$ Score$_{1a}$		
Attribute B	Score$_{1b}$		
Attribute C	Score$_{1c}$		
Attribute D	Score$_{1d}$		
Attribute E	Score$_{1e}$		
Segment Score	Score$_{1a}$ $+ \cdots +$ Score$_{1e}$		

purchasers and with products that are technologically new. Limited problem solving (LPS) occurs when the customer understands the basic functioning of the product and what it competes with, and is concerned with evaluating the alternatives on a small number of attributes. This is generally the approach to most large-ticket purchases when the customer has made purchases in the category before (e.g., consumer durables). The third basic type of purchase is routinized response behavior (RRB), where customers essentially follow a predetermined rule for making decisions. Most routine order purchases fall into this category, but so do many big-ticket items (e.g., some people always buy a Volvo). Since customers who follow this approach can be expected to ignore most information, the implications for marketing strategy are dramatic. Companies with a product that is bought routinely should make it easy for the customer to keep buying. If a product has little market share and the objective is to increase it, the company must "shock" the customer into considering the product to break him or her of the routine. Promotions, significant price breaks, and free samples are useful shock devices.

Why They Prefer a Product

The fourth, and in some ways the most critical, component of customer analysis examines why customers make purchase decisions. Central to this question is the concept of *customer value:* what the product is worth to the customer. Customer value depends on the benefits offered (from the customer's perspective) and the costs involved (price, maintenance, etc.). Value is very different from cost: An item costing only pennies to produce may be worth thousands of dollars if it solves an important problem in a timely and efficient manner, and a product that is costly to produce may have little value. Knowing the value customers place on a product makes it much easier to make key decisions such as setting price.

The customer value of a brand is composed of three basic elements:

1. Importance of the usage situation.
2. Effectiveness of the product category in the situation.
3. Relative effectiveness of the brand in the situation.

Thus, customer value involves two basic notions of value: *category* value, which essentially assumes no competing brand exists (points 1 and 2 above) and *relative* (brand) value, which involves comparison of the product with other products.

Because new markets eventually attract competitors, relative effectiveness determines eventual share and profitability (e.g., most chemical product categories in which formulations vary eventually are chosen based on physical properties such as rigidity and stability under different temperatures).

Sources of Customer Value

Sources of value (benefits) can be classified into three broad categories: economic, functional, and psychological.

Economic A fundamental source of value is the economic benefit a customer derives from using a product. This is a particularly relevant aspect in business-to-business situations and is often formalized as the economic value to the customer (see Appendix 5A). Essentially it is the net financial benefit to the customer from using one product versus another.

Functional Functional value is defined by those aspects of a product that provide functional or utilitarian benefits to customers. In other words, value is provided by the performance features of a product (e.g., luggage capacity, fuel economy).

A particularly important category of functional characteristics involves service. Customers derive value from three kinds of service. Before-sales service involves providing information. Time-of-sales service facilitates purchase, such as reliable and fast delivery, installation and start-up, and convenient financial terms. After-sales service involves providing both routine and emergency maintenance. Even when a product is involved, service often plays a critical role (e.g., when a water heater breaks, most people call a plumber rather than search for low prices on the Internet). Nothing is more likely to cement a long-term customer relationship than speedy and effective reaction to a problem or more apt to destroy one than a slow and bureaucratic response. Monitoring service quality has (appropriately) become a much more important activity.

Psychological This source of value is basically the image of the product, including how the product "feels" (e.g., sporty, luxurious, high-tech) and whether that feeling matches the image the customer wants to project. Price is clearly part of product image; some customers may prefer a high price (either because they view price as a signal of quality or engage in conspicuous consumption), whereas others prefer a low price. The importance of image (as opposed to functional attributes) was highlighted by adverse reaction to Coke's formula change (even though it was preferred in blind taste tests) and the strong positive reaction to the reintroduction of Classic Coca-Cola.

Partly inspired by a wave of corporate takeovers, the value of the brand name per se has received much attention (Aaker, 1991, 1996). To a customer, *brand equity* is the value of a product *beyond* that explainable by economic and functional attributes. (Brand equity also represents value to the manufacturer, as discussed in Chapter 7.) It can be represented by the premium a customer would pay for one product over another when the economic and functional attributes are identical.

A number of methods exist for measuring brand equity at the customer level including Y&R's Brand Asset Valuator, Research International's Equity Engine, and

Millward-Brown's Brand Z. Basically they break down into five broad categories (see also Aaker, 1996; Keller, 2002):

1. *Awareness.* Being aware of a brand is usually a requirement for its purchase (at least for sober customers). It also leads to more favorable opinions due to the reduced risk associated with a familiar option.
2. *Associations.* Images related to overall quality as well as specific product attributes and user characteristics (e.g., young, hip) impact the reaction to a brand.
3. *Attitude.* Overall favorability toward a brand is a critical part of brand equity. A special form of this is inclusion in the consideration set (i.e., the willingness to consider buying the brand, similar to being on an approved supplier list in business-to-business marketing) or, put differently, acceptability.
4. *Attachment.* Loyalty to a brand is the strongest type of equity (although in the extreme case of addiction it has some undesirable consequences), and the most beneficial for sellers. In the extreme (100 percent retention), it guarantees a nonending stream of income. It also may pass from one generation to the next (Moore, Wilkie, and Lutz, 2002).
5. *Activity.* The strongest fans of a brand become advocates, spreading positive word of mouth and encouraging channels to stock the brand as well as participating in brand communities (Muniz and O'Guinn, 2001; McAlexander, Schouten, and Koenig, 2002).

We discuss brand equity and its implications in more detail in Chapter 7.

Manifestations of Customer Value

A variety of signs of the value of a product are evident even without special efforts to measure them:

Price. Price is the company's assessment of the product's value.

Price sensitivity. A product with constant sales when prices increase generally is of greater value than one for which demand slumps.

Satisfaction. Survey-based satisfaction measures are standard practice in our business (e.g., course evaluations).

Complaints and compliments. The number of complaints or compliments the company receives indicates the product's value.

Word-of-mouth. Although often difficult to track, spoken and written comments provide a useful subjective assessment of a product's value. Monitoring chat rooms and bulletin boards on the Web is one way to track word-of-mouth.

Margin/profit contribution. Generally, higher margins indicate partially monopolistic positions due to greater communicated value.

Dollar sales. Total dollar sales provide an aggregate measure of the value of a product as assessed by the market.

Competitive activity. Competitive activity such as new-product introductions indicates that the total gap between customer value and company costs is sufficiently large to allow for profits even when more companies divide the market.

Repeat purchase rate. High loyalty indicates high brand value.

FIGURE 5.11 Personal Computer Product Category Value

Use	(IMP) Importance	Competitive Products	(REL) Relative Effectiveness	Category Value (IMP) × (REL)
Video games	Some 20	TV attachments, board games	Very good	High
Bookkeeping	None 1	Accountant, service bureau, "books"	Marginal	Low
Learning skills	Very low 4	Books, school	Inferior	Low
Data analysis	Large 65	Large-scale computer, time sharing, consultant, calculator	Good	High
Report preparation	A little 10	Typewriter, word processor, secretarial service	OK	Fairly low
	100			

Assessing the Value of the Product Category

Many ways can be devised to estimate the value of a product category. One particularly useful method focuses on the value of different uses or applications of a product:

1. Determine the uses of the product. Like the substitution-in-use approach discussed in Chapter 2 for generating generic competitors, a first step is to determine the present and potential uses to which a particular product category can be put.
2. Estimate the importance of the uses. This estimate could focus on individual customers or market segments and may simply be projected sales to the segment.
3. List competing products for the uses.
4. Determine the relative effectiveness of the product category in each usage situation.

A hypothetical example of this approach, based on the personal computer category, appears in Figure 5.11. Rather than using numbers, this scale uses adjectives since, typically, some of the entries are hard to quantify. However, the main value of the exercise is to generate broad indicators toward which particular uses of the microcomputer should be targeted.

Assessing the Value of the Brand/Product/Service

Assessing the total value of a brand can be done indirectly. A high-value brand has high share, high repeat purchase rate, low elasticity with respect to price, and limited competitive brand shopping.

Using customer responses to estimate the value of a brand generally involves direct ratings. This includes several approaches:

1. *Ratings* (e.g., "How good is X for use Y?") for competing products. Remember we are generally interested in relative and not absolute value. Therefore, an average of 4 on a 5-point scale indicates good value if the other products are getting 2s and 3s, but little value if the other products are getting averages of 4.5 and 4.8.

FIGURE 5.12 Dollar Metric Example: Soft Drink Preference

Pair of Brands (more preferred brand circled)	Amount Extra Willing to Pay to Get a Six-Pack of the More Preferred Brand (cents)
Data	
(Coke) Pepsi	2
(Coke) 7UP	8
(Coke) Dr. Pepper	5
(Coke) Fresca	12
(Pepsi) 7UP	6
(Pepsi) Dr. Pepper	3
(Pepsi) Fresca	10
7UP (Dr. Pepper)	3
(7UP) Fresca	4
(Dr. Pepper) Fresca	7

	Analysis		
Coke:	+ 2 (versus Pepsi) + 8 (versus 7UP) + 5 (versus Dr. Pepper) + 12 (versus Fresca)	=	27
Pepsi	− 2 + 6 + 3 + 10	=	17
7UP	− 8 − 6 − 3 − 4	=	−13
Dr. Pepper	− 5 − 3 + 3 + 7	=	2
Fresca	− 12 − 10 − 4 − 7	=	−33

2. *Constant sum ratings across brands,* such as "Please rate the following brands by dividing 10 points among them":

> Brand A _____
>
> Brand B _____
>
> Brand C _____
>
> Brand D _____
>
> Total   <u>10</u>

3. *Graded paired comparisons,* which require customers to indicate which of a pair of products they prefer and by how much. This is often done in terms of dollar amounts (Pessemier, 1963), as shown in Figure 5.12.

4. *Conjoint analysis* of customer ratings of products described in terms of attributes, including price and brand name. Through analysis (basically regression analysis), the relative importances of the attributes, as well as the values of different levels of these attributes, are determined.

Emotions, Metaphors, and Conceptual Understanding

Of course, not all approaches are as cognitive/rational as implied by the previous discussion. Advances in cognitive science and neuroscience provide both methods and insights into behavior (e.g., Wells, 2003). One approach (Zaltman, 2003) summarizes what products mean to consumers in a collage of pictures, capturing emotional as well as cognitive processes. Such work is increasingly common in practice. Other authors go into considerable detail to demonstrate and interpret the use of emotion/feelings (e.g., O'Shaughnessy and O'Shaughnessy, 2003) and over-all experience (e.g., Schmitt, 1999). Nonetheless, it is still useful to conduct some of the systematic analyses suggested in this chapter if for no other reason than to quantify the potential of different customer types revealed by more qualitative analysis.

Indeed, much effort is being expended to hear "the voice of the customer" (Baraba and Zaltman, 1990). Such efforts not only provide qualitative insight but also a means for communicating the findings of more standard approaches.

How They Respond to Marketing Programs

In addition to the product itself, sensitivity to and preference for prices (and means of payment), distribution and availability (including the effect of direct marketing), advertising, promotion, and service are fundamental aspects of a market. More-over, sensitivity typically varies by customer and at least a segment-level analysis is usually called for. Methods for assessing sensitivity include:

1. *Expert judgment,* using the knowledge of managers, the salesforce, etc.
2. *Customer survey-based methods,* including both direct questioning (e.g., "How important is . . . ?") and more subtle approaches such as conjoint analysis.
3. *Experiments,* in both controlled settings (e.g., in shopping malls or specially designed stores or labs) and actual markets.
4. *Analyses of past data,* comparing results across markets, or where individual customer record data are available (e.g., scanner data) at the individual level. Such analysis often uses techniques such as regression analysis to predict sales as a function of mix elements or logit analysis (basically a type of regression) to assess the impact of mix elements on market share or individual choice probabilities.

Assessing sensitivity to elements of the marketing mix is a large, ongoing task. The output of this assessment has implications primarily for the tactical/programmatic elements of marketing (e.g., how much to spend on advertising). Since this assessment requires specialized data not readily available outside the company, we do not discuss mix assessment in detail here.

Will They Buy It (Again)?

A critical issue involves whether customers will purchase the product in the future, which for current users depends heavily on their satisfaction with past purchases.

Satisfaction

Perhaps the most obvious trend in business in the late 1980s and early 1990s was the religious zeal with which quality programs were promoted, especially in the United States. Providing quality in order to satisfy current customers and retain them in the future is a logical consequence of the basic principle of marketing, to create and maintain customers. So-called relationship marketing also stresses the long-term value of a customer where a single transaction (sale) is not the ultimate goal.

Quality is ultimately measured in terms of customer satisfaction. Further, satisfaction has a strong relative component to it. (Are customers of a certain product category more or less satisfied than those of a different but potentially substitutable one? Are customers of my company's product more or less satisfied than customers of a competitor's?)

Measurement of satisfaction has three key aspects:

1. Expectations of performance/quality.
2. Perceived performance/quality.
3. The gap between expectations and performance.

Much of the early work on satisfaction focused on the gap between expectations and performance, and a widely used scale called SERVQUAL (Parasuraman, Zeithaml, and Berry, 1988) was developed based on it. Subsequently, emphasis has also been placed on the direct impact of expectations and performance on satisfaction as well as the effect of expectations on perceived performance (Anderson and Sullivan, 1993; Boulding, Staelin, Kalra, and Zeithaml, 1992). Thus satisfaction is now typically modeled as a function of (1) expectations, (2) performance, and (3) the difference between expectations and performance (with "negative disconfirmation," when performance falls short of expectations, aka service failure, having a stronger impact than positive disconfirmation).

Of course, indirect measures of satisfaction abound, including word-of-mouth comments, complaints, and, perhaps most importantly, repeat purchase (or lack thereof). The basic reason for caring about satisfaction is that it leads to loyalty and customer retention. Hence, measures of intended or actual repeat purchasing provide a useful way to simultaneously measure satisfaction and its impact. Note that it is possible for customers to be satisfied but not repurchase due to, among other things, poor product supply, variety seeking or multiple sourcing, and large promotional deals. Similarly they may be unsatisfied but continue to purchase, for example, when dealing with a monopoly. Several authors have assembled satisfaction data across industries and demonstrated its link to retention (Fornell, 1992) and profitability (Anderson, Fornell, and Lehmann, 1994).

Intentions

Intentions are imprecise predictors of future purchase (as in he or she "had good intentions but . . ."). Still they provide early signs of future sales. In fact, surveys of customers (asking "Would you buy _____ ?" and/or "How much _____ will you buy?") are a staple input to sales forecasts, especially for industrial products, and we discuss them in greater detail in Chapter 6.

SEGMENTATION

Each customer is unique to some degree. As a consequence, mass marketing (one marketing program for all customers) is typically inefficient. Since it is time-consuming and not very profitable to develop a separate strategy for each customer, some grouping of customers into segments is often useful. Some categories have so few customers that each can be treated as a separate segment and analyzed separately. Examples are passenger aircraft, military products (e.g., battle tanks), and nuclear generators. In addition, there is a trend toward *mass customization,* or one-to-one marketing, which focuses on marketing products and services to individuals rather than to segments. Examples are Levis custom-tailored jeans for women and Internet-based services that the user can customize (Pine, Victor, and Boynton, 1993). Segmentation is a compromise between treating each customer as unique and assuming all customers are equal. Segmentation programs provide insights about different kinds of customer behavior and make marketing programs more efficient. As information technology has advanced and as small retail operators have always known, so-called one-to-one marketing has become a more viable approach, but segmentation is still the norm.

Desirable Criteria for Segments

What makes a good basis for segmentation? While there is no single way to say what is best (anyone suggesting there is probably doesn't understand the problem or is selling a particular method), the following six criteria provide a useful standard for evaluation:

1. *Sizable.* Segments must be of sufficient size in terms of potential sales. While some customers may be large enough to consider on their own, as a rule, billion-dollar companies don't care much about J. R. Smith at 1188 Maple Street, or all the people on Maple Street for that matter.

2. *Identifiable.* Segments should be identifiable so that they can be referred to by more pleasing titles than segment A and segment B (e.g., the 35-to-50 segment, the sports-minded, companies in New York). More importantly, the identity of the segments provides an aid to strategic and tactical decisions.

3. *Reachable.* It may be sufficient for strategic purposes to identify a segment. For purposes of planning the marketing mix (e.g., advertising), however, it is useful to be able to target efforts on a segment. A sports-minded segment tends to be reachable through specific media (e.g., *Sports Illustrated,* ESPN), whereas people who prefer the color blue, though identified, may be harder to reach efficiently (except by labels on blue towels, or by copy that employs the color blue).

4. *Respond differently.* Ideally, segments should respond differently to at least some of the elements of the offering. If all segments respond the same, then no specialized programs can be used. For example, some customers may be sensitive to advertising but not price, whereas others are concerned about price but unaffected by advertising, and still others care about a single attribute such as downtime. The sensitivity to changes in market offering forms a useful basis for both describing the overall market and defining segments. It also makes the "why they buy" part of the analysis particularly crucial.

5. *Coherent.* When interpreting a segment, it is implicitly assumed that all members are homogeneous. This is always violated to some extent. What is important is that the average member of a segment be reasonably close to the rest of the members. Hence, an important conceptual requirement of a segment is that

the within-segment variation in behavior be smaller than between-segment variation. (This desired condition is often operationalized as the basis for statistical tests for determining the number of segments.)

6. *Stable.* Since future plans are based on past data, segments (and hopefully but not necessarily the members of those segments) should be fairly stable over time.

Methods for Market Segmentation

Many of the methods developed for market segmentation, particularly by marketing academics, are highly technical and not in widespread use. In this section, we focus on three that are simple to apply and for which there is easy-to-use computer software: (1) cluster analysis, (2) tabular analysis, and (3) regression analysis. We also briefly describe a fourth approach, latent class analysis. We assume the product manager has customer data from surveys or other sources measuring both descriptive information and information about behavior toward the product in question. Again, we interpret the term *customer* broadly to imply that data should be collected from former and potential as well as current customers.

A useful approach to segmentation analyses relates information about the two kinds of segmentation variables: descriptors and behavioral variables. Neither type by itself is very useful. We know that approximately 50 percent of the population is men and 50 percent women. This information alone is not helpful because it does not indicate whether men or women have a greater propensity to buy our product. Alternatively, suppose we know that 20 percent of the population consists of heavy buyers, 40 percent of medium buyers, and 40 percent of light buyers. Again, this information is not very useful if we do not know who these buyers are (in terms of income, geography, and so forth); that is, we have no way to reach any of the groups. As a result, the methods on which we focus relate descriptor and behavioral data about customers in different ways to form market segments.

Cluster Analysis

One way to generate segments is to collect data about the descriptor and behavioral variables from a sample of customers and then form groups by means of cluster analysis. Cluster analysis examines the values of the variables for each respondent (from a sample of customers) and then groups respondents with similar values. Consider Figure 5.13. Each dot represents a combination of factors, say, age (X_1) and purchase quantity (X_2). In this case, three obvious clusters emerge. These clusters are appealing in that the members of each cluster are similar to one another and different from members of other clusters in terms of age and purchase quantity. A product manager would conclude from this analysis that the youngest customers purchase the most, oldest customers the second most, and middle-aged people are not interested. Cluster analysis programs are widely available in commercial computer software packages such as SAS and SPSS. (Unfortunately, such clear clusters rarely emerge.)

For example, a regional phone company employed cluster analysis to understand its residential customers. The company collected information on descriptors,

FIGURE 5.13 **Cluster Analysis Illustration**

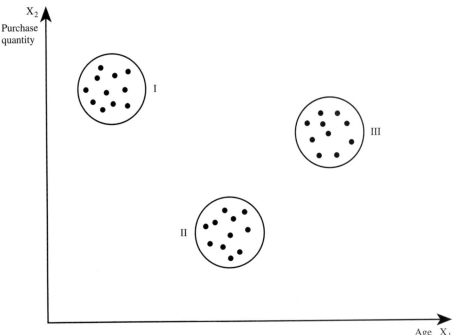

attitudes, and behavior (usage was measured in dollars) and formed six segments based on clustering those households that "looked the same" based on the variables:

1. Low income/blue collar: "Fledglings."
2. Frugal/retired: "Thrifties."
3. Contented middle class: "Contenteds."
4. Aspiring middle-class status seekers: "Climbers."
5. Technology-driven strivers: "Techies."
6. Contented upper middle class: "Executives."

A more detailed profile of the segments is shown in Figure 5.14.

Mobil also applied cluster analysis to gasoline buyers to tailor different stations to neighborhoods with different profiles and needs (Sullivan, 1995). The company identified five segments of gasoline buyers:

1. Road warriors: higher-income, middle-aged men who drive 25,000 to 50,000 miles per year, buy premium gas with a credit card, and buy sandwiches and drinks from the convenience store (16 percent of buyers).
2. True blues: men and women with moderate to high incomes who are loyal to a brand and sometimes to a particular station (16 percent).
3. Generation F3 (fuel, food, and fast): upwardly mobile men and women, half under 25 years old, who are constantly on the go; drive and snack a lot (27 percent).

FIGURE 5.14 Cluster Analysis: Phone Company Market Segmentation Scheme

	Fledglings	Thrifties	Contenteds	Climbers	Techies	Executives
Mean age	37	51	44	43	38	40
Mean income	$26k	$27	$37k	$31k	$40k	$48k
Occupation	Blue collar	Retired/blue collar	Administrative/ professionals	Administrative/ sales	White collar	White collar
Education	14	12	14	16	18	18
Married	60%	72%	76%	65%	33%	72%
Children	44%	38%	51%	54%	75%	33%
Mobility	High	Low	Medium	Medium	High	Low
Home value	$70–85k	$60–80k	$70–85k	$60–80k	$80k+	$90k+
Dual income	Low	Medium	Medium	High	Highest	Medium
Number of phones	Low	Low	Medium	Medium	High	High
Type of phones	Basic/standard	Basic/standard	Medium mix	Medium mix	All types	All types
Monthly bill	Low	Low	Medium	Very high	Very high	Very high
Technology adoption	Late adopters	Laggards	Late adopter	Early adopter	Innovator	Early adopter
Purchase criteria	Value/money	Security	Convenience	Status	Environmental control	Quality
Application	Social interaction	Safety and protection	Social interacton	Social interaction	Personalized systems	Time saving

4. Homebodies: usually homemakers who shuttle their kids around during the day and buy gas from whatever station is along the way (21 percent).
5. Price shoppers: not loyal to a brand or station, rarely buy premium (20 percent).

Many gas companies have targeted the last group. However, Mobil emphasized better service and amenities to customers in the first two segments and was able to charge 2 cents more per gallon than competitors in some markets.

A third example highlights the use of a geodemographic system called PRIZM (Potential Rating Index by Zip Market), marketed by Claritas Corporation. PRIZM's basic analysis is performed on U.S. ZIP codes. Based on the 1990 census, the PRIZM system examined the means of a set of demographic variables for all of the nearly 40,000 U.S. ZIP codes. Using the demographic variables, the ZIP codes were then clustered into 62 different groups. These 62 groups are given catchy names based on the mean levels of the variables, such as "Norma Rae–ville," "Cashmere & Country Clubs," and "American Dreams." The final crucial step, of course, is to relate membership in the geodemographic clusters to purchasing of various products and services (the behavior variable).

One approach uses census data to break neighborhoods into 62 clusters. These are then both profiled and related to specific category usage. Figure 5.15 shows a sample of clusters as well as the number of "wild things members" who reside in each cluster. Figure 5.16 provides another example from Strategic Mapping, Inc.'s ClusterPLUS 2000 for the disposable diaper market. This analysis developed 60 segments using data similar to that used by PRIZM. Figure 5.16 provides the number of households in each segment, the percentage of U.S. households in the

FIGURE 5.15 PRIZM Profile Report by Social Group

PRIZM Clusters Grp	PRIZM Clusters #	PRIZM Clusters Nickname	Households Count	Households % Comp	Wild Things Members Count	Wild Things Members % Comp	Wild Things Members % Pen	Wild Things Members Index
S1	01	Blue Blood Estates	1,238,206	1.20	8,050	3.00	0.70	250
S1	02	Winner's Circle	2,334,557	2.26	12,112	4.51	0.50	200
S1	03	Executive Suites	1,285,478	1.25	3,950	1.47	0.30	118
S1	04	Pools & Patios	1,925,199	1.87	8,326	3.10	0.40	166
S1	05	Kids & Cul-de-Sacs	3,071,716	2.98	12,340	4.60	0.40	154
U1	06	Urban Gold Coast	584,328	0.57	1,271	0.47	0.20	84
U1	07	Money & Brains	1,129,180	1.09	4,768	1.78	0.40	162
U1	08	Young Literati	951,439	0.92	2,251	0.84	0.20	91
U1	09	American Dreams	1,506,981	1.46	4,068	1.52	0.30	104
U1	10	Bohemian Mix	1,516,622	1.47	1,961	0.73	0.10	50
C1	11	Second City Elite	1,948,380	1.89	8,934	3.33	0.50	176
C1	12	Upward Bound	1,871,373	1.81	6,459	2.41	0.30	133
C1	13	Gray Power	2,190,352	2.12	6,384	2.38	0.30	112
T1	14	Country Squires	1,441,183	1.40	8,012	2.99	0.60	214
T1	15	God's Country	2,772,759	2.69	12,126	4.52	0.40	168
T1	16	Big Fish, Small Pond	1,409,739	1.37	5,201	1.94	0.40	142
T1	17	Greenbelt Families	1,569,283	1.52	5,575	2.08	0.40	137
S2	18	Young Influentials	1,360,848	1.32	3,198	1.19	0.20	90
S2	19	New Empty Nests	2,246,499	2.18	8,020	2.99	0.40	137
S2	20	Boomers & Babies	1,047,008	1.01	2,865	1.07	0.30	105
S2	21	Suburban Sprawl	1,452,512	1.41	2,835	1.06	0.20	75
S2	22	Blue-Chip Blues	2,128,142	2.06	5,633	2.10	0.30	102
S3	23	Upstarts & Seniors	1,397,561	1.35	3,207	1.20	0.20	88
S3	24	New Beginnings	1,216,509	1.18	1,431	0.53	0.10	45

S3	25	Mobility Blues	1,516,782	1.47	2,329	0.87	0.20	59
S3	26	Gray Collars	2,002,749	1.94	4,262	1.59	0.20	82
U2	27	Urban Achievers	1,638,535	1.59	3,347	1.25	0.20	79
U2	28	Big City Blend	1,104,724	1.07	2,576	0.96	0.20	90
U2	29	Old Yankee Rows	1,368,473	1.33	1,868	0.70	0.10	52
U2	30	Mid-City Mix	1,120,686	1.09	997	0.37	0.10	34
U2	31	Latino America	1,308,097	1.27	1,460	0.54	0.10	43
C2	32	Middleburg Managers	1,863,879	1.81	5,655	2.11	0.30	117
C2	33	Boomtown Singles	939,270	0.91	1,530	0.57	0.20	63
C2	34	Starter Families	1,572,732	1.52	2,910	1.08	0.20	71
C2	35	Sunset City Blues	1,809,532	1.75	4,150	1.55	0.20	88
C2	36	Towns & Gowns	1,395,701	1.35	1,984	0.74	0.10	55
T2	37	New Homesteaders	1,739,259	1.69	5,623	2.10	0.30	124
T2	38	Middle America	2,358,753	2.29	6,413	2.39	0.30	105
T2	39	Red, White & Blues	1,850,258	1.79	4,549	1.70	0.20	95
T2	40	Military Quarters	437,797	0.42	1,180	0.44	0.30	104
R1	41	Big Sky Families	1,563,136	1.51	6,168	2.30	0.40	152
R1	42	New Eco-topia	919,723	0.89	3,482	1.30	0.40	146
R1	43	River City, USA	1,853,803	1.80	5,618	2.09	0.30	117
R1	44	Shotguns & Pickups	1,991,232	1.93	4,743	1.77	0.20	92
R3	62	Hard Scrabble	2,037,936	1.97	4,140	1.54	0.20	78
Total			103,192,375	100.00	268,337	100.00	0.30	100

Note: Not all 62 clusters are listed above.

147

FIGURE 5.16   ClusterPLUS 2000 Product Potential Report

Item: S1150 Number of Disposable Diapers Used in HH on Avg Day
Market: U.S.
Demographic Base: Households
Group Set: Clusters

Description	Base Count	% Base	Usage	% Usage	Avg Use	Index
Totals: U.S.	96,976,894	100.00	44,435,425	100.00	0.46	100
C54: Young Blacks with Kids	796,378	0.82	656,588	1.48	0.82	180
S45: Low Income Younger Blacks	794,712	0.82	623,785	1.40	0.78	171
C40: Younger Mobile Singles	1,551,509	1.60	1,072,648	2.41	0.69	151
U10: New Families, New Homes	1,794,370	1.85	1,208,366	2.72	0.67	147
S22: Young Families Dual Income	2,545,890	2.63	1,696,654	3.82	0.67	145
S07: High Inc, Young Families	1,582,765	1.63	1,026,304	2.31	0.65	142
T53: Low Income Ethnic Mix	2,408,568	2.48	1,532,643	3.45	0.64	139
U44: Young Black Families	1,097,859	1.13	694,500	1.56	0.63	138
U48: VYng BCollar Hispanic Fams	887,710	0.92	544,265	1.22	0.61	134
C57: Black Lowest Inc Fem Hd HH	1,102,997	1.14	670,655	1.51	0.61	133
S35: Avg Age/Inc Flue Collars	3,111,554	3.21	1,831,753	4.12	0.59	128
C27: Yng Avg Inc, Hispanics Apts	1,606,595	1.66	922,631	2.08	0.57	125
R26: Yngr Settld BCollar Fams	2,202,399	2.27	1,224,826	2.76	0.56	121
U30: Yngr Homeowners L Val Home	1,777,653	1.83	946,531	2.13	0.53	116
R47: Below Avg Inc Work Couples	3,295,708	3.40	1,732,530	3.90	0.53	115
U18: Yngr Hisp/Asian Homeowners	1,336,855	1.38	696,558	1.57	0.52	114
U23: Yngr Families Lo Val Homes	2,342,629	2.42	1,195,549	2.69	0.51	111
C52: Mid-Age Old Apts	1,111,753	1.15	562,416	1.27	0.51	110
T37: Below Avg Inc Blue Collar	2,726,056	2.81	1,343,793	3.02	0.49	108
R28: Settld Couples Lo Val Homes	5,259,551	5.42	2,547,153	5.73	0.48	106
U46: Above Avg Age Low Inc/Rent	1,281,639	1.32	597,541	1.34	0.47	102
C55: Low Inc Mobile Hispanics	1,725,271	1.78	800,347	1.80	0.46	101
R43: Below Avg Inc Blue Collars	3,991,458	4.12	1,802,116	4.06	0.45	99
S03: Well Educated Professional	1,972,176	2.03	877,473	1.97	0.44	97
S50: Very Young Hispanics	560,158	0.58	243,992	0.55	0.44	95
S12: High Inc Settled Families	2,208,503	2.28	960,122	2.16	0.43	95
U08: Hi Inc Urban Professionals	1,390,450	1.43	593,088	1.33	0.43	93
U04: Upscale Urban Couples	1,635,493	1.69	671,429	1.51	0.41	90
C29: Avg Age & Inc Few Kids	1,731,043	1.79	700,570	1.58	0.40	88
C25: Young WCollar Singles Apts	2,472,066	2.55	954,393	2.15	0.39	84
U31: Very Young Apt Dwellers	3,196,517	3.30	1,202,506	2.71	0.38	82
S05: Younger Affluent w/Kids	1,812,746	1.87	676,769	1.52	0.37	81
T19: Above Avg Age White Collar	2,141,629	2.21	793,668	1.79	0.37	81
U24: Avg Inc Apts Fewer Kids	1,728,593	1.78	611,974	1.38	0.35	77
U36: Avg Income Hispanics	1,098,132	1.13	380,782	0.86	0.35	76
U14: High Inc WCollar Apt/Condo	2,741,736	2.83	945,426	2.13	0.34	75
C34: Younger, Hispanics/Asians	2,031,995	2.10	699,422	1.57	0.34	75
S13: WCollar High Value Homes	1,539,106	1.59	519,431	1.17	0.34	74
S21: Suburban Married Couples	1,989,228	2.05	619,096	1.39	0.31	68
S38: Retired Homeowners	1,187,663	1.22	368,475	0.83	0.31	68
R06: Rural Affluents, New Homes	919,158	0.95	281,294	0.63	0.31	67
C15: Single Prof High Rent Apts	2,159,119	2.23	634,909	1.43	0.29	64
S09: Mature Couples Profs	1,139,545	1.18	321,101	0.72	0.28	61
R16: Younger Couples with Kids	2,509,079	2.59	681,097	1.53	0.27	59
S02: Mid-Age Affluent w/Kids	718,314	0.74	194,525	0.44	0.27	59
S01: Established Wealthy	543,731	0.56	135,722	0.31	0.25	54
C17: Prof & Retirees Apt/Condo	1,266,237	1.31	274,325	0.62	0.22	47
C11: Ctr City Affluent Few Kids	968,301	1.00	185,212	0.42	0.19	42
*G59: GQtrs: Military	45,649	0.05	29,083	0.07	0.64	39

*Results should be viewed with caution—insufficient sample size.   Note: Calculations are based on Source Market Usage.
Copyright 1995 Strategic Mapping, Inc. All rights reserved.
Source: Strategic Mapping, Inc. based upon Simmons Market Research Bureau data.

segment (% Base), the estimated number of disposable diapers used in one day in the segment (Usage), the percentage of U.S. daily disposable diaper use (% Usage), the average number of diapers used per household in that segment (Avg. Use), and an index that is the ratio of % Usage ÷ % Base and gives some idea about the usage rate of that segment relative to the size of the segment. While this index obviously is not the only criterion for choosing a target segment (e.g., no data by brand are shown), the information is a useful part of an overall picture of consumer behavior in the disposable diaper category.

Industrial customers can also be segmented on the basis of reactions to marketing mix variables (Rangan, Moriarty, and Swartz, 1992). For example, a large industrial-product company segmented its national accounts based on the trade-offs made between price and service to form four segments:

Programmed buyers: Small customers that do not consider the product important and make routine purchases.

Relationship buyers: Small buyers, loyal to the supplier, that pay low prices and obtain high service levels.

Transaction buyers: Large buyers for which the product is important and that obtain price discounts, expect high service levels, and switch suppliers.

Bargain hunters: Large buyers that get the lowest prices and the highest service.

Using electronic scanner data, a company can segment by store. For example, Kraft can alter the mix of flavors of cream cheeses sold by supermarkets across different neighborhoods. Retailers also use this analysis. Target's store on Phoenix's eastern edge sells prayer candles (the area is heavily populated by Catholic Hispanics) but no child-toting bicycle trailers. The Target 15 minutes away in affluent Scottsdale sells the trailers but no portable heaters. Heaters can be found 20 minutes south in Mesa, which has a cooler climate (Patterson, 1995).

Of course segmentation is not a new topic. In February 1949 critic Russell Lynes produced a conceptual segmentation of American consumers that was both insightful and led to a Broadway show (Figure 5.17).

Tabular Analysis

The simplest analysis uses categorical variables based on customer responses. For example, surveys usually ask respondents to identify the range in which their incomes fall, such as "$20,000–$29,999," "$30,000–$39,999," and so on, or what their favorite brand is. Sometimes surveys ask questions that are continuously "scaled," for example, "How many times did you go to the movies last month?" The answers can then either be analyzed as given or be placed in categories (e.g., 0–2 times, 3–5 times, 6 or more).

As an illustration, consider the data in Figure 5.18. These data were taken from a survey of 1,004 users of cranberry sauce (DeBruicker, 1974). The descriptor variables, located in the leftmost column, are based on some prior analyses of data concerning attitudes toward cooking. These four categories are "convenience oriented," "enthusiastic cook," "disinterested," and "decorator." The descriptor variable is sometimes referred to as the *independent* variable. The behavioral categories,

FIGURE 5.17 Taste Segmentation

	CLOTHES	FURNITURE	USEFUL OBJECTS	ENTERTAINMENT	SALADS	DRINKS	READING	SCULPTURE	RECORDS	GAMES	CAUSES
HIGH-BROW	TOWN Fuzzy Harris tweed suit, no hat / COUNTRY Fuzzy Harris tweed suit, no hat	Eames chair, Kurt Versen lamp	Decanter and ash tray from chemical supply company	Ballet	Greens, olive oil, wine vinegar, ground salt, ground pepper, garlic, unwashed salad bowl	A glass of "adequate little" red wine	"Little magazines," criticism of criticism, avant garde literature	Calder	Bach and before, Ives and after	Go	Art
UPPER MIDDLE-BROW	TOWN Brooks suit, regimental tie, double-breasted suit / COUNTRY Quiet tweed jacket, knitted tie	Empire chair converted to sculpture lamp	Silver cigaret box with wedding ushers' signatures	Theater	Some as high-brow but with tomatoes, avocado, Roquefort cheese added	A very dry Martini with lemon peel	Harper's, Vogue, Gathering Storm	Maillol	Symphonies, concertos, operas	The Game	Planned parenthood
LOWER MIDDLE-BROW	TOWN Splashy necktie, colored slacks / COUNTRY Sport shirt, colored slacks	Grand Rapids Chippendale chair, bridge lamp	his and Hers towels	Musical extravaganza films	Quartered iceberg lettuce and store dressing	Bourbon and ginger ale	Solid nonfiction, the better novels, quality magazines / Book club selections, mass circulation magazines	Front yard sculpture	Light opera, popular favorites	Bridge	P. T. A.
LOW-BROW	TOWN Leather jacket, woven shoes / COUNTRY Old Army clothes	Mail order overstuffed chair, fringed lamp	Balsam-stuffed pillow	Western movies	Coleslaw	Beer	Pulps, comic books	Parlor sculpture	Jukebox	Craps	The Lodge

FIGURE 5.18 Raw Data: Cranberry Sauce Usage

Cooking Attitude	Heavy Users	Medium Users	Light Users	Total (row marginal)
Convenience oriented	81	144	74	299
Enthusiastic cook	97	115	45	257
Disinterested	35	108	127	270
Decorator	45	96	37	178
Column total (marginal)	258	463	283	1,004

located across the top, are divided into three groups based on self-reported usage: heavy, medium, and light. This variable is referred to as the *dependent* variable. Entries in the table or cells indicate the number of consumers who simultaneously belong to both a descriptor group and a behavioral group. In other words, 81 people were both heavy users of cranberry sauce and convenience oriented. The row sums and the column sums are called *marginals.*

Managers have many descriptor variables to choose from, not to mention several behavioral variables. An important task is to sift through the candidate descriptors to find some that are useful to describe the heavy, medium, and light buyers. Is cooking attitude such a variable?

Before analyzing the results in great detail, it is useful to determine if there is a *statistically significant* relationship between the independent variable, cooking attitude, and the dependent variable, usage quantity. The most common and simplest approach is a *chi-square* test. In this test, each cell based on the survey results (e.g., Figure 5.18) is compared to an *expected* cell size or the number of people that would be expected in that cell if attitude toward cooking were independent of usage quantity. The expected cell size can be calculated by multiplying the marginal for the row in which the cell is located by the marginal for the column in which the cell is located and dividing by the total sample size. For example, the expected cell size for the convenience-oriented–heavy-usage cell is $(299 \times 258)/1,004 = 77$. Then the chi-square value is determined by taking the sum over all cells of the (Observed − Expected)^2/Expected. For Figure 5.18, the chi-square value is 86. Combined with the number of degrees of freedom of the table (the number of rows minus 1 times the number of columns minus 1) and the significance level of the test, it is compared to a table of chi-square values found in any statistics book. In this example, the chi-square value of 86 with 6 degrees of freedom exceeds the table value of 12.6 at the 95 percent confidence level. Thus, there is a significant relationship between consumers' attitudes toward cooking and their reported cranberry sauce usage levels.[2]

---

[2] The chi-square tests from different descriptor variables can be compared to see which of these the product manager should consider further in the segmentation analysis. This is more complicated than it sounds, as the chi-square values of tables with different numbers of rows and/or columns (degrees of freedom) cannot be directly compared. One alternative is to standardize all the tables to the same size. A second alternative is to use a computer program such as SAS that prints out the exact level of significance of each chi-square result and rank orders the descriptors by this number.

FIGURE 5.19   Cranberry Sauce Usage Percentages

Cooking Attitude	Heavy Users	Medium Users	Light Users
Convenience oriented:			
Row %	27%	48%	25%
Column %	31	31	26
Enthusiastic cook:			
Row %	38	45	18
Column %	38	25	16
Disinterested:			
Row %	13	40	47
Column %	14	23	45
Decorater:			
Row %	25	54	21
Column %	17	21	13

A second step in the analysis is to better understand the nature of the relationship between the two variables[3] by calculating percentages. The two most common ways to calculate percentages are to divide each cell by its row marginal to obtain row percentages or to divide each cell by its column marginal to obtain column percentages. Figure 5.19 shows the row and column percentages for the cranberry sauce data.

The row percentage indicates what percentage of the row category customers are in the column group. In the example, 27 percent of convenience-oriented consumers are heavy users. The column percentage indicates what percentage of the column category are in the row group. In the example, 31 percent of heavy users are convenience oriented. Of course, the product manager must interpret these two types of percentages differently.[4]

Assume the manager is interested in medium users because heavy users are saturated and light users probably cannot be convinced to consume more cranberry sauce. Which customers should the manager pursue? One obvious group is convenience-oriented cooks, as this group has the largest number of medium buyers (31 percent) and is the second most "concentrated" (48 percent of them are medium users). Enthusiastic cooks might also be targeted, as they are the largest group of heavy users (38 percent).

Regression Analysis

Like cross-tabular analysis, regression analysis is used when a marketing manager can specify an explicit relationship between a dependent (behavioral) variable and one or more descriptor (independent) variables.[5] However, unlike cross-tabular

---

[3] Cross-tabular analysis can easily be extended to tables with more than one independent variable. The same logic for the chi-square test holds.

[4] To see this more clearly, consider the descriptor "men" and the behavioral variable "reads *Playboy* magazine." In this case, a large percentage of *Playboy* readers are men, but a small percentage of men are *Playboy* readers.

[5] We assume in this section that the reader has some working knowledge of regression analysis.

FIGURE 5.20 Cranberry Usage Data by Person

Person	Cranberry Sauce Usage (number of cans)	Cooking Attitudes				Income			Family Size
		CO	EC	DI	DEC	LO	MED	HI	
1	5	0	1	0	0	0	1	0	4
2	2	1	0	0	0	0	0	1	3
3	0	0	0	1	0	1	0	0	5
4	6	0	0	0	1	0	1	0	4
5	3	1	0	0	0	1	0	0	3

analysis, regression theoretically assumes a continuously measured dependent variable. Using the cranberry sauce illustration, if the dependent variable is reported usage in number of cans rather than categories of consumption, then regression will be more appropriate.

Suppose that income and family size are key segmentation variables in addition to the four categories of cooking attitudes. Assume three categories of income (low, medium, and high) are reported on the survey as well as the actual number of people in the family. We can then specify a *model* of the following form:

Usage = f(CO, EC, DI, DE, LOWY, MEDY, HIGHY, FAMSIZE),

where the dependent variable is the reported usage rate of cranberry sauce and the independent variables are the descriptors: convenience oriented, enthusiastic cooks, disinterested, decorator, low income, medium income, high income, and family size, respectively.

Generally, a person can be in only one category of cooking attitude and one category of income. In addition, assume these two variables cannot be represented by continuously measured numbers such as reported usage (number of cans) and family size (number of people). Therefore, we need to create *dummy variables* to represent the cooking attitude and income variables. These variables are simply 0 or 1, indicating membership in one of the categories.

Figure 5.20 provides hypothetical survey responses of five individuals. The first column contains values of the dependent variable, usage of cranberry sauce in number of cans. The next four columns represent cooking attitude. However, each respondent can have a 1 in only one of the columns and must have a 1 in one of them because the categories are mutually exclusive and collectively exhaustive. The next three columns represent the income variable. Finally, family size is reported as the actual number.

Due to statistical (and logical) restrictions, if a dummy variable has n categories, only $n - 1$ are needed in the regression. Therefore, rewriting the regression model in equation form, we obtain

Usage = $a + b$CO + cEC + dDI + eLOWY + fMEDY + gFAMSIZE,

where a to f are regression coefficients estimated using the data in Figure 5.20 and some computer software (e.g., Excel).

The coefficient g is interpreted in the usual way: For a one-person change in family size, usage changes by g units. For example, if g is positive, a one-person increase (decrease) in family size is predicted to increase (decrease) usage by g units. The coefficients $b, c, d, e,$ and f, however, are interpreted differently. Recall that these variables are measured as either 0 or 1 depending on membership in that category. For each set of dummies, a coefficient is interpreted as the *contrast* from the omitted category. For example, b, the coefficient of the dummy variable "convenience oriented," is interpreted as the estimated difference in cranberry sauce usage between a person who is convenience oriented versus one who is a decorator (the omitted category). Likewise, f, the coefficient of "medium income," is the estimated difference in usage between a person who reports having medium income versus one who has high income. (It is irrelevant which category is dropped, as the estimated differences would be the same even though the coefficients themselves would change.)

Suppose we obtained the following results in which all coefficients are statistically significant:

$$\text{Usage} = 10.3 + 2.1 \times \text{CO} - 1.9 \times \text{EC} - 3.5 \times \text{DI}$$
$$- 2.5 \times \text{LOWY} - 1.1 \times \text{MEDY} + 0.9 \times \text{FAMSIZE}.$$

What would be the market segmentation implications? In this case, convenience-oriented cooks have the highest usage rate: 2.1 units more, on average, than the omitted category, decorators. Both of the other categories of cooking attitude use less than decorators, as the negative signs on their coefficients indicate. In terms of income, high-income consumers are estimated to have the highest usage rate (signs on the other income variables are negative). Finally, for every one-person increase in family size, reported usage increases an estimated .9 units (i.e., cans). Thus, the profile of the largest cranberry sauce users is (hypothetically) high-income, convenience-oriented cooks with large families.

One statistic produced with regression is R^2, which measures the degree to which the equation "fits" the data on a 0 to 1 scale, with 1 being a perfect fit. Unfortunately, for frequently purchased products, these kinds of equations tend to have low R^2 values. However, despite the poor fits, these regressions often point to useful bases for segmentation. Figure 5.21 shows that large and significant differences in product consumption can exist even when the R^2 values are low.

Regression approaches also povide information about the response to marketing mix variables. For example, Bolton and Myers (2003) found that price sensitivity depends on various service characteristics (e.g., quality, support). More important, segments in terms of price responsiveness exist across countries and continents, suggesting that segmentation schemes based on responsiveness rather than country boundaries are often useful for global marketing (TerHofstede, Steenkamp, and Wedel, 1999).

Latent Class Analysis

The previous methods begin with individual customers and then aggregate them. Latent class methods, by contrast, begin with the market as a whole and then determine what segmentation pattern best trades off parsimony (few segments) and the ability to explain behavior. This relatively recent approach (see Appendix 5B) is intriguing but requires considerable sophistication, and so it is not yet widely employed. (What this means is you can either (1) ignore it, (2) use it for competitive advantage, or (3) drop the term in conversation to either impress or mystify others.)

FIGURE 5.21 Light and Heavy Buyers by Mean Purchase Rates for Different Socioeconomic Cells

R²	Product	Description		Mean Consumption Rate Ranges		Ratio of Highest to Lowest Rate
		Light Buyers	Heavy Buyers	Light Buyers	Heavy Buyers	
.08	Catsup	Unmarried or married over age 50 without children	Under 50, three or more children	.74–1.82	2.73–5.79	7.8
.07	Frozen orange juice	Under 35 or over 65, income less than $10,000, not college grads, two or less children	College grads, income over $10,000, between 35 and 65	1.12–2.24	3.53–9.00	8.0
.04	Pancake mix	Some college, two or less children	Three or more children, high school or less education	.48–52	1.10–1.51	3.3
.08	Candy bars	Under 35, no children	35 or over, three or more children	1.01–4.31	6.65–22.29	21.9
.08	Cake mix	Not married or under 35, no children, income under $10,000, TV less than 3½ hours	35 or over, three or more children, income over $10,000	.55–1.10	2.22–3.80	6.9
.09	Beer	Under 25 or over 50, college education, nonprofessional, TV less than 2 hours	Between 25 and 50, not college graduate, TV more than 3½ hours	0–12.33	17.26–40.30	—
.02	Cream shampoo	Income less than $8,000, at least some college, less than five children	Income $10,000 or over with high school or less education	.16–.35	.44–.87	5.5
.06	Hair spray	Over 65, under $8,000 income	Under 65, over $10,000 income, not college graduate	0–.41	.52–1.68	—
.09	Toothpaste	Over 50, less than three children, income less than $8,000	Under 50, three or more children, over $10,000 income	1.41–2.01	2.22–4.39	3.1
.03	Mouthwash	Under 35 or over 65, less than $8,000 income, some college	Between 35 and 65, income over $8,000, high school or less education	.46–.85	.98–1.17	2.5

Source: Frank Bass, Douglas Tigerts, and Ronald Lonsdale, "Market Segmentation—Group versus Individual Behavior," Reprinted from *Journal of Marketing Research 5*, published by the American Marketing Association, (August 1968), p. 267.

A simple kind of latent structure analysis focuses on brand switching data. However, rather than estimating share at the individual level and then grouping similar individuals together (e.g., via cluster analysis), this method simply derives segment-level probabilities and market shares. Grover and Srinivasan (1987) provide an example of such segmentation for the instant coffee market. Subjects who always bought the same brand were classified as loyals while the rest (switchers) were then broken into various segments. Figure 5.22 shows the four-segment solution, which appeared to be the best compromise between explanation and parsimony. The results suggest very small hard-core loyal segments (which in total account for 35 percent of the market) and four switching segments with tendencies to favor two or more brands.

Kamakura and Russell (1989) extend this approach to include price sensitivity. They analyze 78 weeks of purchases of a refrigerated (once opened) food product with a 10-week average purchase cycle. The four brands (A, B, C, P) were average priced at $4.29, $3.54, $3.38, and $3.09 and had choice shares of 35.8, 27.8, 23.8, and 12.6 percent, respectively. The resulting segments appear in Figure 5.23. Interestingly, these results also suggest that about one-third (31.4 percent) of the customers are hard-core loyal. In addition, the segments differ in terms of price sensitivity. Segments 1 and 2 (which account for 19 percent of the market) appear to be relatively insensitive to price and fairly brand loyal. By contrast, segments 3 and 4 (which account for 42.2 percent of the market) are quite price sensitive and tend to spread purchases across several brands. Segment 5 appears not to respond to price or be very brand loyal; perhaps this small (7.4 percent) segment represents customers for whom the product is low involvement and who simply pick a brand by reaching for the most readily available one.

Judgment-Based Segmentation

There is a strong tendency to derive segments by examining data. Still, some of the most useful segmentation schemes are simply descriptors on bases selected by managers, such as customer usage rate (heavy users, light users, nonusers) or product preference. While these are not elegant and are unlikely to suggest a new approach, they are often more useful than so-called natural clusters because the segments are readily identifiable and reachable and obviously have responded differently to the product offering. In fact, it is always advisable to use such a segmentation strategy as at least a basis for comparison with the results of more "data mining" oriented approaches.

No simple way exists to tell how to get the best segmentation scheme. In that respect it's a lot like art—you can tell whether you like it or not but never prove it's the best. The problem when segmenting based on intuition, of course, is that given faulty memory and perceptions, it may produce segments for a market that exists only in the mind of a manager.

Summary

The approaches discussed here can be applied to any product, consumer or industrial, low-tech or high-tech, as long as the required data are available. Many other methods have been used. Two methods discussed earlier in this chapter, conjoint analysis and multidimensional scaling, are good examples. In addition, other multivariate techniques (e.g., logit/probit, Automatic Interaction Detector, and CHAID, as well as Bayesian methods) can be applied to obtain information about existing market segments.

FIGURE 5.22 Four-Segment Solution for the Instant-Coffee Market

Brand[a]	Caffeine[b]	Process[c]	Manufacturer[d]	Aggregate Market Share (MS)	Loyal Segment Size	Switching Segments			
						1	2	3	4
							Size (total = .65)		
						.19*	.22*	.18*	.06*
						Within-Segment Market Shares (p̂)[e]			
HP	D	R	PG	.13	.05*	.09*	.20*	.13*	.08
TC	C	FD	N	.10	.04*	.07	.03	.18*	.03
TC	D	FD	N	.07	.01	[f]	—	.32*	.12*
FL	C	R	PG	.12	.04*	.20*	.16*	.04*	—
MH	C	R	GF	.21	.08*	.42*	.15*	.07*	.06
S	D	R	GF	.16	.07*	.04*	.22*	.11*	.15*
S	D	FD	GF	.03	.01*	—	.05*	.03*	—
MX	C	FD	GF	.04	.01*	.04*	.03*	.04*	—
N	C	R	N	.06	.01*	.14*	—	—	.27*
N	D	R	N	.03	.01	—	.07*	—	.27*
B	D	FD	GF	.05	.02*	—	.09*	.08*	.02
Total				1.00	.35	1.00	1.00	1.00	1.00

*Parameter estimate/standard error > 2.
[a]Brand names: HP = High Point; TC = Taster's Choice, FL = Folgers, MH = Maxwell House, S = Sanka, MX = Maxim, N = Nescafé, B = Brim.
[b]D = decaffeinated, C = caffeinated.
[c]FD = freeze dried, R = regular (spray dried).
[d]PG = Proctor & Gamble, GF = General Foods, N = Nestlé.
[e]Underlined numbers denote the two largest choice probabilities within the segment.
[f]Probabilities constrained to zero for model identification.
Source: Rajiv Grover and V. Srinivasan, "A Simultaneous Approach to Market Segmentation and Market Structuring," *Journal of Marketing Research 24* (May 1987), p. 147.

FIGURE 5.23 Preference Segmentation and Price Sensitivity

	Loyal Segments				Switching Segments*				
	A	**B**	**C**	**P**	**1**	**2**	**3**	**4**	**5**
Choice probabilities									
A	1				.790	.219	.152	.095	.192
B		1			.089	.646	.259	.238	.332
C			1		.069	.092	.520	301	.133
P				1	.052	.043	.065	.367	.343
Segment size (% of all households)									
	19.0	5.8	3.9	2.7	9.3	9.7	25.8	16.4	7.4
Price sensitivity									
β					−1.87	−1.44	−3.07	−5.42	.37†

*For switching segments 1 through 4, purchase probabilities greater than .10 are underlined.
†Price coefficient statistically *insignificant* at the .05 level.
Source: Wagner A. Kamakura and Gary J. Russell, "A Probabilistic Choice Model for Market Segmentation and Elasticity Structure," *Journal of Marketing Research 26* (November 1989), p. 385.

ILLUSTRATIONS

Energy Bars

Who the Customers Are

According to SPIN (A.C. Nielsen Consumer Reports),

> 63.7 percent of volume is from households with greater than $40,000 income.
>
> 32.4 percent of volume is from households with greater than $60,000 income.
>
> 72.8 percent of volume is from households with no kids.
>
> 65.8 percent of volume is from households where the Head has some college education.
>
> 39.4 percent of volume is from households with the Head under 35 years old.

Eaten by about 1 in 5 people (Figure 5.24).

FIGURE 5.24 Percent Who Have Eaten Energy Bars in the Last Six Months

Female	20%
Male	18%
65 and over	12%
55–64	10%
45–54	20%
36–44	21%
25–34	21%
18–24	27%

Source: Mintel International Group's March 2002 Survey of 2,026 Adults

Customer segments:

"Hard-core athletes": the original consumer target, who use energy bars, gels, and
other portable food products to maintain a high level of strenuous activity.

"Musclemen": individuals trying to maximize their muscle mass through use
of energy bars, protein powders, and other dietary supplements.

"Dieters": individuals using energy bars as a meal replacement or snack
alternative in an effort to lose or maintain weight.

"Health purists": individuals who insist on the nutritional benefits of organic
and all-natural foods.

"Health conscious and on-the-go": individuals with busy lifestyles who seek a
healthier alternative to traditionally available fast foods.

"Sports enthusiasts": active individuals seeking sustained energy for less
strenuous activity than hard-core athletes.

"Specialty segments": such as women and minorities, who desire specific
nutritional formulations geared to their unique health requirements.

"Nutrition-seeking families": households that actively seek to promote healthier
eating habits among all members of the family, both adults and children.

Overall
Relatively educated, well-off, all ages and genders.

What They Buy
Convenience
Taste
Texture
Health benefits
Performance/energy
Hunger satisfaction
Price (expect to pay $1.00 to $1.50 per bar)
Packaging/buy in bulk
Availability

What Used For
Meal replacements
Snacks
Athletic energy booster

Where They Buy
Health food stores
Outdoor retailers (e.g., REI)
Grocery stores
Drug stores
Convenience stores

Mass merchandizers

Club stores

Odwalla Customers

Tried Odwalla juice first.

Prefer: lighter, fruiter flavors and chewier, whole-grain texture.

Taste matters more than performance.

Personal Digital Assistants

Who the Customers Are

In 2000, the customers for PDAs were primarily upscale mobile professionals. Users were predominantly male, analytical and quantitative in nature, well educated, and over 21 years of age.

Mobile professionals, the key target market, can be segmented as in Figure 5.25. These labels do not help the product manager locate these people, of course. However,

FIGURE 5.25   **PDA Market Segments**

Segment	Size	Characteristics	Distinctive Attribute
Wide Area Travelers:			
Globetrotters	10%	Age 45–54; mostly male Employed in senior positions	Innovators, have modems installed in their portable PCs
Road Warriors	20%	Mostly in corporate management and sales, property management and real estate	High cellular phone usage Overall compuer usage lower than for other mobile pros
Corporate Wanderers	12%	Travel less than Globetrotters or Road Warriors; spend most time visiting employees within their own companies	Employ portable PCs least Heaviest fax users (on PCs) High e-mail users Longest owners of cellular phones
Local Area Travelers:			
Collaborators	8%	Age 25–44 Well-educated young professionals, tend to hold advanced degrees Team leaders, project managers	Innovators High use of pagers (20% of segment) Not very mobile but need mobile products
Corridor Cruisers	15%	Similar profile to Collaborators	Not as likely to adopt new products as Collaborators
Hermits	8%	Least mobile Youngest segment (many under 35) Seldom work with others Mostly finance and telemarketing	Heavy e-mail users Virtually all are PC users but not portable users
Solo Practitioners	16%	Like Hermits but older Diverse collection of technical professionals in small to medium-size companies	Typically connect to corporate network when traveling Highest connect times of any group
Small-Site Bosses	11%	Run small businesses	Highest portable PC purchase intention in next 12 months; shifting to portable PC as primary computer

early adopters of PDAs have a high incidence of purchasing other high-tech consumer products such as personal and laptop computers, home fax machines, cellular phones, and so forth.

What They Buy

Buyers and potential buyers of PDAs seek the following features in decreasing order of importance:

Small size/light weight.

PC connectivity.

E-mail communications capability.

Phone/address book.

Appointment book/calendar/alarm.

One-way paging.

PDAs were initially valued primarily as organizers and less as communications devices by current users (Figure 5.26). This implies that two benefit segments are emerging: (1) those who value PDAs solely for their organizer features and (2) a smaller but growing group who value them for communications. According to a *Forrester Brief,* 63 percent of buyers use PDAs both at home and at work, 31 percent only for personal use, and 6 percent solely for work. As communications capabilities improve, this latter group will grow. At the present time, demand drops to essentially zero when the price of a PDA exceeds $500 and appears to increase steeply as it drops below $500. Also, the Palm operating system still has a greater share than Windows CE.

How They Buy

Advertising and marketing have not been key influencers in PDA purchase decisions to this point. Current users sought out the devices themselves. Again, this is not unusual for a product at the early stage of the product life cycle. Later users,

FIGURE 5.26   **Important PDA Functions**

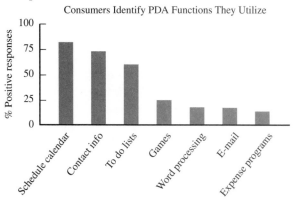

Consumers Identify PDA Functions They Utilize

Source: Forrester Research Inc., July 1999.

however, will rely more on information-based advertising and recommendations from colleagues and friends.

Where They Buy

Customers buy lower-priced, low-feature devices from consumer electronics stores and office supply superstores (e.g., Office Max, Office Depot). Higher-end PDAs are purchased from computer stores or through mail order or via the Internet.

Motorcycles

For those readers who find energy bars and PDAs too tame to be interesting, Figures 5.27 and 5.28 show a segmentation scheme for motorcycle riders.

FIGURE 5.27 Motorcycle Segment Lifestyle Descriptors

Segment	Description
Tour Gliders (13.8%)	I like long-distance touring bikes.
	I use my bike for touring.
	My bike is made more for comfort than for speed.
	I love to ride long distances . . . to me, 500 miles is a short trip.
	I like bikes with plastic farings and engine covers.
Dream Riders (39.8%)	Most of the time, my motorcycle is just parked.
	I like wearing a helmet when I ride.
	I don't know many other people that ride motorcycles.
	My bike is pretty much stock.
	I mainly use my bike for short trips around town.
Hard Core (9.7%)	Some people would call me and my friends "outlaws."
	I have spent lots on speed modifications for my bike.
	Sometimes I feel like an "outlaw."
	Some people would call me a "dirty biker."
	I think it's true that "real men wear black."
Hog Heaven (8.7%)	When I'm on my bike, people seem to be admiring me.
	I really believe that cars are confining, like a "cage."
	Women admire my motorcycle.
	When I ride I feel like an Old Wild West cowboy.
	I feel close to other motorcyclists I see on the road.
Zen Riders (20.3%)	I like dirt bikes.
	When I'm on my bike, people seem to be admiring me.
	I like the attention I get when I'm on my bike.
	Most of the time, my motorcycle is just parked.
	I get excited about motocross or scrambling.
Live to Ride (7.6%)	I love to ride long distances . . . to me, 500 miles is a short trip.
	Motorcycles are a total lifestyle to me.
	Riding, to me, is often a magical experience.
	It's true that "I live to ride and ride to live."
	My bike is everything to me.

Source: William R. Swinyard, "The Hard Core and Zen Riders of Harley Davidson: A Market-Driven Segmentation Analysis," *Journal of Targeting, Measurement and Analysis for Marketing* 4, June 1996, pp. 349–50.

FIGURE 5.28 Summary of Demographic and Motorcycle Ownership
Characteristics, by Segment

	Tour Gliders	Dream Riders	Hard Core	Hog Heaven	Zen Riders	Live to Ride
Demographics						
Average owner age	42.6	42.9	36.2	39.2	36.9	36.6
Sex male	93.8%	95.1%	93.5%	85.4%	94.7%	91.7%
Married	60.0%	68.5%	51.1%	56.1%	75.0%	58.3%
Number of children at home	1.3	1.2	1.0	1.2	1.2	1.2
Education: college graduate	15.4%	24.7%	8.7%	7.3%	19.8%	25.0%
Income of $50,000 and over . . .						
Personal	29.7%	30.2%	4.4%	31.7%	26.3%	25.0%
Household	50.8%	52.0%	26.6%	41.0%	55.4%	55.5%
Average income:						
Personal	$40,438	$40,087	$27,389	$34,744	$38,816	$33,667
Household	$46,563	$46,500	$34,944	$40,397	$47,435	$44,222
Occupation: Professional/ managerial	21.5%	30.1%	0.0%	26.8%	19.8%	29.4%
Motorcycle Ownership						
Motorcycle is 1991 or newer	24.6%	30.7%	7.3%	22.0%	28.7%	15.2%
Owned motorcycle under 2 years	16.7%	22.7%	10.3%	35.5%	30.4%	30.3%
Brought motorcycle new	40.0%	50.0%	15.2%	45.0%	33.0%	55.9%
Model year of principal Harley	1985.9	1985.8	1980.5	1986.2	1983.6	1985.7
This is their first motorcycle	1.5%	9.0%	15.9%	19.5%	9.4%	2.8%
No. of motorcycles owned	9.06	5.34	6.3	6.82	5.7	9.77
No. of Harleys owned	4.74	1.63	2.85	2.13	1.44	2.12
Money spent on motorcycle for . . .						
Purchase of motorcycle	$9,048	$7,460	$5,082	$6,631	$6,966	$8,976
Parts/accessories this year	$ 690	$ 322	$1,260	$ 321	$ 767	$ 860
Parts/accessories in total	$1,571	$1,426	$3,233	$2,419	$1,734	$2,483
Estimated value of motorcycle today	$10,066	$8,414	$8,062	$8,591	$8,827	$10,342
Riding per year . . .						
Number of miles	7351	3675	7099	5051	4169	9662
Number of days	188	109	187	148	112	214
Number years riding	24.1	20.2	16.5	16.9	18	17.7
Type of motorcycle they ride:						
Touring	39.0%	16.4%	0.0%	7.9%	12.6%	31.3%
Full Dress	18.6%	18.6%	11.4%	10.5%	14.9%	18.9%
Cruiser	23.8%	26.0%	36.4%	29.0%	28.7%	31.3%
Sportster	5.1%	30.5%	29.5%	52.6%	35.6%	0.0%
Other type	13.6%	8.5%	22.7%	0.0%	8.0%	18.8%

Source: William R. Swinyard, "The Hard Core and Zen Riders of Harley Davidson: A Market-Driven Segmentation Analysis,"
Journal of Targeting, Measurement and Analysis for Marketing 4, June 1996, p. 351.

SUMMARY

All phases of customer analysis provide potentially useful information. However, a tremendous amount of this information can be summarized in a figure that includes segments across the top and the various aspects of customer analysis as the rows (Figure 5.29). The process of arriving at a useful version of Figure 5.29 is likely to be messy, imprecise, and involve trial and error. The best approach is to try several different schemes for defining segments (e.g., versions of who or why, possibly in combination). The choice of which segmentation scheme to use often depends on the insight gained and the potential for the segmentation scheme to lead to useful strategies (e.g., selecting which segments to serve) and efficient program (e.g., advertising, distribution) determination.

In analyzing customers, it is both natural and useful to look at history. Nonetheless, the reason for doing so is not to be a good historian, but to be a good forecaster. Put differently, one needs to make judgments about what might cause behavior to change (including both your actions and outside influences such as culture, competition, economic conditions, and regulation, as well as natural aging of customers). In addition, some assessment is needed of the likelihood that these causal influences will in fact change. Finally, the impact of likely changes on customer behavior, and consequently on sales, must be analyzed. Then and only then will customer analysis be useful for deciding what to do in the future and what trends to monitor most closely.

FIGURE 5.29 **Summarizing Customer Analysis**

	Segment			
	A	B	C	D
Descriptors				
Who they are				
What they buy				
Where they buy				
When they buy				
How they buy				
Why they buy				
How they respond to marketing				
Will they buy in the future?				
Customer Relationship Stage				
Unaware				
Aware				
Accepting (considering)				
Attracted (like it)				
Active (current customers)				
Advocating (recommend it)				
Lifetime Value				

References

Aaker David A. (1996) *Building Strong Brands*. New York: The Free Press.

Aaker, David A. (1991) *Managing Brand Equity*. New York: The Free Press.

Anderson, Eugene, Claes Fornell, and Donald R. Lehmann (1994) "Customer Satisfaction, Market Share, and Profitability," *Journal of Marketing* 58, July, 53–66.

Anderson, Eugene W. and Mary W. Sullivan (1993) "The Antecedents and Consequences of Customer Satisfaction for Firms," *Marketing Science* 12, Spring, 125–43.

Baraba, Vincent P., and Gerald Zaltman (1990) *Hearing the Voice of the Market*. Boston, MA: Harvard Business School Press.

Bettman, James R. (1979) *An Information Processing Theory of Consumer Choice*. Reading, MA: Addison-Wesley.

Bolton, Ruth N., and Matthew B. Myers (2003) "Price-Based Global Market Segmentation for Services," *Journal of Marketing* 67, July, 108–28.

Boulding, William, Richard Staelin, Ajay Kalra, and Valerie A. Zeithaml (1992) "Conceptualizing and Testing a Dynamic Process Model of Service Quality." Cambridge, MA: Marketing Science Institute Working Paper, 92–127.

Corfman, Kim P., Donald R. Lehmann, and Sundar Narayanan (1991) "The Role of Consumer Values in the Utility and Ownership of Durables," *Journal of Retailing*, Summer, 184–204.

DeBruicker, F. Steward (1974) "Ocean Spray Cranberries (A)" and "Ocean Spray Cranberries (B)," Harvard Business School case studies 9-575-039 and 9-575-040.

Fornell, Claes (1992) "A National Customer Satisfaction Barometer: The Swedish Experience," *Journal of Marketing* 56, January, 6–21.

Green, Paul E., and Yoram Wind (1975) "New Way to Measure Consumers' Judgments," *Harvard Business Review*, July–August, 107–17.

Grover, Rajiv, and V. Srinivasan (1987) "A Simultaneous Approach to Market Segmentation and Market Structuring," *Journal of Marketing Research*, 24, May, 139–52.

Howard, John A. (1989) *Consumer Behavior in Marketing Strategy*. Englewood Cliffs, NJ: Prentice Hall.

Johnston, Wesley J. and Jeffrey E. Lewin (1996) "Organizational Buying Behavior: Toward an Integrative Framework," *Journal of Business Research* 35, 1–15.

Kahle, Lynn P., Sharon E. Beatty, and Pamela Homer (1986) "Alternative Measurement Approaches to Customer Values: The List of Values (LOV) and Values and Life Styles (VALS)," *Journal of Consumer Research*, December, 405–9.

Kamakura, Wagner A., and Gary J. Russell (1989) "A Probabilistic Choice Model for Market Segmentation and Elasticity Structure," *Journal of Marketing Research* 26, November, 379–90.

Keller, Kevin L. (2002) *Strategic Brand Management*, 2nd ed. Upper Saddle River, NJ: Prentice Hall.

Chapter **Six**

Market Potential and Sales Forecasting

Overview

The key document that key outsiders (i.e., those in finance and top management) look for first in evaluating a product plan is the P&L statement. In turn, the key element of the P&L is the top line, revenue. In other words, the revenue (or sales) forecast is the critical element on which the justification for a plan is built. Surprisingly, however, often remarkably little effort is spent scrutinizing this versus, say, the advertising budget, much less considering how the ad budget relates to sales. Therefore, understanding how forecasts are constructed, and how much uncertainty is in them, is critical for both constructing and evaluating marketing plans.

In this chapter, we describe methods for forecasting future sales or market share. Of course, other forecasts such as costs are also required. Fortunately most of the methods described here (e.g., time series extrapolation) apply to other types of forecasts as well.

A critical part of forecasting is the specification of key assumptions. Typically managers make assumptions about factors beyond their control. Most of these are environmentally related factors, such as those covered in Chapter 3. For example, the product manager for Healthy Choice must make assumptions about the likelihood of continued interest in low-calorie entrées and the reaction to carbohydrates. The product manager for Fuji film must make assumptions about the supply of silver as well as the demand for digital photography. Marketing personnel in the home construction business make assumptions about future interest rates. These assumptions both summarize earlier analyses and establish the basis for potential estimates and forecasts.

DEFINITIONS

The terms *potential, forecast,* and *quota* are used in many contexts, and are frequently confused. We use the following definitions:

Potential: The maximum sales reasonably attainable under a given set of conditions within a specified period of time (i.e., what you might or could achieve).

FIGURE 6.1 Forecasts versus Potential

	Expectations	Possibilities
Firm/brand	Sales forecast	Sales potential
Category	Market forecast	Market potential

Forecast: The amount of sales expected to be achieved under a set of conditions within a specified period of time (i.e., what you probably will achieve).

Quota: A related concept, quotas are typically set by senior managers and are what an individual in the company, for example, a salesperson, is expected to achieve (i.e., what you should achieve).

Figure 6.1 shows the distinction between potential and forecast in a sales context. The key difference between the concepts is that *potential* represents what *could* happen in a category if the product in question had full distribution and heavy advertising and promotion, and appealed to all the customers who could possibly purchase the product. Alternatively, *forecasts* represent *expectations,* which (usually) fall far below the potential in a market. Both potentials and forecasts depend on a set of conditions. These conditions can be divided into the four major categories of what customers do, what the firm does, what competitors do, and what occurs in the general environment (economy, culture).

Potentials and forecasts are time dependent. Stated differently, what may not be possible in the short run may be quite attainable in the longer term. While strategic plans depend on long-term potentials, annual plans focus primarily on short-run potentials and forecasts. This suggests a firm can fall into a trap: by optimizing short-run decisions, the firm may make what in the long run is a less than optimal series of decisions. That is one reason why products are often assigned different objectives, such as increasing sales (when the long-term potential seems large and increasing) or maximizing cash flow (when the long-term potential appears low).

MARKET POTENTIAL
Overview

It is hard to estimate the upper limit or maximum of sales. In addition, although managers may perceive potential as a fixed number, it is in fact dynamic and can change dramatically over time. The key to understanding this point is the clause "under a given set of conditions within a specified period of time." In other words, market or sales potential changes depending on market factors such as average category price or general economic conditions.

For example, when Texas Instruments introduced its first handheld calculator, the SR10, which made slide rules largely obsolete, it had four functions (add, subtract, multiply, divide), no memory, and cost over $100. Now calculators and even computers far better than the SR10 are given away as promotions. The market potential of the original calculator was limited to those individuals, usually scientists or college students, who needed to make math calculations and could afford the price. When the number of functions offered dramatically increased and the price rapidly fell, more people could both use and afford one. Consequently both market potential and sales increased.

What Potential Estimates Are Used For

There are five major uses of potential estimates:

1. *To make entry/exit decisions.* Potentials (both market and sales) are key numbers in the strategic decisions of what markets to be in.

2. *To make resource level decisions.* One key aspect of allocation decisions relates to stage in the life cycle. Generally firms are more willing to allocate resources during growth phases. Of course, just because sales have plateaued does not mean they have reached potential. An interesting illustration of the differences between conventional product life cycle thinking and market potential thinking can be found in the running shoe category. In the 1960s, a buyer could get sneakers cut either high or low and in either black or white. The major brands were Keds and Converse. The product life cycle indicated maturity. In the 1970s, the market shot up with the introduction of performance shoes such as Nike, Adidas, and Puma. It became commonplace to wear running shoes to work and then change into work shoes. However, the market again became mature. What happened in the 1980s? Brands such as Reebok and L.A. Gear appealed to segments (e.g., aerobics) and fashion, and again the market jumped. Now a stupefying array of walking shoes, running shoes (for different mileages, degree of pronation, etc.), trail running shoes, cross-trainers, and court shoes are available. One manager's mature market is another's growth market. Thus, as many writers have warned (Dhalla and Yuspeh, 1976), the product life cycle concept must be used carefully.

3. *To make location and other resource allocation decisions.* Both manufacturing plants and distribution facilities tend to be located based on potential estimates, as do retail stores. Similarly sales force efforts and advertising are often allocated across products or regions based on potential.

4. *To set objectives and evaluate performance.* Potentials provide a standard to try to achieve. When actual sales fall below potential, a key question is "Why is there such a difference?" Examining this often leads to changes in market strategy and programs. For example, sales managers use market (or more accurately, area) potential in two ways. First, sales territories are often designed to have equal market potential so that different salespersons can be better judged on the basis of actual sales. Second, sales quotas are often set based on the potential sales in a territory.

5. *As an input to forecasts.* A major use of potentials in annual planning is as a basis for the sales forecast. In this case, a forecast is viewed as the product of potential times the percent of potential expected to be achieved.

Information Sources

Market potential may be estimated in a variety of ways. While the details involved depend on the particular industry and product under consideration, this section suggests some general approaches to assessing potential. Past sales data are useful, and for a stable market provide the key information for both a potential estimate and a sales forecast. In new markets, however, such data may be unavailable,

FIGURE 6.2 **Deriving Potential Estimates**

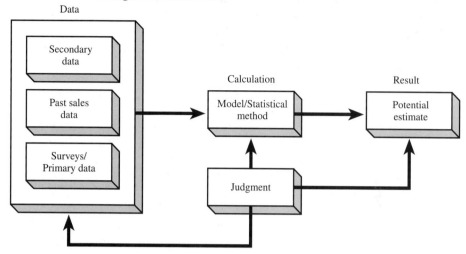

inaccurate, or unduly influenced by isolated events. Even when such data are available, other data should *not* be ignored. Figure 6.2 summarizes a process for deriving potential estimates (which is also useful for forecast development). It is useful to recognize the important role played by judgment not just in directly influencing estimates but also indirectly through data collection and model selection. The exact data and calculations used depend on the situation. Some of the sources useful for potential estimates (and forecasts) are already familiar to readers.

Government Sources

Market size estimates are available for many industries from sources such as the U.S. Department of Commerce and the Bureau of the Census (e.g., *Survey of Current Business, Current Industrial Reports*). Even when specific size estimates for an industry or a product are not available, government data may be useful as inputs to the potential estimate. Examples include breakdowns of industry by location, size, and Standard Industrial Classification (SIC) code, and forecasts of general economic conditions.

Trade Associations

These groups are a good source of information for particular industries or product categories, although they may be a bit optimistic.

Private Companies

A number of private companies track and forecast sales for various industries (e.g., FIND/SVP, mentioned in Chapter 4). Some also survey capital spending plans (e.g., McGraw-Hill), consumer sentiment, and durable purchasing plans (e.g., the Survey Research Center at the University of Michigan).

Financial and Industry Analysts

Industry specialists often provide forecasts or potential estimates for various industries (e.g., Forrester and Gartner for computers).

Popular Press

A substantial amount of material finds its way into the business press (e.g., *Fortune, Forbes, Business Week*) or specialty publications.

The Internet

As in most areas, the Internet provides access to a wide and increasing pool of information.

While many sources exist, their competency and accuracy may not be very high. (It is comforting to assume that published potential estimates and forecasts are accurate and done by experts, but both the accuracy and expertise are often suspect. Think of it this way: The person who prepared the forecast may have been a classmate of yours!) To understand or assess the value of a forecast (whether provided by an outsider or a subordinate), it is important to have at least a rudimentary knowledge of how forecasts are constructed. This chapter therefore goes into some detail on forecasting methods in the hope that the reader will become a more intelligent consumer of forecasts.

New or Growing Product Potential

In considering both the saturation level (ultimate potential) and the time pattern of market development, it is useful to compare the product to its major (and typically older) competitors. This can be accomplished by considering three major dimensions: relative advantage, compatibility, and risk.

Relative Advantage

In terms of benefits provided, is the new product superior in key respects and, if so, to what degree? Noticeably superior benefits increase both the saturation level and the rate at which the level is achieved. Also, in general, the relative advantage of a new product usually increases over time as various modifications and line extensions appear.

Compatibility

The fewer and less important the changes required to understand and use a new product, the faster it will be adopted. Compatibility issues relate not only to customers but also to intermediaries; the company itself (e.g., sales staff); and, if customers use a certain product as a component in another product, their customers as well. Therefore, if a chemical company is planning to manufacture a new product, issues of manufacturing compatibility and sales staff effort arise within the company, along with potential problems regarding the behavior of wholesalers (assuming the product is sold through that channel), and customer problems (is retooling required?). Incompatibility tends to decrease over time. Finally, while incompatibility may be primarily psychological (i.e., "We just don't do things that way here"), failure to consider psychological barriers to adoption is often disastrous, at least in the short run.

Risk

The greater the risk involved (financial, possible impact on product quality if a new component fails, and so on), the lower the probability that someone will buy the new product. Typically, risk—at least in terms of price—tends to drop over time, thus increasing potential.

Overall, the higher the relative advantage (benefits) and the lower the costs (incompatibility, risk), the greater the potential and the faster it is likely to be achieved.

Role of Analogous Products

Examining the pattern of use and adoption of analogous products or services is often quite useful, especially for growing or new products. For either, the previous adoption patterns of similar products provide a clue to the likely pattern and rate of adoption and the eventual saturation level. As will be seen later in this chapter, analogies are also useful for sales forecasting.

The problem with using analogies is that two products are rarely perfectly comparable. To be reasonably comparable, both the newer product and its older analogue should be targeted to a similar market; be similar in perceived value, both in toto and in terms of the major benefits provided; and be similar in price. Under these criteria, a microwave oven could be compared to a dishwasher in that both are targeted at households, stress convenience and time savings, and cost about the same. In contrast, a mainframe computer from 1960, a microcomputer from 1984, and a wireless device linked to the Internet are not analogous, even though one is a direct descendant of the other, because the target market (companies versus individuals), perceived value (number crunching and billing versus convenience and word processing or entertainment and information), and price (a million dollars versus a few hundred) all differ dramatically.

Mature Product Potentials

The more mature products are, the more sales come from reorders from past customers. Reorders in a mature market are of two types. For a consumable product, repurchasing will be in proportion to the market need (if an industrial product) or usage rate (if a consumer product). For a durable product, repurchasing will occur to replace a worn-out product; to upgrade to get new features; or, importantly, to add an additional model (e.g., a second TV; Bayus, Hong, and Labe, 1989).

METHODS OF ESTIMATING MARKET AND SALES POTENTIAL

The role of managerial judgment in deriving potential is crucial and ubiquitous. It influences the type of data examined, the model used to derive the estimate, and often the estimate itself. Although statistical knowledge is useful, logic or common sense is much more important. Therefore, after estimating market potential, a manager should step back and ask, "Does this estimate make sense?"

Analysis-Based Estimates

A formula-based method can be developed based largely on the potential users or buyers of the product in question in a three-step process.

1. *Determine the potential buyers or users of the product.* Buyers should be interpreted broadly as customers who have the need, the resources necessary to use the product, and the ability to pay. This often results in a marketing manager

assessing that almost all customers are in the potential market (and maybe they are). An alternative approach is to work backward: Who *cannot* qualify as a potential customer? This might include apartment dwellers for lawn mowers, diabetics for regular ice cream, and so on. The product manager can determine potential customers judgmentally. In addition, other data sources that could be useful are surveys, commercial sources such as data from Simmons Market Research Bureau or MRI, and government documents.

As an example, consider the problem of estimating the market potential for laptop computers. One judgmental approach for determining the number of potential adult employed users is to divide the market into categories such as: (1) "fleet workers" who are not in an office but need portable computing capabilities in a warehouse or manufacturing line, (2) "road warriors" who are on the road full time and need a virtual office, (3) "office functionalists" who work mainly out of the office but sometimes from home, (4) "corridor cruisers" who need their office computers when they go to business meetings, and (5) "road runners" who need a second office but less intensively than "road warriors" do (Beeh, 1994).

2. *Determine how many are in each potential group of buyers defined by step 1.* Often steps 1 and 2 are done simultaneously. If defined in terms of a particular demographic group, for example, people above age 60, sources such as the *Statistical Abstract of the United States* help determine how many people are in the group. For the previous example of laptop computers, the estimated group sizes were 15 million "fleet workers," 10 million "road warriors," 8 million "office functionalists," 6 million "corridor cruisers," and 5 million "road runners."

The potential U.S. market for ice cream includes most individuals. If we start with a population of 280 million, we might remove diabetics and individuals with lactose intolerance or other reasons not to consume dairy products. Considering the percent who have these conditions would eliminate approximately 16 million diabetics and 30 million with lactose intolerance, leaving about 234 million as the potential market. Of course, many of these are young children, so the size of the buying market is smaller.

3. *Estimate the purchasing or usage rate.* This can be done by taking either the average purchasing rate determined by surveys or other research or by assuming that the potential usage rate is characterized by the heaviest buyers. The latter notion would be based on the assumption that all buyers could be convinced to purchase at that heavy rate. Market potential is then calculated by simply multiplying the number obtained from step 2 by the number from step 3, that is, the number of potential customers times their potential usage rate. For example, if we assume one laptop computer per potential user, the U.S. installed base market potential is simply 44 million units. The market potential estimate derived in this manner usually results in a large number compared to current industry sales. To get annual potential, the installed base potential of 44 million must be multiplied by the percent who buy each year. Assuming purchases are made every four years, this leads to an annual potential of 11 million. This method is often referred to as the successive ratio or chain ratio method. However, the number itself is often not as important as the process of trying to get the number. Estimating market potential using this kind of analysis forces a marketing manager to think about who the potential

FIGURE 6.3 Market Potential: Electric Coil

SIC	Industry	Purchases of Product	Number of Workers	Average Purchase/ Worker	National Number of Workers	Estimated Potential
3611	Electrical measuring	$160	3,200	$.05	34,913	$1,746
3612	Power transformers	5,015	4,616	1.09	42,587	46,249
3621	Motors and generators	2,840	10,896	.26	119,330	31,145
3622	Electrical industry controls	4,010	4,678	.86	46,805	40,112
		$12,025				$119,252

customers for the product are, which can often result in new thinking about untapped segments. A second impact of the market potential estimate is that it usually reveals a significant amount of untapped purchasing power in the market that is waiting for a new strategy, a new product formulation, or perhaps a new competitor.

Two examples help illustrate this method. The first illustration is from the infant/toddler disposable diaper category. The potential users are rather obvious in this case. During the 1990s, an average 4 million babies were born annually in the United States. The average child goes through 7,800 diapers in the first 130 weeks of life (2.5 years) until toilet training, or 60 per week (Deveny, 1990). Thus, the annual market potential for disposable diapers [(2.3)(4 million) babies][60 diapers/week] [52 weeks/year] is 28.7 billion. This figure includes babies who are allergic to the diapers as well as households using cloth diapers or diaper services. Importantly, households using cloth diapers are still potential customers.

A second application shown in Figure 6.3 is typical of estimates of market potential for industrial products (Cox, 1979, Chapter 6). In this case, the potential customers are identified by SIC code. How much they can buy is extrapolated from an activity measure, in this case dollars of purchases per employee. A defect of this approach, however, is that current nonbuying SIC codes that are potential buyers are not included in the analysis.

Now consider again U.S. consumption of ice cream. In 1999, the population was 273,401,000. Of these, 16 million suffer from diabetes (and hence cannot consume regular ice cream) and 30 million are lactose intolerant. Removing these leaves 227,401,000 potential customers (plus those who are both diabetic and lactose intolerant). On average, consumption per person is 46.6 pints per year. This means potential is 10.5 billion pints per year which, at an average price per pint of $3.19, translates into a $33.5 billion dollar market.

For handheld devices (PDAs), market potential in 2000 was based on a total population of 278.1 million. From this we eliminate children under 13 (56.2 million) and those who live below the poverty level (21.1 million) for a potential market size of 200.8 million. Note that this potential assumes each person buys only one and that purchases occur annually, so potential can vary widely as these assumptions are altered. Notice also that it changes each year and hence is not a static concept.

This method has to be used carefully for durable consumer products or industrial products with long interpurchase cycles. In those cases, buyers not in the market because they recently purchased the good must be subtracted from the total. However, sometimes multiple purchases of such products occur; for example, many households have two or three VCRs, DVD players, or even PCs.

This approach to estimating market potential has implications for increasing the sales volume in a category or for a brand. There are two ways to increase sales. First, a firm can increase the number of customers—by pursuing new segments, developing new products, or just getting more customers in existing segments (see Chapter 7). Second, the purchase rate can be increased; that is, a manager can attempt to get customers to buy more through promotions, package size changes, and other tactics. These approaches have been used successfully at General Mills, which has a large number of mature products (e.g., Hamburger Helper, Betty Crocker cake mixes; Sellers, 1991).

Area Potential

Potential is often derived by breaking down total sales by area. When sales data are available for a variety of regions, along with some data on characteristics of the regions, it is common to use a weighted index that combines these characteristics to indicate the relative potential in the area. Many consumer goods companies use the general *Sales and Marketing Management* buying power index, which is 0.2 × (percentage of the population of the area compared to the United States) + 0.3 × (percentage of retail sales of the area of the United States total) + 0.5 × (percentage of disposable income of the area of the United States total). When population, retail sales, and disposable income are input as a percentage of the total United States, this index projects the percentage of the product sold in the various regions. For established products, these weights may be estimated from the actual sales data by, for example, running a regression of sales versus various factors such as the number of schools in the region. Product-related data, such as sales of analogous products, might also be used. In fact, as noted earlier in this chapter, sales of truly analogous products are often the best indicators of potential. An index approach for a hypothetical new copying system might be as follows:

Bases: Percent population in the region (P)

Percent schools in the region (S)

Percent retail businesses in the region (RB)

Percent banks in the region (B)

Percent offices in the region (O)

Percent warehouses in the region (WH)

Percent manufacturing facilities in the region (MF)

Percent other businesses in the region (OB)

Percent Xerox sales in the region (XS)

Percent other copier sales in the region (CS)

$$\text{Index} = W_1 P + W_2 S + W_3 RB + W_4 B + W_5 O + W_6 WH + W_7 MF + W_8 OB + W_9 XS + W_{10} CS$$

Here the *W*s are the weights assigned to each factor.

Sales Potential

Sales potential is the firm-level analogy to market potential. An obvious approach to calculating sales potential is to multiply the estimated potential of the market by some market share figure. This share figure should represent potential share, which the firm could achieve under optimal conditions (but usually not 100 percent).

SALES FORECASTING

Overview

As noted earlier, forecasting deals with expectations of the future, that is, what will happen. The most obvious things for a marketing manager to be concerned about, and the focus of this chapter, are sales, market share, and profits.

Other quantities are of course important to forecast as well. *Resources* used as a factor of production must be forecast (note the earlier discussion about general planning assumptions). Sometimes the key resources are human, making it important to forecast the needed labor pool. *Costs* are also an important factor to forecast. If the product is manufactured and follows the experience curve, costs are somewhat more predictable than in other situations. For many companies, accurate forecasts of the rate of change of *technology* are critical to keeping an edge on competitors. General *economic conditions* have important effects on many types of businesses. Finally, in global businesses currency exchange rates have a major impact on profits.

Forecasts are used in several ways.

1. *To answer "what if" questions.* In considering which strategy and tactics to follow, the key is an estimate of the outcomes of the various strategies and tactics, typically the sales and profit levels. The simplest "what if" question is What will happen next year if everything remains as it has been in the past? This makes the forecast basically an extrapolation.

2. *To help set budgets.* Sales forecasts become the basis of a budget because they specify both sales levels to be attained and, by implication, the resources needed. All pro forma income statements are based on a sales forecast.

3. *To provide a basis for a monitoring system.* Deviations from forecasts serve as warnings to product management to reexamine a market and their strategy in it. Both positive and negative deviations from forecasts can lead to a better understanding of the marketplace through an examination of the underlying causes.

4. *To aid in production planning.* With more companies and their channels moving to just-in-time production and distribution systems with low levels of inventory, accurate forecasting is becoming even more critical. This is particularly important in the personal computer industry. Mistakes in forecasting demand for personal computers cost Compaq $50 million and IBM much more in 1994 (McWilliams, 1995). For several years Apple Computer underestimated the demand for its Powerbook laptop computers, which exacerbated its financial problems.

5. *By financial analysts to value a company.* The huge valuations of the "dot.com" companies at the end of 1999 could be justified only on the basis of large growth rates. Further, deviations from forecasts have a major impact on stock prices (e.g., missing sales or earnings targets).

A good forecast takes into account four major categories of variables, all of which either have been or will be discussed in this book: customer behavior (Chapter 5), past and planned product strategies (Chapter 7), competitor actions (Chapter 4), and the environment (Chapter 3). Company actions are predictable and/or under the control of a marketing manager, although, as noted in Chapter 1, many decisions such as pricing and advertising may be made in other parts of the company. In contrast, customer and competitive actions are much harder to forecast. The general environment consists of such elements as the state of the economy, key industries in it, demographic changes in the population, and costs of basic resources. Although some of these elements can be forecast reasonably well, they are generally derived from secondary sources, such as government projections, and appear in the category analysis or the planning assumptions section of a marketing plan. While environmental changes affect the plan mainly through their impact on competitor and customer behavior, they can be so crucial that we treat them separately here.

Forecasting can be thought of as the process of assessing the possible outcomes under reasonably likely combinations (sometimes called scenarios) of the four basic determinants of outcome. This suggests that forecasting without considering competitive reactions is, unless the competitors are asleep, insufficient. The forecasting process can be viewed as a process of filling out a three-dimensional grid such as that shown in Figure 6.4, with the likely outcomes contingent on values of the three sets of independent variables.

The forecast in each cell should not be a single number but rather a range of possible outcomes. While a forecast of 787.51 may sound better than 800 ± 50, it is likely to be misleading and an example of foolish precision (which puts you out

FIGURE 6.4 Scenario-Based Forecasts

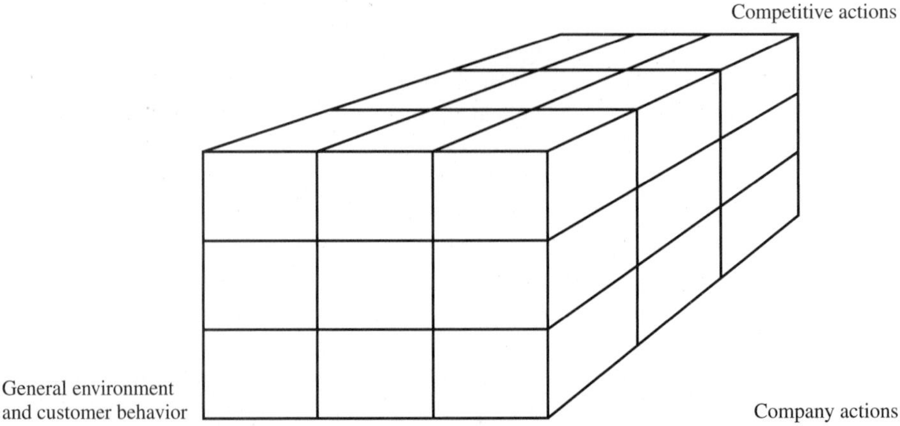

Competitive actions

General environment and customer behavior

Company actions

on a limb with your boss). Do not expect forecasts to six decimal places, especially when such precision is not crucial to making a sound decision.

Knowing the range of likely results is crucial for strategy selection. A manager may be unwilling to undertake a strategy with a high expected result (e.g., a profit of $8 million) that also has a reasonably likely disastrous result (e.g., a loss of $5 million). Conversely, a different manager may be willing to gamble on a possible large return even if the likely result is a small profit or even a loss. It is also useful to know the likely range of outcomes for purposes of monitoring and control. For example, in one situation, a drop of 30 percent below the forecast may be well within the expected range and therefore not necessarily a cause for a major reanalysis, whereas in a different situation, a 15 percent drop below the forecast may signal a serious problem.

At this point, it should be clear that producing a forecast for each possible combination of factors is a tedious task at best. Consequently, it is desirable to limit the task to, say, three environments (expected, benign, and hostile) and a limited number of competitive postures (e.g., status quo, more/less aggressive). This limitation should, however, be made with two points in mind. First, the initial forecasts may suggest a promising avenue or a potential disaster that may lead to refining the scenarios. Second, the assumptions made in forecasting are crucial; therefore, it is desirable to designate them formally as *planning assumptions.*

Level of Accuracy Needed

Obviously, more accuracy in a forecast is better than less. Also, assuming a reasonably intelligent forecasting procedure is being employed (something one should *not* generally assume), then the only way to get a better forecast is to spend more time, effort, and money. Since increasing forecast accuracy has severely diminishing marginal returns (to make the range of a forecast half as large will generally at least quadruple its cost), at some point the cost of improving the forecast will exceed the benefit.

The benefit of a better forecast usually is greater when (1) the price of the product is high in either absolute or relative terms ($40,000 may not be much to IBM but it is to the authors); (2) product demand is relatively volatile; and (3) the cost of an error in forecasting (including reorder cost and the cost of being out of stock—which may include the long-term loss of a disenchanted customer) is high. The cost of a better forecast increases as (1) the number of items or product forms increases (e.g., machine tool A with feature X, with features X and Z, and so on); (2) the method becomes more complicated to use; and (3) the forecast (and its basis) is difficult to communicate to others in the organization. (Generally speaking, review committees prefer not to hear about Fourier series, correlated errors, and so on.)

Judgment-Based Methods

A large number of methods have been developed for forecasting (Chambers, Mullick, and Smith, 1971; Georgoff and Murdick, 1986; Wheelwright and Makridakis, 1985). Figure 6.5 compares a number of methods. Here we discuss four basic

FIGURE 6.5 Summary of Forecasting Methods

Dimensions	1. Time span	2. Urgency	3. Quantitative skills needed	4. Financial resources needed	5. Past data needed	6. Accuracy
Judgment						
Naive Extrapolation	Short/medium term	Rapid turnaround	Minimal	Very low	Some	Limited
Sales Force	Short/medium term	Fast turnaround	Minimal	Low	Not necessary	Highly variable
Executive Opinion	Short/medium term	Depends on whether inside or outside company	Minimal	Could be high if outside experts used	Not necessary	Poor if one individual; better if a group
Delphi	Medium/long	Needs time	Minimal	Could get high	Not necessary	Best under dynamic conditions
Counting						
Market Testing	Medium	Needs time	Moderate level	High	Not necessary	Good for new products
Market Survey	Medium	Needs time	Yes	High	Not necessary	Limited

Time Series	**Moving Average**	Short/medium	Fast turnaround	Minimal	Low	Necessary	Good only in stable environment
	Exponential Smoothing	Short/medium	Fast turnaround	Minimal	Low	Necessary	Good in short run
	Extrapolation	Short/medium/long	Fast turnaround	Basic skills	Low	Necessary	Good for trends, stable time series
Association/Casual	**Correlation**	Short/medium/long	Fast turnaround	Basic skills	Moderate	Necessary	Highly variable
	Regression	Short/medium/long	Moderately fast	Basic skills	Moderate/high	Necessary	Can be accurate if explained variance is high
	Leading Indicators	Short/medium/long	Moderately fast	Basic skills	Moderate/	Necessary	Moderately accurate at best
	Econometric	Short/medium/long	Needs time	High level	High	Necessary	Best in stable environment

Source: David M. Georgoff and Robert G. Murdick, "Manager's Guide to Forecasting," *Harvard Business Review*, January–February, 1986, pp. 110–20.

FIGURE 6.6 Graphical Eyeball Forecasting

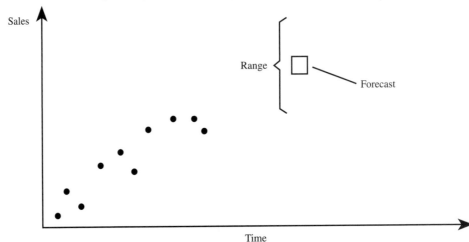

approaches: judgment based, customer based, sales extrapolation, and model based. The first set of methods is referred to as *judgment-based* methods because, unsurprisingly, they rely solely on judgments.

Naive Extrapolation

One method of naive extrapolation uses the last-period sales level and adds x percent, the estimated percentage change in sales. For example, dishwasher sales could be forecast to be last year's plus 6 percent. A related approach might be termed "graphical eyeball." This requires plotting the past sales series and then "eyeballing" the next value to match the past pattern (see Figure 6.6).

Sales Force Composite

Salespeople are often asked to make sales forecasts. Their forecasts can then be aggregated to create a sales forecast for the product or product line. The advantage of this approach is that salespeople are close to customers and thus in an excellent position to understand their purchasing plans. Unfortunately, when the forecast is used to set quotas, such forecasts are naturally on the low side. Alternatively, salespeople can be overly optimistic in an attempt to impress the sales manager.

Jury of Expert Opinion

An extreme example of this method relies on a single expert's opinion. If the expert happens to know the Delphic oracle or be a mystic, the forecast can be excellent. Unfortunately, it is hard to know ahead of time whether someone can predict the future.

Many studies have been published deriding expert forecasts. Consider the following business-related predictions made by "experts" (Cerf and Navasky, 1984):

> With over 50 foreign cars already on sale here, the Japanese auto industry isn't likely to carve out a big slice of the U.S. market for itself. (*Business Week,* August 2, 1968)

A severe depression like that of 1920–1921 is outside the range of probability. (Harvard Economic Society, November 16, 1929)

The phonograph . . . is not of any commercial value. (Thomas Edison, ca. 1880)

TRW sponsored a major technological forecasting project back in the mid-1960s. Some of their predictions were:

- A manned lunar base by 1977.
- Commercial passenger rockets by 1980.
- Undersea mining and farming by 1981.

Despite examples like these, expert forecasts can be useful. The key to the value of expert judgment is the ability of the expert to recall and assimilate relevant data in making a guess. While judgment is often unsystematic, it is an important supplement to other methods and can overcome some of the limitations of quantitative techniques.

The jury approach collects forecasts from a number of experts. The forecasts are then combined in a particular manner, such as a simple or weighted average, in which the weights can be the level of expertise. A variant of the jury approach is the panel consensus method, in which a group of experts is put in a room where they attempt to develop a forecast. Unfortunately a strong, vocal member of the group often drives the result.

An example of the jury approach was provided every month by *Wired* magazine. In each issue, a group of experts in an area were asked for the year in which certain phenomena were likely to occur. For example, in 1995 five experts were asked about the year in which we could expect to be able to purchase custom clothing overnight. The average of the experts was 1999 (*Wired,* 1995).

Delphi Method

The *Delphi method* is a variation of the panel consensus. The process begins by asking a number of individuals to independently produce a forecast. An outside person then collects the forecasts and calculates the average. Next, the outside person returns to each participant both the original forecast and the average and asks the participants to reconsider their initial forecasts. Typically, the participants then change their forecasts to more nearly conform to the average. If the process is repeated several times, consensus is generally achieved. Delphi panels are often established to forecast sales of new technologies (e.g., videotext) for which historical data do not exist.

Customer-Based Methods

A second set of methods relies on customer data.

Market Testing

This category includes a large set of methods involving primary market research. The methods include mall intercept surveys, focus groups, and at-home or at-work situations in which potential customers are asked to respond to a product concept.

Methods such as conjoint analysis, discussed in Chapter 5, are widely used to assess desired product features and ultimate market share.

Market Surveys

Market surveys are a specific form of primary market research in which potential customers are asked to give some indication of their likelihood of purchasing the product. A common approach is to use a 1-to-10 scale, with a 10 implying certainty of purchase. Customers frequently overstate their likelihood of purchase (although for really new products they often underestimate their eventual purchase likelihood). Researchers often use either a "top box" approach (i.e., count only the 10s as purchasing) or some other method based on the past relation between intent and purchase as the basis for the forecast. Alternatively, respondents are asked to indicate the quantity of a product they expect to purchase. These purchase intention surveys are then extrapolated to the population to form demand forecasts. Purchasing agents, for example, are often surveyed to determine demand for industrial products. Standard survey problems, such as nonresponse bias (are the people who do not respond to the survey different from those who do?) and inaccurate responses, exist with this method.

Whom to Survey

When conducting surveys for industrial products, it is not clear whom to talk to within a company even if the company is known. For example, when the Federal Communications Commission (FCC) invited bids for cellular mobile phone licenses in various cities, it required a study of market potential as part of the application. Most applicants attempted to address this by phone surveys, contacting the manager of telecommunications (or someone having a similar title) and asking about how many phones the company would use. However, it is not clear that these managers knew how many were needed or had much authority over such acquisitions.

To determine which companies to survey, first specify the potential segments and then ensure there are enough of each type included to get a reasonable estimate. Unfortunately, if there are 10 target groups and five size variations per group, this leads to a large sample size.

Consider Figure 6.7, which shows the number of firms by employee number in several SIC codes. How would you apportion the sample and still be able to represent each segment accurately? The answer requires a balance between a stratified sample based on assumed variability of demand and getting a reasonable number in each cell.

How to Deal with the Results

It would be preferable if the results "made sense," but sometimes they are inconsistent. For example, assume that the average firm sales for the five size categories in Figure 6.7 were as follows: 192, 181, 490, 360, and 2,000. Do you treat these figures as "truth," or do you smooth them so bigger firms spend more? Moreover, what do you do if total demand comes out three times expected? Do you scale every estimate down by one-third?

FIGURE 6.7 Potential Customers by Industry and Size

SIC	Industry	Percent of 1981 Demand Accounted For	Total Number of Firms	Number of Employees				
				50–99	100–249	250–499	500–999	1,000 or More
28	Chemical	20	7,012	754	610	293	193	123
29	Petroleum	20	444	57	73	53	42	22
33	Primary metals	10	1,889	266	352	181	74	108
12	Bituminous	2	4,050	295	272	166	80	11
20	Food	5	10,032	1,114	957	393	153	57
22	Textile	2	1,786	207	229	187	160	50
26	Paper and allied products	10	1,314	184	235	116	104	58
34	Fabricated metal	3	4,568	310	111	16	2	—
36	Electrical equipment	3	942	90	109	94	43	35
49	Electricity, gas	25	5,250	766	588	214	97	69
	Total		37,287	4,043	3,536	1,713	948	533

Expected Maximum Spending by Size Category

Employee Size	Maximum Spending
50 to 99	$ 100,000
100 to 249	200,000
250 to 499	500,000
500 to 999	750,000
1,000 or more	1,000,000

In summary, then, while surveys may produce a useful number, they are equally likely to produce numbers that, without "creative" manipulation, appear on the surface to be wrong.

Sales Extrapolation Methods

A third set of methods utilizes historical sales data and is referred to as *time-series* methods.

Moving Averages

Moving averages, an old forecasting standby, are widely used to reduce the "noise" in data to uncover the underlying pattern. In doing so, it is important to recognize that past data have at least four major components:

1. Base value
2. Trend
3. Cycle(s) (seasonality)
4. Randomness

Moving averages essentially smooth out random variations to make the patterns (trends and cycles) more apparent.

For purposes of introduction, consider the simple moving-average approach. A three-period moving average of sales at time t is given by

$$\bar{S}_t = (S_{t-1} + S_t + S_{t+1})/3$$

Note that (1) each data point used is weighted equally and (2) no trend or cycle is accounted for. To see how this method works, consider the three-month moving average for the eight periods of sales given in Figure 6.8. The moving average for the first three periods of data is 105, the simple average of 100, 110, and 105. The moving average for periods 2 through 4 is 115, the average of 110, 105, and 130. As can be readily seen by comparing the moving averages to the "Raw Changes" column, the fluctuation in values is much less in moving averages than in the raw data, and a consistent trend of increase of about 10 units per period becomes quite

FIGURE 6.8 Sample Data

Period	Sales	Three-Period Moving Average	Raw Changes	Average Change
1	100	—	—	—
2	110	105	+10	—
3	105	115	−5	10
4	130	125	+25	10
5	140	130	+10	5
6	120	140	−20	10
7	160	152	+40	11.33
8	175	—	+15	—

apparent. Forecasts can now be based on the pattern of moving averages rather than on the raw data.

The basic moving-average method just described can be extended to track trends and seasonal patterns as well. For example, to smooth a trend, simply calculate the period-to-period changes and average them as in Figure 6.8. While other methods, such as regression, are more sophisticated means of developing forecasts, moving averages remain a popular approach.

Exponential Smoothing

A second time-series approach is called *exponential smoothing.* The formula for a simple exponentially smoothed forecast is

$$\hat{S}_{t+1} = aS_t + (1 - a)\hat{S}_t$$

where "^" refers to a forecast. In other words, an exponentially smoothed forecast for period $t + 1$ is a combination of the current period's sales and the current period's forecast. The parameter a is between 0 and 1 and can be determined from historical sales data. In reality, exponentially smoothed forecasts are close relatives to moving-average forecasts in that the former weight past sales using exponentially declining weights.[1] As in the case of moving averages, this approach literally smooths out the random variation in period-to-period values. Trends and cycles are estimated separately.

Regression Analysis

A simple and popular form of extrapolation uses regression analysis with time (period) as the independent variable and is easily accomplished by using Excel or similar programs. Time series regression produces estimates of the base level (intercept) and the trend (slope). Seasonal patterns can either be removed a priori from the data or estimated in the model using dummy variables (see Chapter 5). If we ignore seasonality, the model is simply

$$\text{Sales} = a + b(\text{time})$$

Addressing the same eight-period example from Figure 6.8 produces the graph in Figure 6.9 and the predicted results in Figure 6.10. The forecast for period 9 based on this model would be

$$S_9 = 85.4 + 9.9(9) = 174.5$$

This is represented by the dotted extension to the fitted line in Figure 6.9. Two other useful statistics produced are the R^2, a measure of fit that is the percentage variance in the dependent variable (sales) explained by the independent variable (time), and the standard error of the estimate, which is a measure of the variance of the errors (the differences between the predicted values of sales based on the preceding equation and the actual values) about the line. Rather than just

---

[1] To see this, simply rewrite the equation in terms of period t, that is, $\hat{S}_t = aS_{t-1} + (1 - a)\hat{S}_{t-1}$, and substitute repeatedly for S_t in the equation in the text.

FIGURE 6.9 **Times-Series Extrapolation**

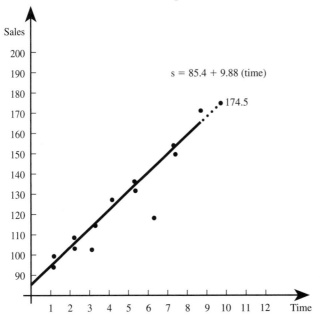

using the point forecast, 174.5, a confidence interval or a range of likely outcomes should be placed around it. For a one-period-out forecast, this is done by multiplying the standard error of the estimate (in this case, 12.3) by 2 to approximate a 95 percent confidence interval. The forecast then becomes 174.5 ± 24.6. Longer-term forecasts can be developed simply by plugging in values for time periods later than 9, extending the line farther out in time, although the confidence interval also grows wider.

Sometimes sales data are highly nonlinear, as in Figure 6.11. This product life cycle curve is clearly not a straight regression line. Figure 6.11 can be estimated

FIGURE 6.10 **Time-Series Regression Example**

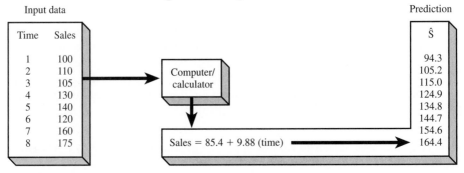

FIGURE 6.11   Trial over Time for a New Product

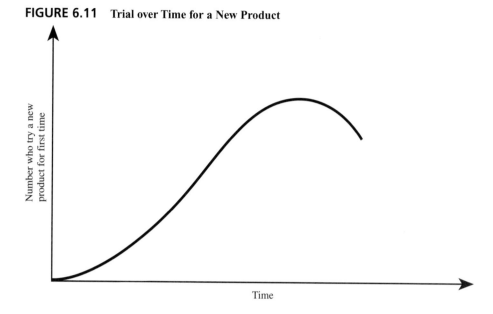

using a variety of functional forms. We discuss one, the Bass model (Bass, 1969), later in this chapter.

Model-Based Methods

The fourth category of forecasting methods is often termed *association* or *causal* because the techniques utilize one or more variables other than time to predict sales (e.g., advertising).

Regression Analysis

This method is a generalization of the time-series model: Instead of having only time as the independent variable, other variables that could affect sales are included. For example, a regression model to predict sales of Pepsi might be the following:

$$\text{Sales} = a + b(\text{advertising}) + c(\text{price}) + d(\text{population age 13–25})$$

Given historical data on sales, advertising, price, and population, the coefficients *a, b, c,* and *d* can be estimated and used to develop a forecast.

Leading Indicators

Economists use certain macroeconomic variables to forecast changes in the economy. When changes in these variables occur before changes in the economy, they are termed *leading indicators.* For example, changes in employment, housing starts, interest rates, and retail sales are often associated with changes in the economy. The construction and real estate industries use leading indicators to forecast demand. Industry-specific leading indicators also exist, such as retail auto dealer inventories for the automobile industry.

FIGURE 6.12 Forecasting Method Usage

Forecasting Technique	Immediate (<1 month)	Short (1 month–<6 months)	Medium (6 months–1 year)	Long (>1 year)
Judgmental				
Manager's opinion	27.9%	39.8	37.1	9.3
Jury of executive opinion	17.5	28.9	40.1	26.2
Sales force composite	28.6	17.5	33.1	8.7
Quantitative				
Moving average	17.7	33.5	28.3	8.7
Straight-line projection	7.6	13.2	12.5	8.2
Naive	16.0	18.5	13.8	0
Exponential smoothing	12.9	19.6	16.8	4.2
Regression	13.4	25.1	26.4	16.5
Simulation	3.4	7.8	11.2	8.3
Classical decomposition	0	6.8	11.9	9.3
Box-Jenkins	2.4	2.4	4.9	3.4

Source: Reprinted by permission, Nada R. Sanders and Kari B. Manrodt, "Forecasting Practices in the U.S. Corporations: Survey Results," *Interfaces*, March–April, 1994. Copyright 1994. The Institute of Management Sciences and the Operations Research Society of America (currently *Informs*), 2 Charles Street, Suite 300, Providence, RI 02904 USA.

Econometric Models

These are essentially large-scale, multiple-equation regression models. During the 1970s they were extremely popular, and companies such as Data Resources, Inc. (subsequently bought by McGraw-Hill) sold these models to companies seeking to develop better forecasts of industry sales. They are less popular today as companies strive to keep their expenditures down. In addition, they never forecasted as well as advertised. A noteworthy failure came during the Arab oil embargo of the early 1970s when the models predicted less damage to the U.S. economy than actually occurred.

What Methods Are Used?

Figure 6.12 shows the results of a survey of 96 companies examining which forecasting methods are actually used in practice (Sanders and Manrodt, 1994). For the short and medium term, judgmental approaches are heavily used. The most frequently used quantitative method is a moving average. The general nature of these results were confirmed by a Product Development Management Association sponsored study based on 168 respondents (Kahn, 2002; Figure 6.13). This is rather discouraging given the length of time more sophisticated methods have been available. However, regression is used quite frequently, particularly for long-run forecasts. Since regression is sufficient for most situations and widely available (e.g., in Excel), we concentrate on it.

Using Regression Models for Forecasting

Given the results from Figure 6.12 and the wide applicability of regression to other marketing contexts (see segmentation research in Chapter 5), we devote significant space in this chapter to showing how it is used in forecasting contexts. Regression

FIGURE 6.13   Use of New Product Forecasting Techniques by All Responding Firms

Forecasting Technique	Average Use Across All Types of New Products (%)
Customer/market research	57%
Jury of executive opinion	44
Sales force composite	39
Looks-like analysis	30
Trend line analysis	19
Moving average	15
Scenario analysis	14
Exponential smoothing techniques	10
Experience curves	10
Market analysis model (including the ATAR model)	10
Delphi method	8
Linear regression	7
Decision trees	7
Simulation	5
Expert systems	4
Other	3
Nonlinear regression	2
Diffusion models	2
Precursor curves (correlation method)	1
Box-Jenkins techniques (ARMA/ARIMA)	1
Neural networks	0

Source: Kahn, Kenneth B. (2002) "An Exploratory Investigation of New Product Forecasting Practices," *The Journal of Product Innovation Management* 19, 133–43.

models are generally developed in three stages. First, the variables assumed to affect dependent variables are specified. For a prediction of unit sales, the variables selected might be

Sales $= f$(our price, competitors' prices, our advertising, competitors' advertising, disposable income)

Next, a model is specified indicating the form of the relation between the independent variables and sales. Most often the nature of the relationship is linear, such as

$$\text{Sales} = b_0 + b_1 \text{(our price)} + b_2 \text{(competitors' prices)} + b_3 \text{(our advertising)} + b_4 \text{(competitors' advertising)} + b_5 \text{(disposable income)}$$

Finally, the model is estimated by means of regression analysis, using commonly available computer programs:

$$\text{Sales} = 1.2 - .3 \text{(our price)} + .4 \text{(competitors' prices)} + 1.1 \text{(our advertising)} - .3 \text{(competitors' advertising)} + .2 \text{(disposable income)}$$

The estimated model serves two primary purposes. First, the model can be used to forecast sales. Notice that to use this regression model to forecast, one must first forecast the values of the independent variables. This is because all the variables are *contemporaneous;* that is, current (say, 2004) sales are determined by current (2004) prices, advertising, and disposable income. We use data from some point in the past through 2003 to estimate the model. However, to forecast sales for 2005, we need 2004 values for the independent variables. While some of the variables may be under someone in the firm's control (price, advertising), several others must be forecasted. If this is difficult, regression becomes less useful as a forecasting device. Put differently, try to use predictor variables that are themselves easy to forecast.

Second, a regression model can answer "what if" questions. In the preceding example, b_1 is the marginal effect of changing our price and b_3 is the marginal effect of changing our advertising. If we are willing to assume the relationships between price, advertising, and sales are causal rather than just correlational, a marketing manager can answer a question such as "What if I increase my price by $5?" In this case, based on the model, an increase in price would be predicted to lead to a change in sales of: $(5)(-.3) = -1.5$.

Developing Regression Models

While developing regression forecasting models is largely a trial-and-error process, certain steps can make the process more systematic and efficient.

1. *Plot sales over time.* It is useful to get a feel for the sales series by simply plotting sales versus time. An important use of this plot is as an aid for identifying key variables that might be useful in predicting changes in sales. Any peaks or valleys in the sales series should alert a good manager to try to uncover the factor that may have caused that sharp change.

   Figure 6.14 shows the (deseasonalized) monthly sales series from 1973 to 1975 of presweetened breakfast cereal purchases made by a sample of households on a dairy panel (Neslin and Shoemaker, 1983). A significant price increase for sugar occurred during 1974 and resulted in a sharp increase in cereal prices. It is difficult to pick out the effect of price alone from the graph. However, it is clear that an overall positive trend in purchases occurred over the three-year period. Some variable accounting for that trend should be included in the regression model.

2. *Consider the variables that are relevant to predicting sales.* The product manager or a team of managers familiar with the product category should brainstorm to develop a set of factors that affect sales. At this stage, the list of variables should be long, allowing for as much creativity as possible. In terms of the type of variables to include, it is generally useful to consider which variables in each of the following categories might be most appropriate:

   a. Customer status and traits (e.g., the size of the population in a particular age category).
   b. "Our" marketing programs (e.g., advertising).
   c. Competitive behavior (e.g., new product introductions).
   d. General environment (e.g., gross domestic product).

   In the case of presweetened cereals, two major factors affecting sales are price and advertising. As noted above, the data are already deseasonalized, so any

FIGURE 6.14 Cereal Sales Data (monthly)

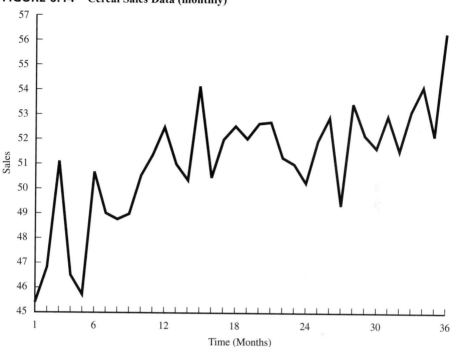

Source: Scott A. Neslin and Robert W. Shoemaker, "Using a Natural Experiment to Estimate Price Elasticity: The 1974 Sugar Shortage and the Ready-to-Eat Cereal Market," *Journal of Marketing,* Winter 1983, pp. 44–57.

winter-versus-summer consumption factors for cold cereals have already been eliminated from the sales series. For simplicity, the upward trend of the data can be accounted for by a trend variable that assumes the values 1 through 36. Finally, advertising may have what is called a lagged effect on sales. In other words, not only may current advertising affect current sales but last month's advertising may also affect current sales through consumer recall. Thus, the general form of the model is

Cereal sales = f(price, advertising, lagged advertising, trend)

3. *Collect data.* Once the variables have been specified, historical values for those variables must be collected. There must be as many historical values for the independent variables as there are for the sales variable. Here, since there are 36 observations on cereal sales, the analyst needs 36 observations on price and advertising (lagged advertising can be computed directly from the advertising series). Figure 6.15 shows the data for this example.

4. *Analyze the data.* There are several aspects to the data analysis step of the model-building process.

First, it is important to examine the *correlations among the independent variables.* Many time series variables are highly correlated because they tend to change over time at the same rate. For example, if the economy is expanding,

FIGURE 6.15   Cereal Data

Sales	Price	Advertising	Time	Lagged Advertising
45.4	29.0	6803	1	—
46.8	28.7	6136	2	6803
51.1	28.1	8850	3	6136
46.5	27.9	6689	4	8850
45.7	27.9	7004	5	6689
50.7	27.6	7801	6	7004
49.0	27.0	7091	7	7801
48.8	26.7	6958	8	7091
49.0	26.6	7357	9	6958
50.6	26.7	7010	10	7357
51.4	26.7	6627	11	7010
52.5	26.7	7350	12	6627
51.0	26.6	6952	13	7350
50.4	26.6	7441	14	6952
54.2	26.8	7519	15	7441
50.5	27.1	8409	16	7519
52.0	27.6	8084	17	8409
52.6	28.3	7830	18	8084
52.1	28.6	7399	19	7830
52.7	28.9	7566	20	7399
52.7	29.3	7076	21	7566
51.3	29.8	7310	22	7076
51.0	30.9	7604	23	7310
50.3	31.6	6793	24	7604
52.0	31.6	7038	25	6793
52.9	31.6	6514	26	7038
49.4	31.7	6439	27	6514
53.5	31.7	6056	28	6439
52.2	31.7	6148	29	6056
51.7	31.1	5787	30	6148
53.0	30.9	6043	31	5787
51.6	30.5	6191	32	6043
53.2	30.3	8034	33	6191
54.2	29.7	8404	34	8034
52.2	29.8	9524	35	8404
56.4	29.9	8973	36	9524

employment and GDP are highly correlated. If a product is being rolled out nationally, the number of distribution outlets and advertising may be highly correlated. If two or more independent variables are highly correlated, computational and interpretation problems can arise. Therefore, an important first step after the data have been collected is to construct a correlation matrix among the variables (remember, we want high correlations between the independent variables and sales, the dependent variable). Note that the diagonal of the matrix

FIGURE 6.16   Cereal Data Correlation Matrix*

	Price	Advertising	Time	Lagged Advertising
Price	1.0	−.28	.76	−.26
	(35)	(35)	(35)	(35)
	.00	.10	.00	.13
Advertising	−.28	1.00	.05	.55
	(35)	(35)	(35)	(35)
	.10	.00	.76	.00
Time	.76	.05	1.00	−.02
	(35)	(35)	(35)	(35)
	.00	.76	.00	.90
Lagged advertising	−.26	.55	−.02	1.00
	(35)	(35)	(35)	(35)
	.13	.00	.90	.00

*The numbers in each cell are presented as: correlation, (sample size), significant level.

(Figure 6.16) contains 1s; the correlation of a variable with itself is obviously 1. The analyst should be on guard against correlations with high absolute values (i.e., above .90, although this number should not be considered a rigid threshold). More generally, you want the correlations between the independent and dependent variables to be larger than the correlations among the independent variables. High negative correlations, which are as harmful as positive ones, are not a major problem here, although time and price are closely related.

Second, *run the regression*. The regression results from the cereal illustration are shown in Figure 6.17, assuming a simple linear form of the model.

Third, determine the *significant predictors* of the dependent variable (i.e., sales). Even when care is taken to choose only those variables thought to be excellent predictors of sales, some often turn out to have little effect. To assess the strength of the effect of an independent variable on sales, look at the ratio of the absolute value of the regression coefficient to its standard error (given on all regression printouts),

FIGURE 6.17   Regression Results: Cereal Data*

1. Model: Sales = 58.528 − .461 (price) + .00044 (advertising) − .00015 (lagged advertising) + .211 (time)
                       (.242)   (.00037)   (.00037)   (.042)
   Standard error of the estimate = 1.479
   Adjusted R^2 = .60

2. Model: Sales = 60.041 − .538 (price) + .00033 (advertising) + .230 (time)
                       (.244)   (.00032)   (.038)
   Standard error of the estimate = 1.468
   Adjusted R^2 = .65

3. Model: ln Sales = 3.193 − .053 (ln price) + .090 (ln advertising) + .044 (ln time)
                          (.095)   (.043)   (.007)
   Standard error of the estimate = .028
   Adjusted R^2 = .68

*Numbers in parentheses are standard errors.

otherwise known as the t statistic. Generally speaking, if this ratio is greater than 2, the variable is referred to as a significant predictor of sales. Examining the first results in Figure 6.17, we can see that price is marginally significant ($t = 1.92$), advertising is insignificant ($t = 1.21$), time is very significant ($t = 5.02$), and lagged advertising is not significant ($t = .41$) at the 5 percent significance level. A decision to be made here is whether to rerun the regression after dropping insignificant variables. *Parsimony* is important in forecasting models, because fewer independent variables must be predicted to develop the ultimate forecast for a "smaller" model. Since lagged advertising is relatively unimportant, regression 2 in Figure 6.17 repeats the regression with that variable eliminated. Price is now significant ($t = 2.45$), as is the time trend, although advertising is still insignificant.

Fourth, check the *signs* of the significant independent variables. This is a logic check and is perhaps the most important test of all. It is important to ensure that the signs on the regression coefficients make sense. For example, a significant positive sign on a price coefficient is a problem; most of the time, these kinds of sign flip-flops are due to what is called *specification error,* the omission of one or more key variables from the model. In the breakfast cereal example, the signs are all in the appropriate direction for the significant variables.

Fifth, check the R^2 of the equation. This is what most analysts gravitate toward first. However, a high R^2 does not guarantee a good forecasting model. This is due to the fact that regression is basically a correlational procedure and it is possible to choose variables that are nonsensical but do explain variance in sales. That is why we stress the combination of spending time a priori in choosing independent variables, checking the signs on the coefficients, *and* looking at the R^2. The R^2 of the breakfast cereal model is .65, as shown in Figure 6.17. This is not particularly high for a time-series model and implies that the forecast confidence interval will be relatively wide.

Finally, develop the forecast and confidence interval. As noted earlier, the forecast is developed by plugging in the appropriate values of the independent variables. In addition, a confidence interval can be constructed using the standard error of the estimate. This produces three forecasts: best guess (the point forecast), optimistic (the high end of the confidence interval), and pessimistic (the low end of the confidence interval).

Taking the results of the second cereal regression from Figure 6.17, we can develop a forecast for the first out-of-sample period, January 1976. If we assume the price will be 30 cents per 10 ounces (remember, this is over 28 years ago) and category advertising will be \$9 million, then, given that the value of the time is 37, the forecast is 55,400 ounces purchased for the panel members (55.4 in the units of Figure 6.15). Given a standard error of the estimate of 1.47, a 95 percent confidence interval around the forecast is ±2,940 ounces, or a range of 52,460 to 58,340 ounces. Thus, 55,400 becomes the best guess, 52,460 the pessimistic and 58,340 the optimistic forecast. Note that this process can and generally should be repeated for different scenarios (e.g., assumptions about price), as we discuss later.

FIGURE 6.18 Format for Reporting a Regression Model Based Forecast

Scenario	Forecast		
	Pessimistic Forecast – 2S_{YX}	Best Guess Forecast	Optimistic Forecast + 2S_{YX}
Pessimistic: No change in GDP Advertising down 10 percent			
Best guess: GDP up 3 percent Advertising up 10 percent			
Optimistic: GDP up 5 percent Advertising up 25 percent			

Recognizing Uncertainty

In order to make forecasts with a regression model, it is necessary to know or forecast the values of the predictor variables (e.g., GDP, advertising) in the next period. When these are known, a reasonable forecast includes a best guess obtained by substituting the known values, a pessimistic forecast (typically the best guess minus two standard errors of estimate), and an optimistic forecast (the best guess plus two standard errors of estimate). Since the predictor variables are rarely known with certainty, it is useful to construct both optimistic and pessimistic scenarios and to generate forecasts based on them. The resulting 3-by-3 table (see Figure 6.18) gives a much clearer picture of the uncertainty inherent in the market (and what it depends on). While managers like to have *the* forecast, they *should* be given information like that in Figure 6.18. (Of course, that is easier for the authors, both of whom have tenure, to say than it is for a junior person facing a demanding boss.)

The impact of uncertainty about predictor variables can be shown more dramatically graphically (Figure 6.19). Notice here that the true range is considerably larger than the range implied by using the standard error of the regression as a basis for estimating uncertainty. What this means is that unless you are fairly certain of what the value of the predictor variable will be, it doesn't help forecast very much. Hence, variables that are easy to predict (e.g., year, GDP) are, *ceteris paribus,* more useful as predictors than variables that are themselves unpredictable (e.g., consumer sentiment, commodity prices).

Nonlinear Relations

Most regression forecasting models are linear; that is, they are of the form

$$\text{Sales} = b_0 + b_1 X_1 + b_2 X_2 + \ldots,$$

where X_1 and X_2 are the independent or predictor variables and the sales total is the dependent variable.

FIGURE 6.19   **The Impact of Uncertain Predictors on Forecasting**

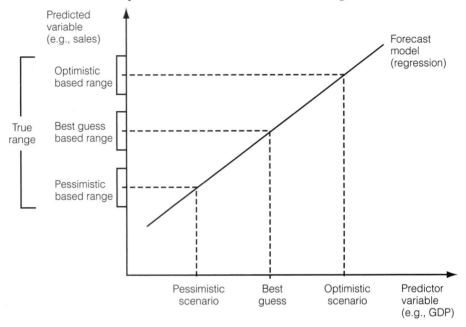

In some cases, there is a nonlinear relationship between the Xs and sales. For example, there may be diminishing returns to advertising. In the linear framework, each dollar of advertising is equally effective. If there are diminishing returns to advertising, the impact of the millionth dollar is less than the tenth. This can be handled in the regression framework by, for example, using a logarithmic function:

$$\text{Sales} = b_0 + b_1 (\log \text{advertising})$$

One model, which has been used fairly extensively, is a multiplicative model (in economics, referred to as a Cobb-Douglas function):

$$\text{Sales} = b_0 X_1^{b_1} X_2^{b_2}$$

which can be written and estimated with a standard regression program by using a logarithmic transformation of the variables:

$$\log \text{Sales} = \log b_0 + b_1(\log X_1) + b_2(\log X_2)$$

An interesting implication of this formula is that the coefficients are interpreted as *elasticities* rather than slopes. Thus, b_1 would be interpreted as the percentage change in sales due to a 1 percent change in X_1.

The results of a logarithmic model of the breakfast cereal data appear in Figure 6.17 (regression number 3). It is interesting that the results differ from those of the linear model. Here the price elasticity is insignificant ($t = .56$), whereas the advertising elasticity is significant ($t = 2.09$), as is the trend. The slope results for price and advertising from the linear model were the opposite. This can happen when two different theories about how sales are created are specified. It also suggests that a third model, using a linear function of price and a logarithmic one for advertising, might be the best.

Share Forecasts

To this point we have focused on volume forecasts. In stable markets, share is critical. Share forecasts are typically based largely on the impact of marketing mix components (price, promotion, advertising) on sales or share. For share modeling, the so-called logit model is now widely applied. Its basic form is:

$$\text{Share Brand } i = \frac{\exp(BX_i)}{\displaystyle\sum_{\text{all brands}} \exp(BX_j)}$$

where $\exp(BX)$ means e to the power BX, and BX is a function such as $B_0 + B_1$ (Advertising \$) $+ B_2$ (Price). Logit models can be used to answer "what if?" questions such as, What will happen if I increase advertising 20 percent and competitors don't match the increase?

Forecasting Really New Products

For many products, the requirement that regression models have a large number of years (or other time period) of data is unrealistic. This is particularly the case for technological innovations or new durable goods. In addition, the demand in the early stages of the product life cycle does not necessarily look very linear. Figure 6.11 demonstrates such a sales curve. For example, the product manager for a PDA in 1995 did not face the same forecasting environment as the product manager for Quaker Oatmeal. PDAs had not been for sale for many years (mainly since 1992), and were in the early growth stage of the product life cycle.

To handle such situations, models have been developed to forecast first purchases of products. The most popular model in marketing is the Bass model (1969). The model assumes two kinds of customers: innovators, who purchase the product early in the life cycle, and imitators, who rely on word of mouth from other purchasers. This results in what is called a *diffusion* process. The model used by Bass has the following form:

$$P_t = p + [q/M]Y(t-1)$$

where

P_t = Probability of purchase given no previous purchase.

$Y(t-1)$ = Total number who have purchased the product through period $t-1$.

M = The market potential (saturation level).

q = Parameter representing the rate of diffusion of the product reflecting the influence of others (also called the *coefficient of imitation*).

p = Initial probability of purchase (also called the *coefficient of innovation*).

Sales in period t is

$$S(t) = [M - Y(t - 1)] P_t,$$

Substituting P_t from the first equation into the sales equation, we obtain

$$S(t) = pM + [q - p]Y(t - 1) - q/M[Y(t - 1)]^2$$

If q is greater than p (the rate of imitation is greater than the rate of innovation), the sales curve will rise and then fall. If q is less than p (the rate of imitation is less than the rate of innovation), the sales curve will fall from its initial level.

The model can be estimated running a regression of the form

$$\text{Sales} = c_0 + c_1 Y(t - 1) + c_2 [Y(t - 1)]^2$$

that is simply using sales as the dependent variable, with the independent variables being the cumulative number of previous adopters and that quantity squared. In other words, all that is needed are historical sales data. Once the c coefficients are estimated, the quantities p, q, and M can be solved for by the following identities:

$$c_0 = pM, c_1 = [q - p], \text{ and } c_2 = -q/M$$

There are three equations and three unknowns, so p, q, and M have unique solutions.[2] Forecasts of sales can also be developed directly from the sales equation.

The Bass model has fit past adoption patterns well. For example, it correctly forecast a downturn in sales of color TVs in the late 1960s, something the "expert" forecasts at the major manufacturers failed to do because they used essentially linear extrapolation. Unfortunately, the model is sensitive to the number of periods of data that are available and can be unreliable when only four or five years of data exist.[3] Also, for example, the market saturation level, M, is probably affected by price, and the imitation parameter, q, is affected by advertising (Horsky and Simon, 1983; Jones and Ritz, 1991). While the preceding model includes no marketing variables, an extended model incorporating these variables has been developed (Bass, Krishnan, and Jain, 1994).

ILLUSTRATIONS

Energy Bar Potential

We assume (optimistically) that consumers eat an average of one bar per day (a real "saturation" level). We then examine how many people are potential customers. Here we start with the entire population and then subtract those we consider not

---

[2] If c_2 is less than zero, p must be solved for using the quadratic formula. It has two solutions, one negative and the positive one that is used.

[3] Reasonable forecasts are obtainable when the results of past studies—essentially the average values of p and q—are combined with data (Sultan, Farley, and Lehmann, 1990).

FIGURE 6.20   Potential Energy Bar Customers

	2003 Potential Consumers (000s)
U.S. population	284,332
Minus children under 5 years old	18,602
Minus 70% of adults over 74 years old	18,014
Minus population allergic to wheat	3,000
Minus population allergic to nuts	3,128
Minus population below poverty level (9.2%)	26,159
Total potential consumers in 2003	**215,430**

to be consumers due to age, allergies, or income level. (Note in doing this we over-adjust since some consumers fall in multiple categories, i.e., are over 74 and poor). The resulting potential number of customers is 215,430 (Figure 6.20). Therefore

$$\text{Potential} = (215 \text{ million})(365 \text{ bars/year}) = 78.5 \text{ billion bars per year}$$

Notice here how critical the usage assumption (bars consumed per week) is to this estimate; if we assume a more realistic 1 bar per week average, the potential estimate drops to a more reasonable, but still hard to attain, 11.2 billion bars per year, a far cry from current levels.

Forecasting Energy Bar Sales via Regression

Forecasting U.S. sales of energy bars is difficult for several reasons. First, there are relatively few years of data to go on (here we use five years, 1997–2001, to forecast 2002). Second, many of the macroeconomic variables one might use (e.g., household income, CPI) are highly correlated, forcing a choice of one (here number of households). Third, causal variables such as price and new product entries are difficult to forecast. For the sake of the example, we use advertising spending of Power Bar, the category creator, partly because it was available. (Note we need to forecast this for 2002, which introduces more uncertainty in the forecast.) The data appear in Figure 6.20. The resulting regression model produced an R^2 of .998, inflated because of the scarcity of data points. The model was

$$\text{Dollar sales} = -7,130,000,000 + 71.29 \text{ (number of households)} \\ + 9,557,467 \text{ (Power Bar Advertising)}$$

with a standard error of 9,314,701.

Households are fairly easy to forecast; here we use 105,458,124 (admittedly ridiculous precision). Power Bar advertising is harder to forecast, so we use three scenarios: an optimistic 26 million, a best guess of 24 million, and a pessimistic 18 million, a decrease from 2001. (Notice how sensitive the forecast

FIGURE 6.21 Power Bar Data

Year	$ Sales	Number of Households	Power Bar Advertising in Millions
1997	85,506,530	99,965,175	9.72
1998	158,197,712	101,042,864	8.36
1999	217,109,706	102,118,600	7.00
2000	353,108,889	103,245,963	14.00
2001	504,000,000	104,344,445	20.00

is to this assumption.) The resulting forecasts, with ±2 standard errors, equal to 18,600,000, used as a conservative estimate of the uncertainty, are the following:

	Power Bar	
Advertising Level	Forecast	Range
18 million	558,100,000	539,500,000 to 576,700,000
24 million	615,600,000	597,000,000 to 634,200,000
26 million	634,600,000	616,000,000 to 653,200,000

Note that, even with R^2 above .99, there is significant uncertainty stemming mostly from uncertainty about the causal market factors (here Power Bar advertising) which drive sales. Notice also how much less this is than the potential estimate, suggesting the result is feasibly attainable.

PDA Sales

Consider the problem of forecasting PDA sales in 1995. The four years of data available at that time (Figure 6.22) provide a limited basis for illustrating the basic Bass model. The results of running the Bass model are

$$\text{Sales} = 78.123 + .783Y(t) - .0007Y(t)^2$$

FIGURE 6.22 Bass Model: PDA Actual versus Predicted

Year	PDA Sales (000s)	Predicted	Percent Error
1992	63	·78.123	24.0%
1993	150	124.674	16.9
1994	200	213.144	6.6
1995	285	282.104	1.1
1996	?	283.614	?

The model predicts historical sales quite well. In addition, q is much greater than p ($q = .798$ and $p = .065$), indicating that the product has favorable word of mouth. The forecast for 1996 is for 284,000 units, or essentially no growth. As we now know, sales have continued to grow. However, a large part of this growth is due to decreased prices and increased quality (i.e., communication capabilities) as well as the explosion of the Internet. In particular, the Palm Pilot was introduced in 1996. This emphasizes the difficulty in forecasting sales early in a life cycle; clearly estimating the Bass model using all data to the present would produce a much higher forecast for future sales.

Forecasts made in early 2000 were much more bullish:

- IDC (via CNETNews.com) suggests sales will increase from 5.4 million in 1999 to 18.9 million in 2000.
- Industry Standard (using analysis by Forrester Research) suggested that by 2000 there could be 15 million PDAs in use and that by 2002 handhelds will outsell PCs.
- Mobile Insights (via Field Force Automation) suggested sales of "mobile information appliances" would be over 25 million and surpass sales of notebooks.

Still upgrades, the influence of Blackberry, technology convergence, and wireless features make even these forecasts seem dated. The point is that in fast-changing markets, forecasts rarely age gracefully.

USING FORECASTS

As noted earlier in this chapter, it is difficult to say which techniques are good and which are bad because success often depends on the circumstances. Accuracy depends on factors such as time horizon, how much money is spent on the forecast, how much time was spent developing the forecast, the volatility of the category, and the like.

Although using quantitative procedures may at times seem tedious, two major reasons encourage their use: (1) they simplify routine, repetitive situations, and (2) they force explicit statements of assumptions. When using quantitative methods, it is best to take the following supplementary steps:

1. *Do sensitivity analysis.* Only when a result seems to be stable over method and data points (e.g., drop one or two years of data and rerun the analysis) can the forecast be advanced with much conviction.
2. *Examine large residuals.* Residuals are individual forecasting errors made for each period. By examining the characteristics of those periods when the forecast was inaccurate, you can often uncover omitted variables.
3. *Avoid silly precision.* This means round off the forecast and give an honest plus or minus range.
4. *Be tolerant of errors.* Expect the methods to improve one's odds of making a good forecast, not guarantee them. Be suspicious of forecasts with very narrow ranges.
5. *Remember that you will generally miss the turning points.* Quantitative (as well as qualitative) forecasting methods work well as long as the patterns that occurred

FIGURE 6.23   Sample Format for Summarizing Forecasts

| | Forecast | | |
Method	Pessimistic	Best Guess	Optimistic
1. Time series extrapolation			
2. Regression model:			
Version A			
Version B			
3. Expert judgment:			
Expert A			
Expert B			
4. Own judgment			
5. Bottom-up forecast			
Average			

in the past extend into the future. Whenever a major change occurs, however, most forecasts will be way off. Stated another way, most forecasting methods are relatively useless for predicting major changes in the way the world operates, and consequently most forecasts do not include the effects of these changes.

Combining Forecasts

So far this chapter has described a number of forecasting methods and their strengths and weaknesses. When you are making an important forecast, it is both common and prudent to make several forecasts and then combine them, perhaps using some averaging method. An average of a set of forecasts using disparate methods will tend to be better than a forecast using only one method that is susceptible to its own particular weaknesses.

The results of several methods can be summarized in a table such as that in Figure 6.23. The range of these forecasts provides a useful indication of the uncertainty faced. Moreover, deciding how to combine these forecasts forces one to make explicit assumptions. In Figure 6.23, a simple average is used as the combination rule (that is, equal weighting), but weights could also be assigned, for example, in inverse proportion to the size of the confidence interval (Wilton and Gupta, 1987).

Gaining Agreement

The previous discussion implies that only one person is involved with developing a forecast. Sometimes forecasts are "top down": A higher level manager develops a forecast for each product's sales. Alternatively, forecasts can be "bottom up," an aggregation of several forecasts made by regional salespeople, country managers, or others. Unfortunately, top-down and bottom-up forecasts rarely agree with either each other or growth targets established for the product. The process of reaching agreement is both useful and frustrating.

In understanding bottom-up forecasts, you should recognize that both personal incomes and budgets depend on the forecast. Personal incomes, especially salespeople's, are tied to quotas, which in turn are derived from forecasts. Therefore, a salesperson will tend to be conservative in his or her forecast to make the sales goal or quota easier to attain. In contrast, certain managers may overstate sales potential to gain a larger budget. Thus, the bottom-up process, though based on the knowledge of those closest to the customer, may well produce a biased estimate. Total reliance on either bottom-up or top-down methods is generally a mistake.

Why Not Just Go to the Web?

An increasingly common approach to forecasting is to search the Internet for forecasts and then combine them, typified by averaging the estimates. This is expeditious but somewhat naive. First, ask yourself where their forecasts came from. Chances are they are influenced by earlier forecasts, creating a snowball or cascade effect where early forecasts have a big impact. Second, consider who did the forecasts and how: Often the person has less training than you do as a result of reading this chapter. If that makes you uneasy, good. The point is that, if the forecast is important, you need to understand the process used to make it and either make it yourself or find a reliable (as opposed to convenient) source.

SUMMARY

Market potential is generally poorly understood, yet very important for different reasons. Low estimates of market potential result in marketing managers declaring categories mature too soon. This tends to create opportunities for ambitious competitors who have different views on the amount of untapped potential. The mere act of trying to calculate potential market size often gives a marketing manager ideas about how to extend the product or service into new segments.

Forecasting is one of the most important jobs facing a marketing manager. The forecast is an input to aspects of marketing strategy. It is also critical to production planning. When forecasts are substantially off on the high side, objectives are overly ambitious; inventories are too large; and senior managers, production personnel, and channel members become upset. When the forecast is much lower than actual, the losses are opportunity costs: lost sales. Multiple methods and logic, plus some knowledge of regression analysis, provides a good basis for forecasts. Luck helps also.

References

Bass, Frank M. (1969) "A New Product Growth Model for Consumer Durables," *Management Science,* January, 215–27.

Bass, Frank M., Trichy V. Krishnan, and Deepak C. Jain (1994) "Why the Bass Model Fits without Decision Variables," *Marketing Science* 13 (Summer), 203–23.

Bayus, Barry L., Saman Hong, and Russell P. Labe, Jr. (1989) "Developing and Using Forecasting Models of Consumer Durables: The Case of Color Television," *Journal of Product Innovation Management* 6, 5–19.

Beeh, Jenny E. (1994) "PCs Are Taking to the Streets," *Advertising Age,* October 31, 28.

Cerf, C., and V. Navasky (1984) *The Experts Speak.* New York: Pantheon Books.

Chambers, John C., Satinder K. Mullick, and Donald D. Smith (1971) "How to Choose the Right Forecasting Technique," *Harvard Business Review,* July–August.

Cox, William E. (1979) *Industrial Marketing Research.* New York: John Wiley & Sons.

Deveny, Kathleen (1990) "States Mull Rash of Diaper Regulations," *The Wall Street Journal,* June 15, B1.

Dhalla, Nariman K., and Sonia Yuspeh (1976) "Forget the Product Life Cycle Concept!" *Harvard Business Review,* January–February, 102–12.

Georgoff, David M., and Robert G. Murdick (1986) "Manager's Guide to Forecasting," *Harvard Business Review,* January–February.

Horsky, Dan, and Leonard S. Simon (1983) "Advertising and the Diffusion of New Products," *Marketing Science,* Winter, 1–18.

Jones, J. Morgan, and Christopher J. Ritz (1991) "Incorporating Distribution into New Product Diffusion Models," *International Journal of Research in Marketing,* June, 91–112.

Kahn, Kenneth B. (2002) "An Exploratory Investigation of New Product Forecasting Practices," *The Journal of Product Innovation Management* 19, 133–43.

McWilliams, Gary (1995) "At Compaq, a Desktop Crystal Ball," *Business Week,* March 20, 96.

Neslin, Scott A., and Robert W. Shoemaker (1983) "Using a Natural Experiment to Estimate Price Elasticity: The 1974 Sugar Shortage and the Ready-to-Eat Cereal Market," *Journal of Marketing,* Winter, 44–57.

Sanders, Nada R., and Karl B. Manrodt (1994) "Forecasting Practices in US Corporations: Survey Results," *Interfaces,* March–April, 92–100.

Sellers, Patricia (1991) "A Boring Brand Can Be Beautiful," *Fortune,* November 18, 169.

Sultan, Fareena, John U. Farley, and Donald R. Lehmann (1990) "A Meta-Analysis of Applications of Diffusion Models," *Journal of Marketing Research,* February, 70–77.

Wheelwright, Steven C., and Spyros Makridakis (1985) *Forecasting Methods for Management.* New York: John Wiley & Sons.

Wilton, Peter C., and Sunil Gupta (1987) "Combination of Forecasts: An Extension," *Management Science,* March, 356–72.

Wired, November 1995, p. 76.

Appendix 6   Time Series Regression with Seasonal Factors

Consider the following data on quarterly fuel oil shipments to the United Kingdom in 1964–66 (Figure 6A.1). In plotting these data, we see that there is, as expected, a very strong seasonal effect (Figure 6A.2). Clearly, ignoring the seasonal component would be a major error. (It would also produce significant autocorrelation.) Running four separate regressions is impractical because there would only be three observations per regression. It would be possible to deseasonalize the data before performing the regression, using an adjustment factor for each quarter such as

$$\frac{\text{Average sales for the particular quarter}}{\text{Average sales for all quarters}}$$

Possibly the most appealing approach, however, is to employ dummy variables. This would consist of first creating ("dummying up") a variable for each of the four quarters (Figure 6A.3). The following equation would then be estimated by regression:

$$\text{Shipments} = B_0 + B_1 (\text{Time}) + B_2 (\text{Winter}) + B_3 (\text{Spring}) + B_4 (\text{Summer})$$

Note that one of the possible dummy variables must be left out so the computer program will run. If all the independent variables are included, the independent variables are perfectly multicollinear. In this case it is impossible to invert a key matrix, and the program will bomb. (Alternatively, we could drop the constant B_0 and retain all four dummy variables if that were an option of the computer program being used.) In general, if a categorical variable has c categories, $c - 1$ dummy variables must be employed. Here, fall was excluded. This does

FIGURE 6A.1   Fuel Oil Shipments to the United Kingdom

Quarter	Year	Sales
1	1964	210
2		120
3		140
4		260
1	1965	220
2		125
3		145
4		270
1	1966	225
2		128
3		149
4		275

FIGURE 6A.2 **Graph of Fuel Oil Shipments**

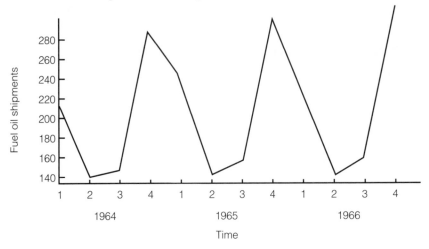

not affect the forecasts, which are independent of the variable deleted. The results were:

$$B_0 = 256.5$$
$$B_1 = 1.468$$
$$B_2 = -45.6$$
$$B_3 = -141.1$$
$$B_4 = -122.2$$

Predictions for each of the quarters are thus:

Winter: Shipments $= B_0 + B_1 \text{(Time)} + B_2(1) + B_3(0) + B_4(0)$
            $= (B_0 + B_2) + B_1 \text{(Time)}$
            $= 210 + 1.468 \text{(Time)}$

FIGURE 6A.3 **Seasonal Dummy Variables**

| | | Dummy Variables | | | |
Shipments	Time	Winter	Spring	Summer	Fall
210	1	1	0	0	0
120	2	0	1	0	0
140	3	0	0	1	0
260	4	0	0	0	1
220	5	1	0	0	0
125	6	0	1	0	0
145	7	0	0	1	0
270	8	0	0	0	1
225	9	1	0	0	0
128	10	0	1	0	0
149	11	0	0	1	0
275	12	0	0	0	1

FIGURE 6A.4 Predicted Shipments by Season

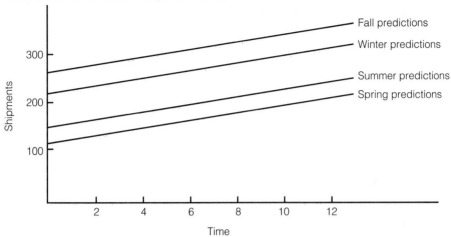

Spring: Shipments $= (B_0 + B_3) + B_1 \text{ (Time)}$
             $= 115.5 + 1.468 \text{ (Time)}$

Summer: Shipments $= (B_0 + B_4) + B_1 \text{ (Time)}$
             $= 134.4 + 1.468 \text{ (Time)}$

Fall: Shipments $= B_0 + B_1 \text{ (Time)}$
             $= 256.6 + 1.468 \text{ (Time)}$

The results are shown graphically as Figure 6A.4. The coefficients of the dummy variables are interpreted as the difference in the average value of the dependent variable between the category of the dummy variable and the category of the variable that has no dummy variable (in this example, fall). Thus,

$$B_2 = \frac{210 + 220 + 225}{3} - \frac{260 + 270 + 275}{3} + 3(1.468)$$
$$= -50 + 3(1.468) = -45.6$$

If this model were used to predict shipments in the second quarter of 1968, the "best guess" prediction would then be

$$\text{Predicted shipments} = 155.5 + 1.468(18) = 142$$

Developing Marketing Strategy

Overview

The previous chapters gave a detailed view of the background analysis homework helpful to developing a marketing plan.[1] This chapter addresses the reason for doing all the analysis, the selection of marketing strategy (i.e., an action plan for the product). That action plan should address three related questions:

1. *Where are we headed?* Here the focus is on basic objectives such as growth versus profits.
2. *How will we get there?* This is the core of marketing/product strategy that addresses issues such as whether to focus on existing versus new customers. It is summarized in a Targeting and Positioning statement defining (*a*) customer targets, (*b*) competitive targets, and (*c*) the proposition (general offering) that will enable the firm to succeed in capturing the targeted customers in the face of competition.
3. *What will we do?* This addresses specific programs or tactics to be employed in order to implement the core strategy. Basically it entails describing the marketing mix (product, pricing, promotion, distribution, service).

This chapter focuses primarily on number (2), targeting and positioning.

Benefits of Strategy

A successful strategy leads to at least three key outcomes:

First, it *enhances coordination* among functional areas of the organization as well as within marketing. Different areas of the organization have different perspectives on how to make a product successful. Product managers often like to increase advertising spending. Sales managers favor (more) flexible pricing policies. Production personnel typically advocate longer production runs and fewer products. Financial/accounting analysts require quantitative justification of expenditures and favor quick results.

---

[1] Much of our thinking about marketing strategy has been influenced by James "Mac" Hulbert, Columbia Business School; William Brandt, Impact Planning Group; and Abraham Schuchman, long-time marketing professor at Columbia.

For example, suppose a computer manufacturer wishes to target a specific industry with unique product features. The image or "positioning" of the product is high quality and technological superiority. In such a case, a sales manager's flexible pricing orientation is inconsistent with the strategy. The production people may be upset with the approach because it means lower volume and more customization. The brand-building activities of the advertising agency are difficult to evaluate in financial terms for the accounting personnel. One purpose of strategy is to ensure that all members of the team are working together (i.e., on the same proverbial page). Of course, a strategy that is not accepted, poorly articulated, or not well understood cannot provide the necessary coordination.

Second, strategy *defines how resources will be allocated.* Resources are limited. Typically some resources, such as manufacturing or service capacity, sales force time, money, and so forth, will be more limited than others. In addition, these resources are often shared. For example, a single sales force often sells many products. The lower the level of the organization, the more resources are typically shared. Therefore, at the product level it is essential that the strategy provide clear guidance for the allocation of resources across activities.

Third, strategy should *lead to a superior market position.* Chapter 2 showed how the definition of competitors is critical to market success. A good strategy takes cognizance of existing and potential competitors and their strengths and weaknesses (see Chapter 4). A *competitively sensible* marketing strategy has at least one of four main characteristics:

1. It is something a competitor *cannot* do. A competitor's inability could be based on patent protection (e.g., the pharmaceutical industry), extra capacity, or some other proprietary or technological advantage. For example, until the release of Windows 95, Apple Computer was the only personal computer supplier with a truly easy-to-use graphical user interface. Other operating systems, notably DOS and earlier versions of Windows, could not match the Apple interface. Note, however, that cannot do does not mean forever, as Apple found out as Windows 98, NT, etc., eroded its position.

2. It is something a competitor *will choose not to do.* Often smaller companies pursue small segments of the market in the hope that large companies will ignore them due to financial criteria. For example, Silicon Graphics, Inc., a manufacturer of computer workstations, specialized in computers that manipulate three-dimensional images on screen for jet design, movie special effects, and other applications. The other major suppliers of workstations, Sun, IBM, and Hewlett-Packard, built more general-purpose computers that did not perform as well as those made by Silicon Graphics for the segment's needs.

3. Competitors *would be at a disadvantage if they do it.* Sears's marketing strategy of "everyday low pricing" was an unsuccessful attempt to emulate the success of Wal-Mart because the company was not prepared to fully integrate a low-cost and low-price orientation in the entire organization.

4. *It causes us to gain if the competitor does it.* Campbell Soup Company ran an advertising campaign around the theme "Soup is good food." Such a theme is clearly generic and is aimed at increasing soup consumption in general. Since

Campbell has a dominant position in the market, it benefits from such generic promotion. However, Heinz or Lipton could not afford such a strategy because it seems likely to primarily cause Campbell's sales to increase.

In sum, a good marketing strategy coordinates functional areas of the organization, helps allocate resources efficiently, and helps the product attain the market position management desires. It also identifies an advantage over the other products and services pursuing the same customers.

ELEMENTS OF A PRODUCT STRATEGY

A more complete statement of marketing strategy for a product consists of seven parts (Hulbert, 1985):

1. Statement of the objective(s) the product should attain.
2. Selection of strategic alternative(s).
3. Selection of customer targets.
4. Choice of competitor targets.
5. Statement of the core strategy.
6. Description of supporting marketing mix.
7. Description of supporting functional programs.

The first two elements, objectives and strategic alternatives, establish the general direction of the strategy. The next three elements, selection of customer and competitor targets and description of the core strategy, are the essence of marketing strategy.[2] Taken together, they are often referred to as positioning, that is, how the product is to be differentiated from the competition in the minds of the target customers. Finally, the supporting marketing mix and functional programs relate to the implementation of the strategy.

A systematic approach to developing strategy helps achieve the coordination and integration referred to earlier. There is a logical order to the aspects of the strategy: It is clear that marketing mix decisions such as price and advertising logically depend on the basic strategy. For example, the strategy of a high-quality positioning to upscale customers, such as Ralph Lauren's Polo clothing line, is logically implemented by high price, exclusive distribution, and classy advertising to obtain consistency between the strategy and implementation.

SETTING OBJECTIVES

An organization has a variety of objectives, beginning with mission or vision and ranging from corporate to product. The type of objective that is our concern addresses the question "Where do we want to go?" Clearly, the answer to such a

---

[2] Product selection is also part of the marketing strategy as well, that is, "which products" to "which markets?" Because we assume the role of a product manager in this book, the basic product choice is taken as given.

FIGURE 7.1 **Hierarchy of Objectives**

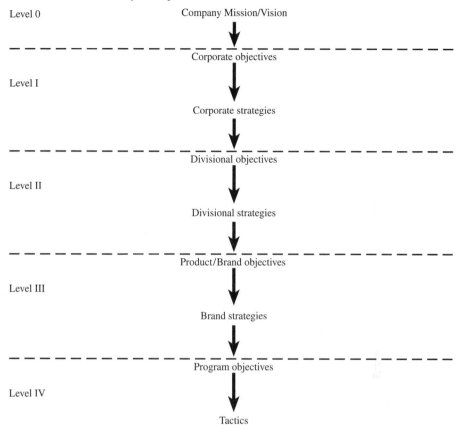

Level 0   Company Mission/Vision

Corporate objectives

Level I

Corporate strategies

Divisional objectives

Level II

Divisional strategies

Product/Brand objectives

Level III

Brand strategies

Program objectives

Level IV

Tactics

question will differ depending on the level of the organization. At the corporate level, objectives related to return on investment, stock share price, and business mix are common. However, they are not very useful for the marketing manager because they give little guidance at the product level for how to proceed.

Figure 7.1 represents the different levels of objectives and strategies in an organization, that is, a *hierarchy of objectives*. Objectives at different levels of the organization should mesh to achieve overall corporate objectives. The job of ensuring that individual product objectives add up to the organization objective usually falls to corporate personnel who are responsible for negotiating both business unit and product objectives to achieve the overall objective.

In this chapter, we are concerned primarily with level III, product objectives. The two objectives most commonly set for specific products or services are growth—in terms of sales revenues or market share—and profitability. It is usually not possible to optimize both simultaneously during the time span of an annual marketing plan. The kinds of activities necessary to achieve an ambitious market share objective work against satisfying an ambitious profit objective.

For example, to reach a market share objective, the usual actions include price reductions, increased spending on advertising, increasing the size of the sales force, and so forth. Significant growth in share is, at the margin, achievable only by increasing expenditures or lowering profit margins per unit. The trade-off between profits and share is exemplified by Japanese auto manufacturers that shifted to a profit orientation from a share objective, partly due to losses suffered when the yen rose to 80 to the dollar in 1995. The result was the introduction of upscale cars (e.g., Lexus) and SUVs (*Business Week,* 1996).

Few managers employ a growth objective without some consideration of its impact on the product's profits (although several Internet firms did so, disastrously in many cases). Likewise, profitability may be the main goal but subject to share maintenance or controlled decline (i.e., harvesting). The objective to be maximized might be called the *primary* objective and the objective acting as the constraint the *secondary* objective. A third objective that can be set for a product is cash flow. When a company is bought through a leveraged buyout (as was the rage in the 1980s), cash flow to pay down debt is a primary concern, and thus the company's products are often charged with generating cash.

Other characteristics of good objectives are the following:

1. They should have *quantified standards* of performance. In other words, every objective statement should include a metric on which to evaluate performance such as "increase market share two share points."
2. They should be ambitious enough to be *challenging,* but not unrealistic. Objectives act as motivators. If regularly set too high, employees treat them as meaningless. Unrealistic objectives also lead to missed earnings targets, an event punished fairly harshly by the stock market. If set too low, the organization is not sufficiently challenged to reach its potential.
3. They should have a *time frame* within which to achieve the objectives. For annual planning purposes, the year serves as the primary time frame, with perhaps quarterly checkpoints.

Two key questions to be answered with respect to objectives are (1) which one should be pursued and (2) how high a target should I set?

To answer the first question, product managers should consider industry, competitor, and customer analyses and the company's current and anticipated financial resources. For growth objectives to be feasible, there must be some competitor vulnerabilities that can be exploited (competitor analysis), a customer segment with remaining potential (customer analysis), or general category growth anticipated (industry analysis).

Some industries have traditional objectives. For example, in consumer products, the focus for many years was market share and sales volume. Product managers have been under constant pressure to "move cases" of products. However, a recent trend emphasizes profits over traditional volume targets. This is difficult to implement for two reasons. First, information systems at most companies do a good job of measuring share and sales volume on a regular basis but not of measuring profits. Second, and perhaps more important, companies do not always reward product managers on the basis of profits; the key to fast-track careers has been to increase volume and share.

The second issue is how ambitious to be: If a manager is pursuing increased market share, how much increase is appropriate? In some cases, no growth in share is challenging enough: If a product has had declining share, halting the decline could be considered ambitious. The size of the gain to be expected depends on the market size forecasts and the anticipated activities of competitors. If the competitors are going for profits, it can be a good time to gain significant share. Still, if all companies plan to increase share (i.e., share goals total 130 percent), some will clearly be disappointed.

A number of noneconomic or nonquantitative objectives are also pursued, although not necessarily as primary product objectives. For example, it is difficult to find a U.S. company that has not made a major push for quality, and many firms have specific customer satisfaction objectives (e.g., to increase satisfaction from 70 to 75 on a 100-point scale). Similarly, maintenance of brand equity is a concern in a growing number of companies. There is an obvious link between these "enabling" objectives and economic objectives: Achieving the former should eventually lead to reaching the latter.

In sum, the task of setting objectives involves choosing the appropriate objective, quantifying the objective, and setting a time frame for its achievement.

SELECTION OF STRATEGIC ALTERNATIVES

The choice of strategic alternatives follows the selection of the primary objective. This is the first step in developing the marketing strategy for the product or service that provides broad guidelines for the ultimate strategy selected. Figure 7.2 presents alternative strategies in a treelike structure. The diagram assumes the long-run objective of a marketing manager is to maximize long-run profits (which in turn should maximize shareholder value). We link the description of the alternatives to the selection of whether the primary objective is growth in sales/share and hence long-run profits or short-term profitability. The options available depend on the objective. If a manager chooses growth, the two main ways to achieve it are market development and market penetration, often via the introduction of new products or extensions. Market development strategies are directed toward selling the current product to current noncustomers; market penetration aims at current or past customers of the product category. If the manager chooses the profitability path, the primary focus is on either decreasing inputs (basically cutting costs, also known as denominator management) or increasing outputs (sales revenue).

Increasing Sales/Market Share

Market Development Strategies

These strategies are aimed at noncustomers of the product (i.e., customer acquisition). One approach is to pursue nonusers in segments already targeted. For example, if an Internet service is targeted to law firms, a development strategy would pursue those law firms that have not yet purchased the product (as well as pursuing current customers with value-added). Essentially, this approach tries to tap

FIGURE 7.2 **Strategic Alternatives**

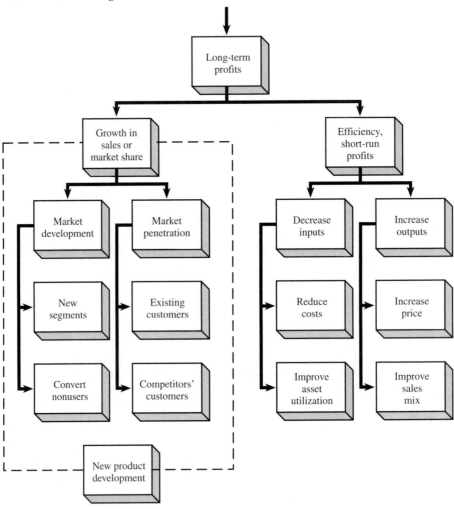

remaining market potential from those segments identified as prime prospects. One example is the increased attention small business owners have received from large banks such as Wells Fargo. While the banks already have customers from that segment, the lack of growth from lending to larger clients gives the banks more incentive to expand their marketing efforts to get more customers from entrepreneurial companies.

A second approach is to enter new markets, developing segments previously ignored by the product category. An example of this strategy is the attempt by Kodak and Fuji to attract children to photography using a variety of promotions and special programs (Bounds, 1994). Another example is the seed company that put small containers of vegetable seeds in plastic wheelbarrows at garden supply stores to try to get children to begin gardening at a young age. Similarly, antacids such as Tums have been positioned as not only solving stomach acid problems but also as a calcium additive. The classic example is Arm & Hammer baking soda, which has been marketed as useful for several purposes.

Market Penetration Strategies

An alternative, and often overlooked, way to increase market share or sales volume is to increase the usage rate of the brand's existing customers (i.e., customer expansion). The biggest asset a company has is its customer base, and it should be leveraged as much as possible. A company can obtain more volume from existing customers by, for example, using larger package sizes, promoting more frequent use, or getting a larger share of the business if the customer uses several vendors (i.e., share of wallet).

Many firms have successfully taken this track. Banks try to get a larger share of commercial customers' business by cross-selling other services, such as cash management and annuities. Coupons are often used to induce customers to buy larger package sizes in the hope of increasing the consumption rate (Wansink, 1996; Chandon and Wansink, 2002). Marketing managers should always ask themselves: Is the actual consumption rate equal to the *potential* rate?

A second route to increasing sales or market share is to attract competitors' customers (i.e., customer acquisition), that is, to induce brand switching. This is a difficult strategy when the switching costs are high (e.g., mainframe computers, nuclear generators). In addition, the strategy could be risky. First, it can incur the wrath of a larger, more formidable competitor. Second, it may involve substantial use of sales promotion, which could make the strategy unprofitable. Third, a strategy inducing brand switching may call for comparative advertising, which is not only expensive but also risky; if poorly executed, it may call attention to the competitor's brand, particularly if the brand is the market leader. Because of the increase in credit card issuers (e.g., AT&T, General Electric, "affinity" cards), category participants resorted to stealing the best customers from one another (Pae, 1992). AT&T was heavily involved in defending its long-distance phone calling business from MCI, which developed new services (e.g., "Friends and Family") and launched price comparison ads to steal AT&T customers, as well as the Baby Bells, Sprint, and other newer entrants. The 2002 "churn" (switching) rate in cell phone customers was 20 percent a year *before* it became possible to keep your same phone number when switching companies.

Increasing Profitability

Decreasing Inputs

One way to increase profits is cost reduction. Obvious candidates for reduction are costs of marketing such as advertising, promotion, selling expenses, marketing research, and so forth. Unfortunately, reducing these inputs may have adverse long-run effects. A possible danger in stressing variable cost reduction is that a reduction in the inputs can cause a commensurate reduction in the outputs. Aluminum Company of America (Alcoa) restructured its operations in 1992 and reduced its workforce; the result was a rejection rate at one of its can manufacturing facilities of 25 percent and a drop in customer satisfaction to below 50 percent (Milbank, 1992). At the same time, some minor product changes can save a substantial amount of money. For example, Ford reduced its costs $8 million to $9 million per year by decreasing the number of carpeting options from nine to three and saved $750,000 by using black screws rather than color-matched screws on Mustang side mirrors (Schwartz, 1996).

A second way to decrease inputs is to improve the utilization of the assets. This might mean keeping down accounts receivable and, for a manufactured product, the costs of inventories. Other, related activities include running production equipment more efficiently and, at a more aggregate level, investing idle cash on hand in overnight interest-bearing securities.

Managers choosing the profit branch of the tree must, of course, also choose customer targets. The probable approach for this objective would be to concentrate on current customers. In fact, one of the most obvious ways to improve profits is to reduce customer turnover/churn, (i.e., increase customer retention).

Increasing Outputs

The easiest way to increase revenues from existing unit sales is to improve prices. This can be done in a variety of ways, including increasing the list price, reducing discounts (think rebates on car purchases), reducing trade allowances, and so forth. Of course this can lead to a substantial drop in unit sales and hence lost revenue. There is also the issue of competitive reaction, which has doomed many airline price increases and hurt P&G's attempt to institute everyday low pricing (EDLP; Ailawadi, Neslin, and Lehmann, 2001).

The other way to increase revenues is to improve the sales mix. The 80/20 rule often holds: 20 percent of the product variants (sizes, colors, etc.) produce 80 percent of the sales or profits. In such an instance, it may make sense to emphasize selling more of the profitable items. Alternatively, if we apply the rule to customers, a company may want to de-emphasize unprofitable customers and concentrate resources on those producing 80 percent of the profits (i.e., customer deletion).

Summary

We have presented two broad strategic options available to a marketing manager in terms of strategic alternatives.[3] This does not mean that a manager is limited to either growth or profits. For example, it is common to seek reductions in variable costs while pursuing market share gains. In addition, a manager may attempt both to increase the consumption rate of current customers and to introduce product-line extensions.

---

[3] A similar view of the alternatives in a high-tech context is provided by Kadanoff (1995), pp. 24–26. She labels current customers in the installed base as "Low-hanging fruit," new customers in current segments as "Juicy fruit," new customers in "adjacent" markets as "Ripe fruit," new customers in new segments as "Fruit on the vine," and new customers in developing segments as "Seedlings."

The marketing manager's dilemma is that while several of the options may appear to be equally attractive, it is very difficult and expensive to successfully implement multiple strategic alternatives. Part of the difficulty arises from the multiple positionings different alternatives may require. For example, to simultaneously obtain new customers and get current customers to buy more, different advertising campaigns may have to be run, projecting different images and confusing customers. Multiple strategies prevent economies of scale from advertising copy, increase the use of more expensive media (i.e., spot versus national TV), and so forth, thus increasing expenses. It also creates confusion within the organization about what the goals really are. Hence, there is pressure on managers to select a subset of the options available and concentrate resources on them.

POSITIONING: CHOICE OF CUSTOMER TARGETS

In selecting a customer target, three key considerations are critical:

1. *Size/growth of the segment.* An important part of customer analysis focuses on which customer groups are growing and how fast.
2. *Opportunities for obtaining competitive advantage.* Competitor analysis assesses which market segments competitors are pursuing and their claimed competitive advantages, the resources they can put into the market, and their likely future marketing strategies.
3. *Resources available.* This is covered in the self-analysis part of the assessment of competition analysis.

As mentioned earlier, positioning entails a specific statement of how the product differs from the competition in the minds of a specific set of customers, and encompasses (1) customer targets, (2) competitor targets, and (3) some attribute(s) by which the differentiation will occur. The choice of which customer group(s) to target follows immediately from specification of the strategic alternatives and the segments developed in the customer analysis. If the profit route is taken, the customer targets are generally current ones, for example, "men 18 to 25" or "banks with assets between $100 million and $1 billion." The task is similar for any of the growth alternatives. For a market penetration strategy aimed at the product's own customers or a market development strategy aimed at nonusers, the customers of the current strategy would again be selected. For the market penetration strategy aimed at stealing competitors' customers, the specific descriptors of those customers would be used. Finally, for the market development strategy aimed at new segments, the descriptors from the new segments chosen would be specified.

Consider Handspring's strategy in the PDA market in 2000. Given that their basic product was strong on convenience and low in price, their target segments differ from the traditional PDA customer: upscale, price-insensitive business professionals. One can identify three segments worth pursuing (Figure 7.3). Why choose to serve customers who currently provide little profit? In the case of such acquisition strategies, this means ensuring that the value of acquired customers is greater than their acquisition cost.

FIGURE 7.3 Target Segments for Handspring

Factor	Price-Sensitive Business Professionals	Nonbusiness Professionals	Nonprofessionals
Benefits, key attributes of PDA	• Functionality, expandability • Status • Design, sleek, small, nice screen • Price • Memory, speed	• Ease of use, convenience • Design, sleek, small, nice screen • Price • Functionality, expandability • Status • Durability	• Ease of use, convenience • Price • Fun/Enjoyment (music, games) • Design, nice screen • Battery life • Status, sense of belonging (cool product)
Main factors affecting PDA purchase	• Price • Functionality • Memory	• Ease of use • Functionality • Price	• Ease of use • Price • Design, sleek, small, nice screen
Where do they purchase?	• Through company, possibly buy themselves at consumer electronics retailers • Over Internet	• Through company, possibly buy themselves at consumer electronics retailers • Over Internet	• Consumer electronics retailers • Over Internet
When do they buy?	• When colleagues buy	• When colleagues buy	• When friends, neighbors, or classmates buy • Receive or purchase as gift

POSITIONING: CHOICE OF COMPETITOR TARGETS

Even if the competition is not explicitly mentioned in any of the product's communications programs, it is still important to consider which competitors are the primary targets of the strategy. For a penetration strategy that involves stealing competitors' customers, the targeted customers should be identified based on an analysis of which competitor's customers are both valuable and the most easily pried away. However, all strategic alternatives at least implicitly involve competition because of the necessity to position the product *against* major competitors.

Positioning involves some prioritization of the competitors, both direct and indirect. Again, the chief source of information about this choice is the situation analysis in Chapter 4, which details the strengths and weaknesses of the competition. The hope is to identify a weak or docile company with significant sales that can be easily overcome. Unfortunately such targets are not always available (Ries and Trout, 1986; Czepiel, 1992). Market leaders often take defensive steps and therefore focus on the strong second competitor and perhaps the third one. The followers in the market take different competitor stances depending on their market share relative to the leader. A strong second might focus on offensive warfare and target the leader. Weak followers often try to avoid the major competitors and seek market niches that have either few or weak rivals. For example, in banking they might be a "boutique," offering customized services targeted at individuals with high net worth, thus avoiding full-scale competition with large banks.

POSITIONING: CORE STRATEGY

The core strategy defines the differential advantage to be communicated to the target customers, often referred to as *product positioning*. The advantages that can be employed fall into two basic categories: (1) cost/price (economic) differential advantage and (2) differentiation based on product offering or service features.[4] (Note that differentiation can include psychological as well as functional benefits.) In other words, you either have to have a lower price that can be supported in the long run only with lower costs or be better on some element of the product offering customers recognize as a benefit.

As several examples show, being "stuck in the middle" can be disastrous. In 1991, Compaq Computer was in deep trouble. The previously high-flying computer company, known for its high-priced, high-quality personal computers, showed its first-ever quarterly loss. The loss occurred because it was neither the low-price nor the quality/performance leader in an increasingly competitive market. United Airlines' shuttle ("express") service failed to significantly affect Southwest Airlines in the large California market since it was not lower priced nor perceived to be of higher quality.

In general, the positioning decision has four steps (Day, 1990, Chapter 6):

1. Identify alternative positioning themes by consulting the advertising account team, the product team, and past marketing plans.
2. Screen the alternatives according to whether each is (*a*) meaningful to customers, (*b*) feasible given the firm and product resources and customer perceptions, (*c*) competitively sensible (see the definition in the overview of this chapter), or (*d*) helpful for meeting the product objective.
3. Select the position that best satisfies these criteria *and* can be sold to the marketing organization.
4. Implement programs (e.g., advertising) consistent with the product position selected.

This systematic approach ensures that alternative positionings are considered and diverse constituents consulted.

The core strategy should be easy to summarize and communicate in paragraph form. Sometimes this statement of the core strategy is referred to as the *value proposition*. The value proposition for Southwest Airlines, for example, could be the following:

> To provide travelers with the lowest-cost air transportation with an enjoyable, fun atmosphere.

---

[4] See, for example, Porter (1985). Porter actually advocates a third basic strategy, market segmentation. However, we believe market segmentation is a necessary part of any strategy.

This clearly states that Southwest's differential advantage is price and fun, not food, frills, and nonstop routes.

Cost/Price (Value) Strategy

Almost every product category has a competitor that focuses on price or "value," as opposed to product features or on some aspect of the product other than price. Wal-Mart made Sam Walton the richest man in the United States. Charles Schwab invented the discount brokerage business. Private labels have become very popular in many supermarket product categories, and are often the number one brands in their categories (e.g., frozen juices, drinks, and cookies). Mail-order personal computers stressing price constitute a huge business, and for a time Packard-Bell (now aligned with NEC) was the largest vendor of personal computers in the United States largely through its low-price, mass distribution channel approach.

Not all products can be the low-price leader. Many firms lack the required size, capital, or other resources. First, a high volume of a single product or family of products should be produced or sold. Focused production hastens cost reduction, which must be continuously pursued. Second, investment should focus on efficient facilities and market share. Again, efficiency does not apply just to production equipment. The lowest-cost companies pay strict attention to corporate overhead, including size of staff, perks such as jets and limousines, fancy offices, and so on. Finally, control should focus on cost in manufacturing products and delivering services, as well as activities such as advertising and promotion.

In pursuing lower costs, a marketing manager should focus on important activities in which their cost is high. The important costs involved vary widely over different products. For a personal computer, decreased cost of semiconductors, microchip boards, video screens, and the like all bring the cost of the product down significantly. However, for a laundry detergent, the major cost items might be the thickness of the plastic package and the size of the label.

The low-price core strategy poses real risks. One is that customer tastes shift, and the product being produced in large quantities may no longer be desired (e.g., Atari and other video games before the Nintendo era). A second is that technological shifts can either make it easier for competitors to have the same costs or make the product obsolete. Competitors can also leapfrog in cost cutting, which eliminates the cost differential advantage. One advantage of a low-price strategy is that there is probably always room in a product category for a low-priced, "value" option because some segment of customers will always be price sensitive. The key question, of course, is how large the price-sensitive segment is, how many competitors will target it, and, therefore, whether it is worth the investments necessary to be a cost leader.

Nonprice Strategy

One way to think about the nonprice differential advantage is as a product characteristic, not necessarily tangible, that allows the product manager to obtain a price higher than the price that would be allowed under perfect competition. As every student of microeconomics (and, it is hoped, every reader of this book) knows, with many suppliers of undifferentiated commodities, the market price tends to approach marginal cost. Therefore, a differential advantage that creates added value in the

FIGURE 7.4 Total Product Concept

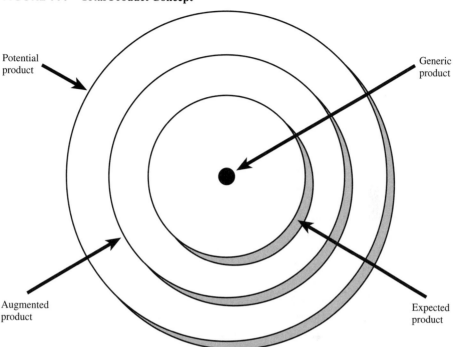

minds of customers enables the producer to obtain a higher price than the pure competition case; with a significant differential advantage, customers focus on product attributes other than price.

From where can a differential advantage be obtained? Figure 7.4 portrays what is called the *total product concept* (Levitt, 1986). The *generic* product is the bundle of characteristics—the functional aspects of a product. For example, an automobile could be described by quality of tires, miles per gallon, engine size, and so forth. The *expected* product is described by other benefits delivered by the product that customers have come to take as routine. For cars, the expected product includes some degree of reliability and warranty coverage. The *augmented* and *potential* products are often what give rise to differential advantage. The augmented product includes features or benefits that can be delivered now to go beyond expectations—for example, a satellite-based global positioning system (GPS) for tracking. The potential product contains those features or benefits that can be added to a product or service some time in the future. Customers remember restaurants that offer free meals when a customer is dissatisfied or the retail clerk who pays special attention to a customer when the store is busy. Actions which enhance the customer's purchasing and consumption experience generally lead to repeat buying.

The point here is that differential advantages are often obtained by going beyond what customers expect, to provide unanticipated product benefits. It may take some creative thinking, but one important aspect of providing differential advantages is to move away from asking, "How can I make this product different?" to asking, "What am I selling?" By focusing on what customers are buying—that is, benefits, and more broadly, customer experience—managers can better determine how to make their products or services different from the competition.

Firms typically use five areas for differentiation (Schnaars, 1991).

1. *Quality.* Product quality has many dimensions. For example, particularly for technologically based products, enhanced quality can mean improved performance. Intel originally differentiated its products by being technologically ahead of other semiconductor companies. Quality can also mean superior design. Automobile brands such as Lexus, computers such as Apple, stereo manufacturer Bang & Olufsen, and consumer product companies such as Sony emphasize superior design in their products. Customer service is also an area for differentiation based on quality. Manufacturers such as Timken (bearings) and Caterpillar (farm equipment) are well known for their customer service. For service businesses, product quality and customer service are virtually synonymous. Airlines such as Singapore and retailers such as Nordstrom differentiate on this basis. For manufactured products, quality can also mean reliability and durability. Brands marketed by the appliance manufacturer Maytag, for example, are advertised on this dimension (the "lonely repairman").

2. *Status and image.* In the bottled water category, brands such as Evian and Perrier have claimed this point of differentiation from other bottled waters. Many consumer fashion brands, such as Rolex watches and Polo clothing, use this approach.

3. *Branding.* A particular aspect of image involves brands. Brand names and their values communicated to customers, brand equity, can serve as a point of differentiation. IBM, McDonald's, and Nestlé are leading brands worldwide. It is particularly interesting when a product that had previously been considered a commodity is differentiated and becomes successful after branding, such as Perdue chickens. A more recent illustration is the campaign by Intel using ads touting "Intel Inside."

Perceptual mapping, described in Chapter 5, has been extensively used by marketers to assess the current perceptual positions of brands among customer and competitor targets and to help determine if the current positioning is effective or whether repositioning can help. Figure 7.5 shows what is called a *joint space* because it not only indicates brand locations versus competition on the two axes but also displays *ideal points,* the preferred bundle of attributes of clusters of households. Note that the map incorporates all three aspects of positioning. Customers are represented by the ideal points (the segments are numbered according to size), competitors are located on the map, and the differential advantage can be assessed using the brand attributes represented by the axes.

Consider the joint space figure from the perspective of RC Cola. RC is perceived as a nondiet cola, but it is equidistant from segment 1, which is close to Coke and Pepsi, and segment 3, which seems to want a lower-calorie cola. RC can position itself more within the mainstream, where it would encounter heavy competition from Coke and Pepsi. Alternatively, it can pursue segment 3 with a "lighter" image where it would find fewer competitors, but also fewer potential customers.

FIGURE 7.5 **Joint Space for Colas**

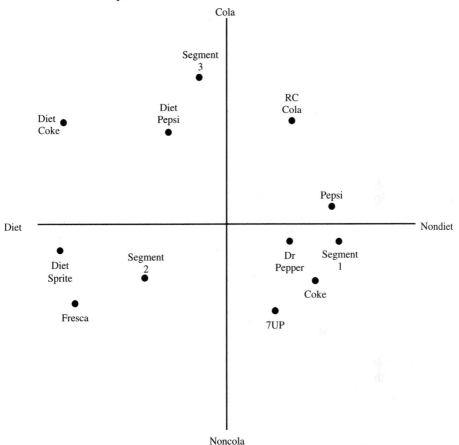

4. *Convenience and service.* Many consumer products are differentiated on the basis of convenience. Lexus and Infiniti differentiated themselves from other luxury car brands by making it easier for customers to have their cars serviced, giving free loaner cars, and sometimes making arrangements to pick up the car at the customer's home. Home shopping grocery services focus on convenience to entice people with home computers and modems to change their buying habits and purchase their weekly supermarket orders from home.

5. *Distribution.* A marketing manager can sometimes gain differential advantage by reaching customers more efficiently and effectively than competitors. Federal Express, through its Powership terminals, allows its customers to determine for themselves where their packages are in the system and to order the "product." Thus, Federal Express becomes, in effect, the customers' shipping department.

The requirements for a nonprice differential advantage core strategy are naturally quite different from those for a cost/price strategy. First, the strategy requires searching for continuous product improvements (or improvements in perceptions) to maintain the differential advantage. Second, a differential advantage core strategy requires flexibility in both production and management to keep up with changes in customer tastes and competition.

The risks involved in the differential advantage core strategy are also considerable. First, the cost/price differential may become so great that customers are willing to pay less to get less. Perhaps the biggest problem is that the differential can often disappear due to imitation. Witness the quick adoption of frequent-flier programs by almost all the major airlines. Who remembers—or cares—that American was the first with such a program?

MANAGING BRAND EQUITY

Managing a product's reputation is one of the most important strategic jobs facing a marketing manager. Like objects owned by a firm such as manufacturing equipment and buildings, a brand name is an asset, and a potentially valuable one.

For several years, the growth of private label brands and higher spending on price-oriented promotions led pundits to predict the "death" of national and international brands. This belief was given further credence when "Marlboro Friday," the Friday in April 1993 on which Philip Morris reduced the price of its venerable Marlboro brand by 40 cents per pack to combat private label cigarettes, caused sharp drops in the stock prices of manufacturers of national brands. This action was replicated by the cereal manufacturers, led by Post (also owned by Philip Morris) and Kellogg's in April 1996.

There is no question that many private labels have in effect become brands (as President's Choice, originally a house brand of Loblaw's, formally did). Yet many brands remain powerful and profitable. Several companies have decided that the best way to combat lower-priced competitors, whether private labels for supermarket products or clones for computers, is to reemphasize their brand names. Companies such as Coca-Cola, Hewlett-Packard, and P&G invest in advertising and attempt to reduce harmful price-oriented promotions. Such efforts caused the sales of private labels to plateau and made 12 out of the 15 *Fortune* most admired companies household brand names (Morris, 1996). Of course, branding alone is not enough: during 1999 and 2000, new Internet companies poured massive dollars into ads designed to attract customers and build brand recognition (the first level of brand equity), with at best mixed success.

Brands are also engaged in global warfare against counterfeiters and "knockoffs," products that are almost identical to the originals with very similar (or the same) brand names and packaging but substantially lower prices. Knockoffs mislead customers into thinking that the product is the well-known global brand. Counterfeiting is particularly prevalent in the music CD, computer software, and clothing industries (the U.S. government has sent numerous trade missions to China to try to persuade them to crack down on these activities to little effect). The problem is not just the lost revenues but the potential for the reputations of the global brands to be damaged by poorly made substitutes.

In Chapter 5 we described brand equity in terms of awareness, associations (image), attitude (overall quality), attachment (loyalty), and activity (e.g., word of mouth). A slightly different version developed by Aaker (1996) appears in Figure 7.6 and includes five categories:

1. *Brand loyalty.* The strongest measure of a brand's value is the loyalty (repeat buying, word of mouth) it engenders among customers. Sometimes the loyalty is circumstantial: Repeat buying comes from a lack of reasonable alternatives. Circumstantial loyalty includes what are called *proprietary* assets (e.g., patents, copyrights, trademarks, control of an airport) that give a firm at least a temporary monopoly position (the impact of generic drugs when an ethical drug comes off patent suggests that much of the advantage is in fact circumstantial and hence temporary). In other situations, loyalty reflects an *efficiency* motive: The brand is good, so we automatically select it to minimize effort. Notice that an important special case of efficiency loyalty occurs when a customer relies on an "expert" (e.g., a dealer) to make the choice for her or him and the expert has a preferred alternative. In this case, loyalty is really channel-created loyalty.

   The strongest form of loyalty is *attachment.* In this case, the customer doggedly seeks out a product, often out of deference to its role in a previous situation (e.g., "They were there when I needed them") and sometimes in an almost ritualistic manner (e.g., stopping at a certain ice cream store as a rite of summer). This level of loyalty insulates a brand from competitive pressures such as advertising and price promotion and leads to higher margins and profits.

2. *Brand awareness.* The simplest form of brand equity is familiarity. A familiar brand gives the customer a feeling of *confidence* (risk reduction), and hence it is more likely to be both considered and chosen. There is also convincing evidence that, on average, customers *prefer* brands with which they are familiar. Finally, choosing a known brand gives the customer a *justification* for the decision, an explanation for his or her actions. This justification also serves a *social* role, indicating that the person has bought something of value.

3. *Perceived quality.* A known brand often conveys an aura of quality (good or bad). A quality association can be of the general halo type; for example, Levi Strauss for years had an outstanding reputation both for its products and as a place to work. Associations can also be attribute or category specific: Gillette makes fine-quality razors, Apple produces user-friendly products, and Samsonite products last forever. In some cases, a brand becomes synonymous with a category (e.g., Xerox, Kleenex, FedEx). Further, a brand often has strong price associations that influence quality perceptions (e.g., a Kmart brand product is expected to be low in price and probably low in quality as well).

4. *Brand associations.* More subjective and emotional associations are also an important part of brand value. These include *personal* associations; Gatorade's "Be Like Mike" campaign was a blatant example, but every celebrity endorsement contains elements of it. Other associations are more emotional, relating to such lifestyle or personality characteristics as *stability* (see many Kodak ads, as well as Prudential's "A piece of the rock"), being *"hip"* or *"with it"* (a standard appeal of fashionable clothing companies, soft drinks, beer, and liquor), and

FIGURE 7.6 **Brand Equity**

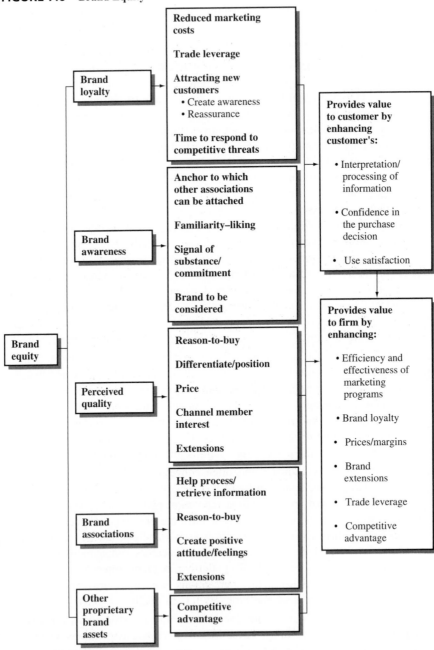

Source: Reprinted with permission of The Free Press, a division of Macmillian, Inc. from *Building Strong Brands* by David A. Aaker. Copyright 1996 by David A. Aaker.

FIGURE 7.7   **Some Brand Attribute and Image Dimensions**

Attributes	Image Dimensions
Flavor/taste	Reliable—unreliable
Caffeine content	Old—young
Price	Technical—nontechnical
Packaging	Sensible—rash
Size	Interesting—boring
Calories	Creative—noncreative
Brand name	Sentimental—nonsentimental
Sweetness	Impulsive—deliberate
Weight	Trustworthy—untrustworthy
Warranty	Conforming—rebellious
Durability	Daring—cautious
Convenience	Forceful—submissive
Color	Bold—timid
Style	Sociable—unsociable
Comfort	
Freshness	
Construction material	
Availability	
Serviceability	
Compatibility	
Energy efficiency	
Instructions	
Automation	
Ease of use	

Source: Rajeev Batra, Donald R. Lehmann, and Dipinder Singh. "The Brand Personality Component of Brand Goodwill: Some Antecedents and Consequences," in David A. Aaker and Alexander L. Biel, eds., *Brand Equity and Advertising: Advertising's Role in Building Strong Brands* (Hillsdale, N.J.: Lawrence Erlbaum Associates, 1993), pp. 83–96.

being *responsible* (e.g., environmentally conscious, currently both an important issue and the subject of much hype). Other strong associations may be with the type of customer or user of the product (e.g., white shirts and bald heads with business executives) or geographic region (e.g., country of origin for Japanese cars, Swiss watches). Figure 7.7 provides a general list of both product attribute and user images. Taken together, these associations form a *brand personality* that suggests situations for which a brand is (and is not) suitable (Aaker, 1997).

5. *Other brand assets.* Other assets, such as patents and trademarks, are clearly valuable. However, we exclude these from brand equity since they are tied to the physical product or process and not to the brand *per se.*

Brand equity creates value for both customers and the firm. Customers can use brand names as simplifying heuristics for processing large amounts of information: Awareness of the brand name Lexus and the brand associations generated can act as a substitute for reading *Consumer Reports,* talking to friends, and using other information sources. Dannon introduced its brand of bottled water under the assumption that consumers who view its yogurt positively will transfer that good feeling to the new product. Over-the-counter cold and headache remedies by well-known companies such as Bayer and Johnson & Johnson command significantly higher prices than their private label counterparts because of the trust customers have in those companies. Thus, firms benefit enormously from having strong brand names. Investment in a brand name can be leveraged through brand extensions and increased distribution. High brand equity often means less price sensitivity, which allows higher prices to be charged, a significant competitive advantage. Similar efficiencies can exist for other marketing activities such as advertising and promotion.

An example of the power of brand names is the ill-fated Audi 5000, which was accused on a widely viewed edition of TV's *60 Minutes* of having a problem with sudden acceleration. The program claimed the car suddenly lurched forward although the driver's foot was not on the gas pedal. Audi failed to view protecting the brand name as one of its chief marketing jobs. As a result, the company handled the problem by accusing U.S. drivers of making mistakes and stepping on the accelerator rather than the brake. Regardless of the truth (it was eventually concluded that the cars did not have a problem), protecting the asset—the company's brand name—should have been Audi's priority. The sales of *all* Audi products dropped two-thirds between 1985 and 1989. As a consequence, the manufacturer introduced new models (Quattro, 100, etc.) and eliminated the problem-ridden 4000 and 5000 lines. This problem of how to handle disasters and their impact on the brand name continues to surface. Consider the problems faced by Ford and Firestone over tread separation in their tires. Another example is Intel's initial reaction to problems with its Pentium processor.

The importance of brand equity raises three important issues for marketing managers. First, it is particularly important for packaged goods manufacturers that face increasing competition from supermarkets' "own label" brands. The price difference a national brand can support relative to a private label is a direct function of the level of brand equity of the national brand. Even more basic, high brand equity helps get the brand into distribution channels, an obviously critical step in selling the product.

A second question is: How far can a successful brand name be stretched? Clearly Toyota, Nissan, and Honda believed luxury cars could not be sold with cars with a cheaper image; hence, the development of Lexus, Infiniti, and Acura, respectively. Not only are the brand names different but the cars are sold in separate dealerships. Mitsubishi believed otherwise. It marketed a new luxury coupe, the Diamante, along with the rest of its product line, to limited success.

Third, marketing managers should view the management and sustenance of brand equity as an important task. This suggests the desirability of both measuring and setting objectives for brand equity. Aaker (1996) provides 10 guidelines for building strong brands:

1. *Brand identity.* Each brand should have an identity, a personality. It can be modified for different segments.

2. *Value proposition.* Each brand should have a unique value proposition.

3. *Brand position.* The brand's position should provide clear guidance to those implementing a communications program.

4. *Execution.* The communications program needs to implement the identity and position, and it should be durable as well.

5. *Consistency over time.* Product managers should have a goal of maintaining a consistent identity, position, and execution over time. Changes should be resisted.

6. *Brand system.* The brands in the portfolio should be consistent and synergistic.

7. *Brand leverage.* Extend brands and develop cobranding opportunities only if the brand identity will be both used and reinforced.

8. *Tracking.* The brand's equity should be tracked over time, including awareness, perceived quality, brand loyalty, and brand associations.

9. *Brand responsibility.* Someone should be in charge of the brand who will create the identity and positions and coordinate the execution.

10. *Invest.* Continue investing in brands even when the financial goals are not being met.

Measuring Brand Value

In order to manage brand equity, it is helpful to measure it. Such measurement is not only the concern of product managers, however. The board of governors of the United Kingdom's Accounting Standards Board held public hearings on rules to require all companies to value their brands, and some companies in the United Kingdom and the United States carry brands on their balance sheets. Grand Metropolitan, for example, carried specific brand equities for Smirnoff, Pillsbury, and Burger King.

Given the large amount of attention paid to brand equity in the last few years, it is not surprising that a variety of consulting firms, advertising agencies, and other interested parties have developed their own approaches to measuring the value of brands and, as a result, rankings of relative brand equities (e.g., Research International's Equity Engine, Milward-Brown's Brand Z, and Y&R's Brand Asset Evaluator). These measures focus on the image of brands (i.e., the customer's view). For example, Y&R's BAV assesses a brand in terms of stature (knowledge and esteem) and strength (differentiation and relevance) and has shown, along with Stern, Stewart & Co., that the ratings are related to profits, specifically EVA.

Interbrand assesses the financial value of a brand in two steps. First, it computes the revenue premium vs. a generic competitor. It then adjusts this with a multiple which attempts to account for differences in industry growth and other factors. Based on this, Coca-Cola was the most valuable brand in 2002, worth about $70 million followed by Microsoft ($65 million), IBM ($52 million), GE ($42 million), and Intel ($31 million). (For more, see its website, *Interbrand.com.*)

An example of a survey-based approach is Landor's ImagePower. The 1999 study on consumer perceptions of technology brands was based on over 6,000 respondents from a mailing to 50,000 Internet users. Each respondent had to provide information for at least 50 of the 250 brands evaluated. Landor used four primary measures: appropriateness (how relevant the brand is to everyday life), share of heart (how highly the person regards the brand), distinctiveness (how unique and different the brand is from competition), and share of mind (how familiar the person is with the brand). Based on its survey, the top five technology brands in 1999 were the following:

1. Windows
2. Microsoft

3. Yahoo!

4. Pentium

5. Microsoft Word

Obviously, Microsoft has been an effective marketer.

An example from the technology area is a quarterly survey conducted by Techtel Corporation. The firm surveys business buyers of computer equipment including software and hardware on measures such as awareness, trial, purchase, and repurchase intention. The survey also measures the percentage of the buyers who have a positive opinion about a brand. An illustration of the results is shown in Figure 7.8 for IBM notebook computers. The squares represent the opinion measure while the vertical bars represent those who bought recently (within the previous quarter). The obviously high correlation between positive opinion and purchasing measures gives some assurance that brand strength converts into actual buying behavior. Further, opinions such as these turn out to be predictors of stock price movements (Aaker and Jacobsen, 2001).

A company can measure overall brand value through a variety of means. Basically, measuring brand value requires answering the question "How much more value does the product have with the brand name attached?" A variety of direct methods questioning can be used to measure brand value. One other method already discussed, conjoint analysis, can also be used. By simply using brand name as an attribute and using the different brand names in the market or fictitious brand names being considered for a new product, the part-worths estimated are quantitative measures of the value of a brand name relative to the others used in the experimental design. (Recall that in the example in Chapter 6 we found different values for Dell and HP.)

A related method relies on so-called hedonic regression. This technique regresses market price (or the amount customers say they are willing to pay for various products) against product features and brand name:

$$\text{Price} = B_0 + B_1 \,(\text{Feature 1}) + B_2 \,(\text{Feature 2}) + \cdots$$
$$+ \, C_1 \,(\text{Brand A}) + C_2 \,(\text{Brand B}) + \cdots$$

The output gives a dollar value for each brand. (Of course, when actual prices are used, this analysis ignores the sales volume of each brand, so it may present a somewhat distorted view of the value to those customers who choose to buy each product.)

The various components of brand value can also be assessed in relatively straightforward ways. Different levels of awareness measurement (e.g., aided or unaided) are possible. Attribute associations can be directly assessed ("If ABC Inc. made a product with X amount of attribute A, how much of attribute B would you expect it to have?").

A simple product-market level measure is the extra revenue a brand receives vis-à-vis private label products of equal quality, which is driven by two components: price premium and share premium. Brand equity realized in a particular year is thus simply the additional revenue the brand received, assuming both its share and price are greater than those of the private label (Ailawadi, Lehmann, and Neslin, 2003). For example, according to Mediamark data, in 1996. Dreyer's price premium

FIGURE 7.8 IBM Notebook Computers: Purchase versus Positive Opinion

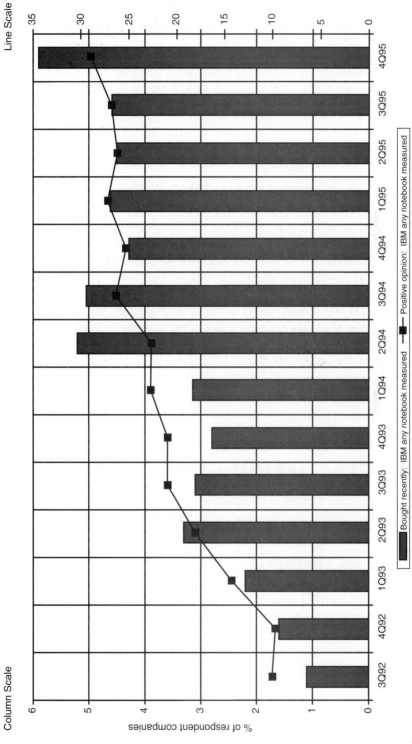

Techtel Corporation, Emeryville, CA.
Source: Developed by Techtel Corp. T-MAS™ © 1992–1996 and data © 1987–1996 by Techtel Corp. and others.

versus private label was $0.90 - 0.53 = 0.37$ and its volume was approximately $(14.29\%)(36.83)(100$ million households), so an estimate of its realized equity in 1997 is $(\$0.37)(526.3$ million$) = \$194$ million. This measure does not explicitly include additional costs—variable and fixed—associated with the brand or its growth and extension potential (i.e., future value). Still, it provides a simple measure that is easy to calculate and hence monitor (and serves as the core of the Interbrand method).

RELATION TO CUSTOMER STRATEGY

As suggested earlier, different product strategies suggest different approaches to customers. Four basic customer strategies are available:

1. Customer acquisition (i.e., getting new customers by market development or market penetration by capturing competitors' customers).
2. Customer retention (i.e., keeping current customers satisfied via enhancing brand loyalty or through superior service).
3. Customer expansion, either getting customers to buy more of what they are currently buying (increasing usage) or "cross-selling" other products (i.e., market potential via increasing business with existing customers).
4. Customer deletion, dropping customers that are not profitable (both now and potentially in the future) in such a way as to not generate legal problems or public relations disasters.

Taken together, the results of these activities determine sales and form a high-level implementation of basic strategy (i.e., growth versus profit).

MARKETING STRATEGY OVER THE LIFE CYCLE

We have repeatedly mentioned the importance (and weaknesses) of the product life cycle concept. One way the life cycle can be used is to conceptualize different general approaches to developing core strategies and tactics.

Introduction Strategies

Up to this point, this book has focused mainly on existing products, but the introductory phase of the life cycle is a useful place to begin this analysis (more will be said about new products in the next chapter). This stage in the life cycle has several characteristics. First, there are often few competitors, perhaps only one. Second, sales volume increases slowly due to the small number of firms marketing the product and the reluctance on the part of customers to purchase it. Early on, selling and advertising focus on selling the generic product; the effort is on product form benefits. Distributors also have the power in the relationship because the product is still unproven with customers, so securing distribution is a major issue. (In the Internet world this means developing links from other sites, etc.) Prices can be high or low depending on the entry strategy of the firm(s) marketing the product.

What are the core strategy options at this stage? There are two well-known options: *skimming* and *penetration*. The skimming strategy assumes a product feature–based differential advantage that allows a company to enter and stay in the market during the introductory period with a high price. Target customers are the least price sensitive, that is, the pioneers or early adopters of the product. A penetration strategy is just the opposite: The marketing manager uses a low-price core strategy and attempts to get as many customers and establish a significant market share position as quickly as possible. This is particularly beneficial if purchase by one customer makes the product more attractive to others.

A skimming strategy is useful when the cost structure of the product is largely variable costs, usually the case when the product is a manufactured good. A high margin can be sustained because the product manager is not under intense pressure to cover large fixed costs. Distribution outlets should be limited to protect the high price. This strategy is most effective when high entry barriers exist because the high price and high margins make the category very attractive to potential competitors. The margins can then be used to fund investment in research and development, leading to new products which can be skim priced when the inevitable competition arrives in the current product category.

A penetration strategy is more appropriate when fixed costs are high (e.g., many services, general purpose computer software). When a broad segment is being pursued, it is important to obtain wide distribution and thus spend heavily on trade-oriented promotion. The manager is also under pressure to make the market as large as possible, which involves generic or product category marketing. This is a more expensive strategy due to the lower margins and higher marketing costs. A marketing manager generally should use a penetration strategy when the lead in the market will likely be short-lived.

There are strategic advantages to being first in a market and establishing a strong position early, consistent with a penetration strategy. Much empirical research shows that the first "mover" (or, more precisely, the first to achieve substantial market position) in a category has an advantage (called, not surprisingly, the *first-mover advantage*) in that it tends to maintain its lead through the product life cycle (Urban et al., 1986). Some of this advantage is obvious: Early movers get first access to distribution channels, establish awareness, and have the first opportunity to establish brand loyalty and create preferences (Carpenter and Nakamoto, 1989). However, followers often overtake leaders, so first movement itself is no guarantee of success (Golder and Tellis, 1993).

Several examples illustrate the different core strategies available. Consumer electronics and industrial product companies almost always pursue a skimming strategy. When VCRs, camcorders, flat screen TVs, and similar products were introduced, they were priced high initially and then fell in price over time. Since usually only one brand was on the market for some months and the early customers for such products (electronics nuts) are generally price insensitive, there was little rationale for pricing low initially. In addition, the products needed word of mouth to help spread information about their utility. Alternatively, penetration pricing is often used for consumer packaged goods because market share is very important for retaining shelf space in super markets. This is clearly evident in Internet strategies that give away the product for free, hoping (often unreasonably) to recoup costs with advertising revenues and future sales.

Growth Strategies

The growth phase of the product life cycle encompasses two different kinds of market behavior: early growth—the phase just following the introductory phase—and late growth—the phase in which the rapid increase in sales begins to flatten out. The growth phase has several features beyond the obvious fact that product category sales are growing. First, the number of competitors increases. This puts pressure on managers to hold distribution channels and changes the focus of sales and communications to the superiority of the product over others in the category. As customers become more knowledgeable about the product and the available options, this puts pressure on price. Finally, with the increased competition, market segmentation begins to be a key issue.

The general strategic options relate to the product's position in the market: whether it is a leader (the brand with the leading market share) or a follower. The leader can choose either to fight, that is, keep the leadership position, or to flee, which cedes market leadership to another product. If the leader chooses to fight, it can attempt to either simply maintain the current position (a dangerous approach, since it is difficult to know exactly what it takes to maintain the position) or keep enhancing the product or service. Why would the leader flee? It is possible that the new entrants in the market are just too strong (as indicated by the competitive analysis) and raise the stakes for competing to a level the incumbent cannot sustain. Witness Minnetonka, which established the liquid soap category. When Lever Brothers and Procter & Gamble jumped in, Minnetonka sold out. Exit is always an option. Other options are to attempt to reposition the product so it can be a strong number two or three brand, which can be accomplished through resegmenting the market, or to retreat to a specific niche.

The follower also has a number of options, the choice of which depends on the strength of the leader, its own strength, and market conditions. One option is to exit quickly and invest in some product that has better long-term potential. A follower can also be content to be a strong number two or three by fortifying its position. The riskiest move is to try to leapfrog the competition. Some companies do this successfully through pure marketing muscle and an imitative product. For example, Johnson & Johnson often allows another company to establish the market and then becomes number one through superior marketing. Specifically, in over-the-counter yeast infection drugs: Schering-Plough established the market and J&J followed with its Monistat 7 brand, which quickly obtained more than half of the market (Weber, 1992).

Other companies attempt to leapfrog through technological innovation. A good example is Docutel Corporation in the 1970s (Abel, 1977). Docutel was the first company to develop and market automated teller machines (ATMs) to banks in the United States. The company was very small at the time, with only $25 million in sales in 1974. The market for ATMs grew rapidly during the 1970s as banks discovered they could use ATMs to differentiate themselves from other banks in a geographical area. However, new competitors entered the market, including mainframe computer manufacturers IBM, Burroughs, and NCR, as well as two firms in the bank vault and security information business, Diebold and Mosler. In addition, customers became more concerned about cost savings from the machines as opposed to marketing advantages. Thus, Docutel, the market leader, had to make a fight-or-flight decision. Fighting would mean making substantial investments in marketing and product development, particularly in developing software compatible with banks' computer systems. In addition, the company would have to decide which market segments to target. Alternatively, the company could be a strong number two or three given the potential size of the market. Unfortunately, Docutel did not make a clear decision to pursue any strategy and was ultimately surpassed in the market by Diebold.

Maturity Strategies

The maturity stage of the life cycle is characteristic of most products, particularly consumer products. Product categories exhibiting fierce battles for market share and access to distribution channels, large amounts of money spent on trade and customer promotion, and aggressive pricing are often in this stage of the product life cycle.

In maturity, the sales curve has flattened out and relatively few new buyers enter the market. While some untapped market potential usually remains, it is difficult and/or expensive to reach. Buyers are sophisticated and well versed in product features and benefits. Where differential advantage can be obtained, it is usually through intangible benefits such as image or through the extended product concept discussed earlier (e.g., service, distribution). Market segments are also well defined, and finding new ones that are untapped is a struggle.

The general strategies in mature markets are similar to those in growth markets, and depend on the relative market position of the product in question. A focus on key products and brands has been the hallmark of P&G's rejuvenation at the beginning of the 21st century. However, leaders sometimes look at the time horizon for "cashing out" the product. If management is committed to a product for an extended time period, the objective is usually to invest just enough money to maintain share. An alternative objective is to "harvest" the product, that is, set an objective of gradual share decline with minimal investment to maximize short-run profits. Other firms have alternatives that depend on the leader's strategy. If the leader is harvesting the product, the number one position may be left open for an aggressive number two brand. If the leader is intent on maintaining that position for a long time (many leading consumer packaged goods brands have been number one for over 50 years!), the follower may choose to be a profitable number two or to exit the category.

Strategies for the Decline Stage

In the decline stage of the life cycle, sales of the category are dropping. So is the number of competitors. Markets reach the decline stage for a variety of reasons. Perhaps the most obvious is technological obsolescence. The demise of the buggy whip is such a case. However, shifts in customer tastes also can create declining categories. The decline of brown alcohol consumption can be related to changing tastes for "white" alcohol such as gin and vodka, and subsequently, for wine and microbrewed beer.

Perhaps the clearest strategy is to try to be the last in the market. By being last, a product gains monopoly rights to the few customers left. This, of course, results

FIGURE 7.9   Strategy over the Life Cycle

	Life Cycle Stage			
	Introduction	Growth	Maturity	Decline
Competitive Position:				
Leader/Follower				
Objective				
Positioning				
Customer targets				
Competitor targets				
Differential advantage				

in the ability to charge commensurately high prices. For example, Lansdale Semiconductor was the last firm making the 8080 computer chip introduced by Intel in 1974. While most applications of computer chips are well beyond the 8080, the 8080 was still used in military systems that were typically built to last 20 to 25 years, such as the Hellfire and Pershing 2 missiles and the Aegis radar system for battleships. Where did the Department of Defense go when it needed 8080s? There was only one supplier: Lansdale.

Summary

A useful way to think about strategic issues over the life cycle is to use a table such as Figure 7.9 which encourages both an audit of current position (share; leader–follower) and change in objectives, positioning, and programs as the industry situation changes.

ILLUSTRATIONS

Odwalla Energy Bar

Objective

Grow 10 percent faster than the category.

Customer Targets

Existing juice customers

Health conscious and on-the-go

Sports enthusiasts

Health purists

Nutrition-seeking families

Competitive Targets

Clif Bars and Clif Luna

Kashi Go LEAN

Balance (Outdoor, Plus, Oasis)

Core Strategy

Increase distribution to 80 percent ACV in mainstream grocery stores.

Focus on natural health.

Leverage brand name, Minute Maid resources.

Handspring

Objective

To capture 15 percent of the PDA market by the end of year 2.

Customer Targets

As in Figure 7.3, there are three main targets:

Price-conscious professionals (including buyers for company salesforces, etc.).

Nonbusiness professionals (e.g., teachers).

Nonprofessionals (e.g., stay-at-home spouses, students, retired people).

Competitive Targets

Palm

Sharp

Core Strategy

Focus on:

Simplicity/convenience.

Low price.

Expandability (via expansion slot).

SUMMARY

This chapter provides the reason for doing the background analyses described in Chapters 2 through 6. The central component of the marketing plan is objectives and strategies for the product that synthesize the current market situation into a recommended plan of action. The strategy, which can be summarized as in Figure 7.9, then leads to specific marketing programs, such as pricing and advertising. The success of a strategy is largely dependent on the integration of the situation analysis and programs in providing a coherent direction for the product.

Strategy can be organized in multiple ways. Here the focus was on a key strategic alternative, growth versus efficiency. Other perspectives include customer strategy, brand equity, new products, and stage in the life cycle. While at first this may be confusing, closer inspection reveals a close relationship among them. Growth strategies tend to be preferred during growth states of markets, require new products, focus on customer acquisition and expansion, and involve building brand equity. Efficiency strategies, by contrast, tend to be preferred later in life cycles and involve focusing on retaining and/or expanding current customers, making minimal or simple product changes, and leveraging brand equity, often through licensing or selling the name. Figure 7.10 describes these likely contingencies.

FIGURE 7.10 Linked Strategic Issues

		Strategic Alternatives	
		Growth	Efficiency
Customer Strategy	Acquire	✓	
	Retain		✓
	Expand	✓	
	Delete		✓
Brand Strategy	Build	✓	
	Leverage	Brand Extensions	Line Extensions
	Milk		License
Product Strategy		New Products	Prune Product Line
Life Cycle Stage	Introduction	✓	
	Growth	✓	
	Maturity		✓

References

Aaker, David A. (1996) *Building Strong Brands.* New York: The Free Press.

Aaker, David A. (1991) *Brand Equity.* New York: The Free Press.

Aaker, David A., and Robert Jacobsen (2001) "The Value Relevance of Brand Attitude in High Technology Markets," *Journal of Marketing Research* 38, November, 485–93.

Aaker, Jennifer (1997) "Dimensions of Brand Personality," *Journal of Marketing Research* 34, August, 347–56.

Abel, Derek F. (1977) "Docutel Corporation," Harvard Business School case study 9-578-073, 1977.

Ailawadi, Kusum, Scott Neslin, and Donald R. Lehmann (2001) "Market Response to a Major Policy Change in the Marketing Mix: Learning from Procter & Gamble's Value Pricing Strategy," *Journal of Marketing* 65, January, 44–61.

Ailawadi, Kusum L., Donald R. Lehmann, and Scott A. Neslin (2003) "Revenue Premium as an Outcome Measure of Brand Equity," *Journal of Marketing* 67, October, 1–17.

Batra, Rajeev, Donald R. Lehmann, and Dipinder Singh (1993) "The Brand Personality Component of Brand Goodwill: Some Antecedents and Consequences," in David A. Aaker and Alexander L. Biel, eds., *Brand Equity and Advertising: Advertising's Role in Building Strong Brands.* Hillsdale, NJ: Lawrence Erlbaum Associates, 83–96.

Bounds, Wendy (1994) "Photography Companies Try to Click with Children," *The Wall Street Journal,* January 31, B1.

Business Week (1996) "Japan Turns a Corner," February 26, 108–9.

Carpenter, Gregory S., and Kent Nakamoto (1989) "Consumer Preference Formation and Pioneering Advantage," *Journal of Marketing Research,* August, 285–98.

Chandon, Pierre, and Brian Wansink (2002) "When Are Stockpiled Products Consumed Faster? A Convenience-Salience Framework of Postpurchase Consumption Incidence and Quantity," *Journal of Marketing Research* 39, August, 321–35.

Czepiel, John A. (1992) *Competitive Marketing Strategy.* Englewood Cliffs, NJ: Prentice Hall, Chapter 1.

Day, George S. (1990) *Market Driven Strategy.* New York: The Free Press, Chapter 7.

Golder, Peter N., and Gerard J. Tellis (1993) "Pioneering Advantage: Marketing Logic or Marketing Legend," *Journal of Marketing Research* 30, May, 158–70.

Hulbert, James M. (1985) *Marketing: A Strategic Perspective.* Katonah, NY: Impact Planning Group.

Kadanoff, Marcia (1995) "Customers Who Are Ripe for the Picking," *Marketing Computers,* December, 24B26.

Keller, Kevin L. (2002) *Strategic Brand Management.* Upper Saddle River, NJ: Prentice Hall.

Lefton, Terry and Weston Anson (1996) "How Much Is Your Brand Worth?" *Brandweek,* January 29, 43–44.

Levitt, Theodore (1986) *The Marketing Imagination.* New York: The Free Press.

Mehegan, Sean (1996) "A Picture of Quality," *Brandweek,* April 8, 38–40.

Milbank, Dana (1992) "Restructured Alcoa Seeks to Juggle Cost and Quality," *The Wall Street Journal,* August 25, B4.

Morris, Betsy (1996) "The Brand's the Thing," *Fortune,* March 4, 72–86.

Pae, Peter (1992) "Card Issuers Turn to Stealing Customers," *The Wall Street Journal,* August 18, B1.

Porter, Michael E. (1985) *Competitive Advantage.* New York: Free Press.

Ries, Al, and Jack Trout (1992) *Marketing Warfare.* New York: McGraw-Hill.

Schnaars, Steven P. (1991) *Marketing Strategy: A Customer-Driven Approach.* New York: The Free Press.

Schwartz, Karen (1996) "Pennies Saved, Millions Earned," *San Francisco Chronicle,* March 24, D1.

Urban, Glen L., Theresa Carter, Steven Gaskin, and Zofia Mucha (1986) "Market Share Rewards to Pioneering Brands: An Empirical Analysis and Strategic Implications," *Management Science,* June, 645–59.

Wansink, Brian (1996) "Does Package Size Accelerate Usage Volume?" *Journal of Marketing* 60, July, 1–14.

Weber, Joseph (1992) "A Big Company That Works," *Business Week,* May 4, 124–29.

Appendix A

Measuring the Value of Customers

Consistent with the view of a customer as an asset, the value of an individual customer is simply the net discounted margin over time derived from that customer. The expected value depends on the retention probability (r) and margin (m) over time as well as the annual cost to maintain that customer as an account (A). This can easily be set up as a standard spreadsheet (Figure A.1) and the value calculated accordingly.

In addition to the direct value of customers relationship to a firm, of course, there is value in simply having customers (who serve as an ad, in particular when they are celebrities) and in what customers communicate to other customers (word-of-mouth and, now, critically, word-of-web) and to influentials (e.g., government regulators, watchdog groups). These can overwhelm the direct impact of a particular company–customer relationship. For this section, however, we focus on the direct value customers.

The aggregate value of customers is simply the value of an average customer multiplied by the number of customers. More generally, the net aggregate value is

Value of customers = Sum over time of:

$$\begin{pmatrix} \text{Number of} \\ \text{customers} \\ \text{in time t} \end{pmatrix} \begin{pmatrix} \text{Average net} \\ \text{margin} \\ \text{in time t} \end{pmatrix} - \begin{pmatrix} \text{Acquisition} \\ \text{costs}_t \end{pmatrix} - \begin{pmatrix} \text{Retention} \\ \text{costs}_t \end{pmatrix} - \begin{pmatrix} \text{Expansion} \\ \text{costs}_t \end{pmatrix}$$

In a *very* special case, the value of a customer can be reduced to a simple formula. Specifically, if (1) the retention rate is constant over time and (2) the growth/expansion rate is constant over time (a generally untenable assumption if the growth rate is positive since growth eventually slows), the value of a customer reduces to a formula. For an infinite time horizon[1].

$$\text{VOC} = \sum_{K=1}^{\infty} \frac{(M - A)r^{K-1}(1 + g)^{K-1}}{(1 + d)^{K-1}} = \frac{(M - A)}{1 - \dfrac{r(1 + g)}{1 + d}} = \frac{(M - A)(1 + d)}{1 + d - r(1 + g)}$$

[1] Note: These formulas only work when $\dfrac{r(1 + g)}{1 + d}$ is less than 1.

FIGURE A.1 Calculating the Value of a Customer: Spreadsheet Format

	Value in Year					
	1 (current)	2	3	4	...	n
Retention probability (r)	1	r_2	$r_2 r_3$	$r_2 r_3 r_4$	...	$r_2 r_3 \ldots r_n$
Gross margin (m)	m_1	m_2	m_3	m_4	...	m_n
Expected margin (r)(m)	m_1	$r_2 m_2$	$r_2 r_3 m_3$	$r_2 r_3 r_4 m_4$	...	$r_2 r_3 \ldots r_n m_n$
Annual account maintenance cost	A_1	A_2	A_3	A_4	...	A_n
Net margin	$m_1 - A_1$	$r_2(m_2 - A_2)$	...			
Discount factor	1	$\dfrac{1}{1+d}$	$\left(\dfrac{1}{1+d}\right)^2$	$\left(\dfrac{1}{1+d}\right)^3$	...	$\left(\dfrac{1}{1+d}\right)^{n-1}$
Discounted value						

where:

M = Margin.

A = Constant annual account maintenance (retention) cost.

r = (Constant) retention rate.

g = (Constant) growth in margin rate.

d = Constant discount rate.

For a finite time horizon (n years) this becomes:

$$\text{VOC} = \sum_{K=1}^{n} \frac{(M - A)r^{K-1}(1 + g)^{K-1}}{(1 + d)^{K-1}} = (M - A)\frac{1 - \left[\dfrac{r(1 + g)}{1 + d}\right]^K}{1 - \left[\dfrac{r(1 + g)}{1 + d}\right]}$$

In the case when the growth rate is 0 (i.e., margin is constant over time) over an infinite horizon, this reduces to the simple formula for an annuity:

$$\text{Value of a customer} = \frac{(M - A)(1 + d)}{1 + d - r}$$

EXAMPLE

For an interesting example, consider Federal Express when they began introducing Courier-Pak (Lovelock, 1976). In the dark old days of 1976, they sold

FIGURE A.2 Value of Advertising Account: Spreadsheet Approach

	Margin	Retention	Discount Factor $\left(\frac{1}{1.12}\right)$	Present Value
1	1,617	1	1	1,617
2	1,617	.9	.89	1,299
3	1,617	.81	.80	1,037
4	1,617	.729	.71	840
5	1,617	. . .	. . .	. . .
6	1,617			
7	1,617			
8	1,617			
9	1,617			
10	1,617	.387	.360	225
Total				

Courier-Paks for $12.50 and had a variable cost of $4.00 for a margin per pak of $8.50. One type of account was firms in the advertising business. Specifically, 140 advertising accounts accounted for 2,285 paks per month. To these facts we add the following assumptions:

1. Margin remains constant (i.e., the number of paks per account times the margin per pak stays the same).
2. The retention rate is 90 percent (which seems reasonable for satisfied customers).
3. The appropriate discount rate is 12 percent.

The typical advertising account thus generates 2,285/140 = 16.32 paks per month or (16.32)(12) = 196 paks per year. This translates into a margin per year of (196)(8.50) = $1,617. Using the spreadsheet approach and a 10-year horizon would then produce Figure A.2, and thus a value of about $7,200. Of course we could use an infinite horizon, but since the margin is constant, this will add little to the total discounted value as the following shows:

1. Infinite horizon: $\text{VOC} = \left(\dfrac{1,617}{1 - \dfrac{0.9}{1.12}}\right) = \$8,085$

2. 10-year horizon: $\text{VOC} = 1,617 \dfrac{1 - \left(\dfrac{0.19}{1.12}\right)^{10}}{\left(1 - \dfrac{0.9}{1.12}\right)} = 1,617\left(\dfrac{1 - .11}{.20}\right) = \$7,196$

DRIVERS OF VALUE

The key drivers of the value of a particular customer are (1) the retention rate and (2) expansion (i.e., the growth rate). In the previous example, assume the retention rate was 80 percent instead of 90 percent. Using an infinite horizon, the value decreases to

$$\frac{1,617}{1 - \dfrac{0.8}{1.12}} = \$5,660$$

or 70 percent of the value at a 90 percent retention rate. Similarly if retention could be increased to 95 percent, the value becomes:

$$\frac{1,617}{1 - \dfrac{0.95}{1.12}} = \$10,653$$

which is 32 percent greater than its former value. Thus the value of a customer is very sensitive to the retention rate.

The expansion (or contraction) rate similarly has a major impact on the value of the customer. For example, if we assume a negative 10 percent growth rate, the infinite horizon value becomes

$$\frac{1,617}{1 - \dfrac{(.9)(.9)}{1.12}} = \$5,842$$

or 28 percent less. Similarly at the aggregate (firm) level, expansion comes from a combination of new customer acquisitions and expansion of same-customers' sales (margin).

There is both good news and bad news in these sensitivities. The good news is that it is clear what can be done to improve value: increase retention (e.g., through satisfaction if not barriers to exit) and expand relations with customers (e.g., cross-sell or improve the product mix). Further, small changes make a big difference, thus potentially justifying marketing activity as cost effective. On the other hand, the bad news is that since small changes in the parameters lead to big changes in valuation, there is an obvious opportunity to alter the numbers to justify a particular decision.

Index

A

A. C. Nielsen, 18, 30, 40, 158
Aaker, D. A., 136, 137, 165, 229, 230, 232, 234, 242
Aaker, Jennifer, 231, 242
Abel, Derek F., 238, 242
Abell, D., 28, 49
Acura, 27
Adidas, 172
AdRelevance, 87
Advertising Age, 53
Aerial reconnaissance, 91
Ailawadi, K., 220, 234, 242
Airbus, 60, 93
AK Steel Inc., 60
Aluminum Company of America (Alcoa), 219
Amazon.com, 26, 44
AMD, 60
American Association of Retired Persons
    (AARP), 59
American Demographics, 86
American Express, 47, 48
Analysis-based estimates, for buyers, 175–178
Anchor Hocking, 108
Anderson, E., 141, 165
Andrews, Edmund L., 68, 75
Andrews, Rick L., 44, 49
Angwin, Julia, 53, 75
Annual reports, 83
Ansoff, H. Igor, 38, 49
Anson, Weston, 243
Apple Computer, 18, 19, 29, 80, 179, 213, 226
Area potential, and sales forecasting, 178
Arm & Hammer, 129
AT&T, 18, 55, 60, 219
Audi, 27, 66, 232
Autobytel, 27, 33, 34
Avon, 91

B

Backer Spielvogel Bates Worldwide, 124
Balance Bar Inc., 17, 110–114, 240
Bang & Olufsen, 35, 226
Baraba, Vincent P., 140, 165
Barnesandnoble.com, 44
Bass, Frank, 155, 202, 207
Bass model, 204, 205

Batra, R., 231, 242
Bayer, 232
Bayus, Barry L., 175, 207
Beatty, Sharon E., 124, 165
Beeh, Jenny E., 208
Behavioral data, using, 40–42
Benchmarking, 90
Berry, Leonard L., 141, 166
Best Buy, 129
Bethlehem Steel, 108
Bettman, James R., 130, 165
Bic, 47
BiggerBooks.com, 44
Billboard, 85
Bittar, Christine, 104, 118
Blackberry, 205
BMW, 27, 31, 66, 90
Boeing, 60
Bolton, Ruth N., 154, 165
Boston Consulting Group, 5, 51, 96
Bottom-up planning, 8
Boulding, William, 165
Bounds, Wendy, 218, 242
Bourgeois, Jacques, 43, 49
Boynton, Andrew C., 142, 166
Brand equity, managing brand, 136, 228–233
Brandt, William, 212
Brand value, measuring, 233–236
Brandweek, 20
Braniff, 104
Browder, Seanna, 93, 118
Brown, Monica, 16
Burger King, 79, 233
Burroughs, 238
Business 2.0, 85
Business Week, 20, 83, 184, 216
Buyers
    bargaining power of, 58–59
    vs. users, 121–122

C

Campbell Soup Company, 70, 213
Capital requirements, 57
Capon, Noel, 7, 22
Carpenter, Gregory S., 237, 243
CarPoint, 27
CarsDirect, 27

Carter, Theresa, 75, 243
Casio, 18, 27, 37, 73, 114–117
Category analysis, in situation analysis, 11–12
Category attractiveness
    and aggregate market factors, 52–56
    bargaining power of buyers, 58–59
    bargaining power of suppliers, 59–60
    category capacity, 61–62
    category factors, 56–58
    current category rivalry, 60–61
    environmental analysis, 62–70
    overview of, 51–52
    pressure from substitutes, 61
Category size, 52–53
Caterpillar, 226
Cerf, C., 184, 208
C4U, 87
Chambers, John C., 181, 208
Chandon, Pierre, 219, 243
Charles Schwab & Company, 56, 107
Chemical Week, 85
Chen, Ming-Jer, 109, 118
Chi, Caroline, 18
Chi-square test, 151
Chrysler, 27
Cingular, 60
Cisco Systems, 51
Citibank, 47, 63
Claburn, Thomas, 30, 44, 49
Claritas Corporation, 145
Clark, Bruce H., 39, 49, 109, 118
Clif Bar Inc., 17, 49, 110–114, 240
Cluster analysis, 143–149
ClusterPLUS, 145
CNET News.com, 20, 205
CNN.com, 20
Coca-Cola Company, 17, 28, 29, 35, 41, 53, 57, 78,
    79, 95, 107, 110–114, 136, 160, 228, 233, 241
Cohen, William A., 13, 22
Colgate-Palmolive, 58
Colloquy, 85
Comdex, 89
Commodore, 54
Company Sleuth, 87
Compaq, 29, 37, 179, 223
Competition
    defined, 28–33
    determining, 38–45
    levels of, 28–38
    selection, 45–47
Competitive analysis
    assessing a competitor's current objectives, 93–95
    assessing a competitor's current strategies, 95
    assessing a competitor's will, 106–107
    creating a product features matrix, 92–93

differential advantage analysis, 102–106
    marketing strategy, 95–102
    overview, 76–81
    predicting future strategies, 107–110
    sources of information, 82–92
Competitive Intelligence Guide, 86
CompUSA, 129
CompuServe, 83
Computer Reseller News, 20
ComScore MediaMetrix, 42
Conjoint analysis, 132–133
Conner Peripherals, 26
Consultants, as information source, 85, 89
Consumer Reports, 59, 129, 231
Converse, 172
Cooper, Lee, 42, 49
Core strategy, 95
Corfman, Kim P., 124, 165
Corning Glass, 108
Cost/price strategy, 224
Cox, William E., 177, 208
Cravens, David W., 51, 75
Cray Computer, 59, 97
Cricket, 47
Cross-tabular analysis, 152
Currency exchange rates, 65
Customer analysis
    overview, 120–121
    what we need to know, 121–141
Customer-based measures, and market structures,
    39–44
Customer-based methods, of sales-forecasting,
    185–188
Customer judgments, 42–44
Customers, as sources of information, 88
Customer value, 135
    manifestations of, 137
    sources of, 136–137
Czepiel, John A., 222, 243

D

Data Resources, Inc., 192
Day, George S., 4, 22, 39, 50, 223, 243
Day Timer, 37, 73
Dean Witter, 107
De Beers, 31, 32
DeBruicker, F. Steward, 149, 165
De Lisser, Eleena, 92, 118
Dell, Michael, 39, 89
Dell Computer Corporation, 29, 39, 60, 70, 89,
    129, 133, 234
Delphi Method, 185
Deshpandé, Robit, 4, 22

Deveny, Kathleen, 177, 208
Dhalla, Nariman K., 172, 208
DHL, 129
DIALOG Information Services, 86
Diebold, 239
Distribution, 57–58, 98
Docutel Corporation, 238
Dreyer's, 234
Dummy variables, 153
Dun & Bradstreet, 83, 86
DuPont, 98
Dvorak, Phred, 31, 50

E

E. F. Hutton, 108
Eastern Airlines, 104
Eastman Kodak, 26, 218, 229
Econometric models, 192
Economies of scale, 56
Edison, Thomas, 185
Edmunds.com, 59
Egghead, 129
Electronic data services, 86–87
Electronic News, 20
Ellison, Larry, 61
Emerson Electric, 90
Emery Air Freight, 94, 129
Employee communications, 85
Employees, as information sources, 89
Enterprise competition, 47–49
Entrants, threat of new, 56
Eraso, Juan, 18
Ericsson, 26
E*Trade, 56
Everyday low pricing (EDLP), 220
Executive summary in marketing plan, 11
Expedia, 28
Exponential smoothing, 189
Exxon's Office Systems Division, 107

F

Farley, J. U., 7, 22, 202, 208
Federal Communications Commission (FCC),
    85, 186
Federal Express (FedEx), 57, 94, 121, 227, 229
Federman, Josef, 27, 28, 50
Fidelity Investments, 47
Field Force Automation, 205
Financial Times, 86
FIND/SVP, 85, 173
Firestone, 232
First-mover advantage, 237

Fitch, Stephane, 30, 50
Food and Drug Administration (FDA), 66, 85
Forbes, 20, 83, 98, 174
Ford Motor Company, 27, 47, 51, 232
Fornell, C., 141, 165
Forrester Research, 20, 205
Fortune, 20, 83, 174, 228
Freshdirect, 63
Frontier Airlines, 78
Frost & Sullivan, 20
Fuji, 218
Fulford, 76

G

Gartner Group, 20
Gaskin, Steven, 75, 243
Gates, Bill, 61
Gateway 2000, 29, 129
GE Global Exchange Services, 30
Genentech, 66
General Electric (GE), 5, 28, 39, 47, 48, 78,
    219, 233
General Foods Corporation, 104
General Mills, 57
General Motors (GM), 27, 47, 48, 60, 79, 90
Generic competition, 30
Georgoff, David M., 181, 208
Gerber, 90
Geyelin, Milo, 80, 118
Gillette, 47, 57, 100
GlaxoSmithKline, 108
GLOBALSCAN, 124
Golder, Peter N., 237, 243
Gomes, Lee, 78
Google, 87
Government sources, of information, 85
Grand Metropolitan, 233
Green, Paul E., 132, 165
Green, William, 76, 78, 118
Grimm, Curtis M., 109, 118
Grover, Rajiv, 156, 157, 165
Gruner, Stephanie, 78
Gupta, S., 82, 118, 166, 206, 208
Guthrie, Julian, 91, 118

H

Hager, Bruce, 91, 119
Haines, George, 43, 49
Handspring, 20, 70, 114–117, 221, 222, 241
Hauser, J. R., 44, 50
Help-wanted advertisements, as information
    sources, 89

Hershey Foods, 90
Hewlett-Packard (HP), 20, 47, 55, 60, 78, 87, 91, 133, 213, 228, 234
Hoenig, Scott, 1, 22
Homer, Pamela, 124, 165
Honda, 232
Hong, Saman, 175, 207
Hoover's Online, 86
Hopkins, David, 22
Horsky, Dan, 202, 208
Howard, John A., 130, 134, 165
Huang, Eleanor, 16
Hubert, James, 22
Hulbert, J. M., 7, 22, 212, 214, 243

I

IBM, 29, 34, 37, 38, 47, 59, 78, 96, 97, 179, 181, 213, 226, 233, 238
The Industry Standard, 20
Information Resources, Inc. (IRI), 30, 40
Information sources
    with ethical considerations, 91–92
    other sources, 89–91
    primary sources of, 88–89
    secondary sources of, 82–87
Intel, 59, 60, 78, 108, 233
Interest rate fluctuations, 65
International Data Corporation, 20
Internet, and market potential, 174
Investment bankers, as information source, 89
Ito-Yokado, 31

J

Jacobsen, Robert, 234, 242
Jaguar, 90
Jain, Deepak C., 202, 207
JetBlue, 31
Johnson, Philip, 44, 50
Johnson & Johnson, 232, 238
Johnston, Wesley J., 130, 165
Jones, J. Morgan, 202, 208
Judgment-based methods, of sales forecasting, 181–185
Judgment-based segmentation, 156
Jury of expert opinion, 184–185

K

Kadanoff, Marcia, 220, 243
Kahle, Lynn P., 124, 165
Kahn, Kenneth B., 192, 208
Kalra, Ajay, 165

Kalwani, Manohar, 40, 50
Kalyanaram, G., 54, 75
Kamakura, Wagner A., 156, 158, 165
Kashi Co., 110–114, 240
Keds, 172
Keller, K. L., 137, 165, 243
Kellogg's, 57, 90, 228
Kim, W. Chan, 31, 50
Kimberly Clark, 47, 53
Kirsner, Scott, 108, 118
Kleenex, 229
Kmart, 213, 229
Knight, Charles, 5, 22
Koenig, H. F., 137, 166
Kohlberg Kravis Roberts (KKR), 94
Kotler, Philip, 123, 125
Kraft/General Foods, 2, 49, 57
Krishnan, Trichy V., 202, 207

L

L. A. Gear, 172
Labe, Russell P., Jr., 175, 207
Landor's ImagePower, 233
Lanktree, Patricia, 1, 7, 8, 22
Lansdale Semiconductor, 55, 240
Latent class analysis, 154–156
Latent class methods, 169
Lattin, James, 41, 50
Leading indicators, 191
Lee, Jennifer, 18
Lee, Louis, 64, 75
Lefton, Terry, 243
Lehmann, D. R., 1, 22, 40, 50, 82, 118, 124, 141, 165, 166, 202, 208, 220, 231, 234, 242
Lever Brothers, 238
Levitt, T., 30, 50, 225, 243
Lewin, Jeffrey E., 130, 165
Libby-Owens-Ford, 108
Linux, 78
Litton Industries, 39
Loblaw's, 228
Lock-in, 57
Lonsdale, Ronald, 155
Lorge, Sarah, 94, 118
Lovelock, Christopher H., 166
Lutz, Richard J., 137, 166
Lynes, Russell, 149, 166

M

Macadam, Stephen E., 90
Magazine Total Audiences Report, 98
Maidique, Modesto A., 100, 118

Main, Jeremy, 90, 118
Makridakis, Spyros, 181, 208
Managerial judgment, 38–39
Manrodt, K. B., 192, 208
Marigold, Lys, 70, 75
Market development strategies, 217–219
Marketer's Guide to Media, 100
Market growth, 53
Marketing mix, 97–98
Marketing objectives, 12
Marketing plan
  approaches to planning, 8–9
  components of, 11–16
  mistakes in the process, 4–7
  objectives of, 1–4
  outline, 23–24
  planning process, 8–11
  summary, 12
  vs. strategic plan, 3
Market penetration strategies, 219
Market potential
  information sources, 172–174
  methods for estimating, 175–179
  overview, 171–172
  uses for estimates, 172
Market testing, 185–186
Martin, Justin, 166
Mary Kay Cosmetics, 91
Mass customization, 142
Matsushita, 60
Mauborgne, Renée, 31, 50
Maytag, 226
McAlexander, J. H., 137, 166
McAlister, L., 41, 50
McCartney, Scott, 78
McDonald's Corporation, 79, 97, 226
McDonnell Douglas, 60
McGraw-Hill, 77, 173, 192
MCI, 39, 85, 107, 219
McKinsey & Company, 5
McNealey, Scott, 61
McWilliams, G., 179, 208
Means, Howard B., 70, 75
Mediamark Research, 98, 100
Mehegan, Sean, 243
Mei, Mei, 18
Memorex, 100
Mercedes, 90
Merrill Lynch, 47, 48, 107, 108
Metamediaries, 33
MicroPatent, 83, 84
Microsoft Corporation, 53, 61, 78, 91, 233, 234
Milbank, Dana, 220, 243
Miller, Annetta, 67, 75
Miller Brewing Company, 95

Milward-Brown, 137, 233
Minnetonka, Inc., 58, 238
Model-based methods, of sales forecasting,
  191–192
Monster.com, 89
Montgomery, David B., 39, 49
Moody's, 86
Moore, Elizabeth S., 137, 166
Moore, Marian C., 109, 118
Moriarty, R. R., 149, 166
Morris, Betsy, 228, 243
Morrison, D., 40, 50
Mosaic, 53
Mosler, 239
Motorola, 26, 78
Moving averages, 188–189
MRI, 176
Mucha, Zofia, 75, 243
Mullick, Satinder K., 181, 208
Multiattribute model, of consumer decisions,
  130–134
Multidimensional scaling; *see* Perceptual mapping
Muniz, A., Jr., 137, 166
Murdick, Robert G., 181, 208
Myers, Matthew B., 154, 165

N

Naisbitt, John, 75
Naive extrapolation, 184
Nakamoto, Kent, 237, 243
Narayanan, Sundar, 124, 165
Navasky, V., 184, 208
NCR, 238
NEC, 26, 59, 224
Nedungadi, Prakash, 4, 22
Neslin, S., 194, 195, 208, 220, 234, 242
Nestlé S. A., 49, 226
NetBank, 48
Net-Generation, 67, 68
Netscape, 53
NewDirectory, 86
Newspapers, 82–83
Nike, 70, 96, 172
Nintendo, 35, 57, 224
Nissan, 232
Nonprice strategy, 224–228
Nordstrom, 97, 226
Nortel, 26

O

Office Depot, 162
Office Max, 162

O'Guinn, T. C., 137, 166
Okanes, Jennifer, 16
OneSource, 20
Oracle, 60, 61, 91
Osborne, 54
O'Shaughnessy, John, 140, 166
O'Shaughnessy, Nicholas Jackson, 140, 166

P

Pacific Bell, 85
Packard-Bell, 224
Pae, Peter, 219, 243
PaineWebber, 107
Palm Computing, 26, 78, 114–117, 205
Pan Am, 104
Panasonic, 35
Parasuraman, A., 141, 166
Parker-Pope, Tara, 31, 50
Patch, Peter, 100, 118
Patent filings, 83
Patterson, Gregory A., 149, 166
Patzer, Gordon L., 82, 118
Peapod, 63
Pen Computing, 20
Penetration strategy, 237
PepsiCo, 27, 35, 41, 53, 57, 79, 95
Perceptual mapping, 42–43, 131–132
Pessemier, E. A., 139, 166
Peters, Tom, 4
Petersen, Laurie, 75
Pettersson, Frederik, 18
Pezzullo, M. A., 8
Philip Morris Co. Inc., 94, 228
Phillips, 20
Pine, B. Joseph II, 142, 166
Pioneer, 35
Planning assumptions, 12
Plant tours, as information sources, 90
Popcorn, Faith, 70, 75
Pope, Kyle, 60, 75
Porsche, 27, 66
Porter, Michael E., 56, 75, 92, 96, 118,
    223, 243
Port Import Export Reporting Service
    (PIERS), 86
Positioning
    choice of competitor targets, 222–223
    choice of customer targets, 221–222
    core strategy, 223–228
PowerBar Inc., 17, 110–114
Premier Industrial Corporation, 97
Pricing, 97
PRIZM, 145, 146–148

Procter & Gamble, 6, 31, 35, 39, 47, 53, 58, 78,
    91, 104, 120, 220, 228, 238, 239
Product Development Management
    Association, 192
Product differentiation, 57
Product life cycle, 53–55
Product/service capabilities, 98
Product strategy
    benefits of strategy, 212–214
    elements of, 214
    implications, 33–36
    managing brand equity, 228–236
    over the life cycle, 236–240
    overview, 212
    and positioning, 221–228
    relation to customer strategy, 236
    selection of strategic alternatives, 217–221
    setting objectives, 214–217
Profits, 55–56
Promotion, 97
Prudential, 47, 48, 107, 229
Psion, 20
Puma, 172

Q

Quaker Oats, 57, 201

R

Ralph Lauren, 214
Rangan, Kasturi, 149, 166
Rangan, U. Srinivasa, 92
Rao, V., 41, 50
Ratneshwar, S., 44, 50
RC Cola, 226
Reebok, 96, 172
Regression analysis, 152–154, 189–191, 202–205
Regression models
    developing, 194–198
    for forecasting, 192–194
Research International, 136, 233
Reverse engineering, as information sources, 90
Ries, Al, 4, 22, 78, 222, 243
Ritz, Christopher J., 208
RJR Nabisco, 94, 104
Robinson, William T., 54, 75
Robock, Stefan H., 64, 75
Rochester Electronics, 55
Rolex, 56, 98, 99, 226
Rolm, 39
Rolodex, 37
Royal, 37

Rubber Age, 85
Russell, Gary J., 156, 158, 165

S

Sabavala, Darius, 41, 50
Sales, increasing, 217–219
Sales and Marketing Management, 178
Sales cyclicity, 55
Sales extrapolation methods, 188–191
Sales force, as information source, 88
Sales force composite, 184
Sales forecasting
    definitions, 170–171
    illustrations, 202–205
    overview, 170, 179–181
    summary of methods, 182–183
Sales potential
    methods for estimating, 175–179
    and sales forecasting, 179
Sandberg, Jared, 53, 75
Sanders, Nada R., 192, 208
San Francisco Chronicle, 20, 107
Sanyo, 35
Schelling, Thomas, 79, 119
Schering-Plough, 238
Schmitt, Bernd, 140, 166
Schnaars, Steven P., 70, 75, 226, 243
Schonfeld, E., 67
Schouten, J. W., 137, 166
Schuchman, Abraham, 212
Schwartz, Karen, 220, 243
Scott Paper, 47
Sculley, John, 80
Seagate Technology, 26
Seasonality, 55
Seegers, Harvey, 30
Segmentation
    desirable criteria for, 142–143
    methods for, 143–158
    variables, 125–126
Sellers, Patricia, 178, 208
SERVQUAL, 141
Shapiro, Carl, 57, 75
Sharp, 18, 20
Shell Petroleum, 5
Shocker, Allan D., 39, 44, 50
Shoemaker, R. W., 194, 195, 208
Siebel, Tom, 61
Siebel Systems, 60, 61
Silicon Graphics, Inc., 47, 213
Simmons Market Research Bureau, 176
Simon, Leonard S., 202, 208
Singh, Dipinder, 231, 242

Situation analysis in marketing plan, 11–12
Six Flags, 60
60 Minutes, 232
Skimming, 237
Slotting allowances, 58
Smith, Donald D., 181, 208
Smith, Ken G., 109, 118
Society of Competitive Intelligence
    Professionals, 92
Sommers, Montrose, 43, 49
Sonesta Hotels, 13–16
Song Airlines, 31
Sony Corporation, 20, 27, 31, 35, 57, 60, 87
Southwest Airlines, 31, 33, 223
Sprint, 60, 85, 219
Srinivasan, V., 156, 157, 165
Srinivasen, T. C., 44, 49
Srivastava, Rajendra V., 39, 50
Staelin, Richard, 165
Staples, 78
Stasch, Stanley, 1, 7, 8, 22
Steckel, Joel H., 82, 118, 166
Steenkamp, J. B., 154, 166
Stefflre, Volney, 44, 50
Stern, Steward & Company, 233
Sternburg, T., 78
Strategic Mapping, Inc., 145
Strategic Planning Institute, 4
Strategy Software, 87
Substitution in use, 44
Sullivan, Allanna, 166
Sullivan, Mary W., 165
Sultan, Fareena, 202, 208
Sun Microsystems, 26, 47, 61, 213
Suppliers, 57
    bargaining power of, 59–60
    as information source, 89
Sutton, Howard, 2, 6, 15, 22
Swartz, Gordon S., 149, 166
Swinyard, William R., 162, 163
Switching costs, 57

T

Tabular analysis, 149–152
Tapscott, Don, 68
Target, 149
Taylor, Jim, 70, 75
Technology strategy, 100–102
Technology substitution, 39
Techtel Corporation, 234
Teinowitz, Ira, 94, 119
Teitelbaum, Richard S., 119
Tellis, G. J., 237, 243

10K Statements, 83
TerHofstede, Frankel, 154, 166
Test and Measurement World, 85
Test markets, 90
Texas Instruments, 171
Thomas, Philip S., 63, 75
Thomaselli, Rich, 28, 50
Threat of new entrants, 56
3Com Corporation, 18, 19, 20, 37, 73
Tigerts, Douglas, 155
Times series regression, 190, 209–211
Timex, 27
Timken, 226
Top-down planning, 8
Toshiba, 29, 37
Total product concept, 225
Toyota, 79, 232
Trade associations, 85
Trademark filings, 83
Trade press, 85
Trade shows, as information sources, 89–90
Trash, buying/stealing, 91
Trout, Jack, 4, 22, 78, 222, 243
TRW, 185
Tupperware, 26

U

United Airlines, 33, 57, 78
United Parcel Service (UPS), 129
Upton, David M., 90
Urban, Glen, 44, 50, 54, 75, 125, 166, 237, 243
Urbany, Joel E., 109, 118
Users, vs. buyers, 121–122

V

VALS (Values and Lifestyles) typology, 122–124
Value chains, 96–97
Value proposition, 95, 223, 232
Vanguard, 47
Varian, Hal R., 57, 75
Verizon, 60
Victor, Bart, 142, 166
von Hippel, Eric, 125, 166

W

Wacker, Watts, 70, 75
The Wall Street Journal, 79, 83
Wal-Mart, 120, 129, 213
Walt Disney Co., 39, 60
Wansink, B., 219, 243
Wasserman, Todd, 78
Waterman, Robert, 4
Weber, Joseph, 238, 243
Wedel, Michel, 154, 166
Wells, Melanie, 139, 166
Wells Fargo, 218
Wernerfelt, Birger, 44, 50
Wheelwright, Steven C., 181, 208
Wickland, Jennifer, 16
Wilkie, W., 130, 137, 166
Williams, Jeffrey, 27, 50
Wilton, Peter C., 206, 208
Wind, Yoram, 132, 165
Winer, R. S., 97
Wired, 85, 185
Women's Wear Daily, 85

X

Xerox Corporation, 58, 90, 229

Y

Yahoo!, 234
Yip, George, 27, 50
Young & Rubicam Brand Asset Valuator, 136, 233
Yovovich, B. G., 119
Yuspeh, Sonia, 172, 208

Z

Zachary, Pascal, 80, 119
Zaltman, Gerald, 140, 165, 166
Zeithaml, V. A., 141, 165, 166
Zellner, W., 91, 119